A PARISIENNE IN CHICAGO

Translated and with an introduction
by Mary Beth Raycraft

Essay by Arnold Lewis

A

Parisienne

in Chicago

Impressions of the World's Columbian Exposition

MADAME LÉON GRANDIN

UNIVERSITY OF ILLINOIS PRESS
Urbana, Chicago, and Springfield

Library of Congress Cataloging-in-Publication Data
Grandin, Léon, Madame, 1864–1905.
[Impressions d'une Parisienne à Chicago. English]
A parisienne in Chicago : impressions of the World's
Columbian Exposition / Madame Léon Grandin;
translated and with an introduction by Mary Beth Raycraft;
essay by Arnold Lewis.
p.   cm.
Originally published as: Impressions d'une Parisienne à Chicago.
Paris: E. Flammarion [1894]
Includes bibliographical references and index.
ISBN 978-0-252-03513-5 (cloth : acid-free paper)
1. Chicago (Ill.)—Description and travel. 2. French—
Illinois—Chicago. 3. Grandin, Léon, Madame, 1864–1905—
Travel—Illinois—Chicago.
I. Raycraft, Mary Beth. II. Title.
F548.5.G7513   2010
917.73'1103—dc22   2009034554

Contents

ILLUSTRATIONS FOLLOW PAGE 76

Acknowledgments

A number of friends and colleagues have provided intellectual and moral support during this project. Special thanks go to Arn Lewis, first for urging me to consider a translation of Madame Grandin's account and, second, for providing expertise and encouragement along the way. Bénédicte Monicat's exemplary work on French women travelers and her careful reading of the manuscript helped shaped the entire project. The incisive comments of the anonymous reviewers were very helpful, as were Patricia Ward's suggestions. Librarians and staff members at the Chicago Historical Society, the Art Institute of Chicago Archives, the Bibliothèque Nationale, Yale University's Beinecke Library, and the Staten Island Historical Society responded quickly to my questions and gave useful research suggestions. The tireless efforts of Jim Toplon and the staff of the Interlibrary Loan Department at Vanderbilt University in tracking down a long list of obscure volumes greatly facilitated my research. Laure de Margerie at the Sculpture Archive at the Musée d'Orsay, Katherine Bourguignon and Vanessa Lecomte at the Musée d'Art Américain at Giverny, and Mary Smart all expressed enthusiasm about the work and provided information and documentation concerning Léon Grandin's career. The family of Marie Gélon Cameron generously agreed to allow the publication of excerpts from her correspondence. Todd Hughes shared his expertise in genealogy, and Matthew Guzman kindly assisted with formatting the text. At the University of Illinois Press, Joan Catapano took an early interest in the manuscript, and her enthusiasm for the project was encouraging. Rebecca McNulty provided gracious assistance throughout the process, and Mary Giles improved the quality of the manuscript through her editing. Norma Santurri, Patricia Hannon, and Marianne Hinds Wanamaker listened to my stories about Madame Grandin and kept me company during research trips to Paris, New York, and Chicago. Finally, I thank my husband, Raul Guzman, and our children, Matthew, Will, and Claire, for their patience and support.

Introduction to Chicago

The Shock City of the Age

Arnold Lewis

Marie Lédier Grandin and her husband, Léon, arrived in New York on July 30, 1892. They were on their way to Chicago, where he would work for ten months on a sculptured fountain for the international exposition that opened there in 1893. Thousands of foreign tourists and observers, mainly from northwestern Europe, visited the United States that year. Like many who described their experiences and reactions, Madame Grandin published her account after returning to Paris, but her story was atypical, distinctive in its focus, tone, themes, and, ultimately, in the transformative discoveries she made during her stay.

The majority of European visitors who made the trip to the United States in these years were curious and relatively well-educated. They made the journey for various reasons. Some of these were obvious. They wanted to see the New World, and most restricted their travels to the East and Midwest. Niagara Falls was an obligatory stop. They also wanted to know how the energetic and optimistic Americans were transforming their spacious land and shaping their centers of population and industry. Some, like the French novelist Paul Bourget, came for more subtle reasons. He acknowledged that Europeans knew their own histories and priorities but were not well informed about developments in the United States and their implications for Western civilization. Would democracy honor art and thought above the utilitarian level? Would science destroy mystery and poetry? That Americans seemed to pay little attention to these questions was another reason, he added, why "this country is so intensely interesting to us."[1]

In 1893 the focal city of the United States was Chicago. Shortly after the Paris Exhibition of 1889 closed, observers abroad began to speculate about the coming American exhibition, initially scheduled for 1892. Some Europeans were wary; the Yankees would probably try to "lick all creation." Some suggested that an exposition sponsored by the United States could be informative. The British journal *Engineering*, for example, valuing the exposition as an important event, called for demonstrations of contemporary possibilities in engineering and architecture that would be both responsible and innovative.[2] The majority thought the choice of Chicago as the host city was fitting. No city on either side of the Atlantic appeared to be in a stronger position to summarize the astounding achievements of a marvelous century.

We do not know if foreign observers who traveled to Chicago in 1893 went primarily to see the exposition or primarily to see the city. Nor do we know if the unexpectedly conservative designs of the exposition's major buildings, first publicized abroad in the fall of 1891, encouraged or discouraged foreign attendance. What is clear, however, is that Chicago had become one of the wonder cities of the late-nineteenth century, not a wonder city like Paris, celebrated for its beauty and organization, but one of both wonder and shock, startling for its sudden appearance, perplexing transience, and daring material innovations.

Chicago did not exist when the nineteenth century began, but by 1870 it was processing more lumber, grain, and livestock and serving more railroad lines than any city in the world. By 1893 it was the globe's sixth-largest city. This rise to international prominence was first recognized abroad in 1861, when *Chamber's Journal* referred to Chicago as "something of a wonder."[3] In the next two decades the city's Herculean engineering feats were the focus of foreign attention. To ensure better drainage, downtown roadways and sidewalks were elevated four to ten feet and existing buildings were either jacked up and reset on higher supports or relocated. Europeans thought the 1871 project to protect the city's water source in Lake Michigan by reversing the direction of the Chicago River was more startling, although the attempt to make the river run uphill seemed typical of Chicago. During the 1870s the foreign press often commented on the rebuilding of the business district after the great fire of October 1871, another demonstration of Chicago's aggressive response to seemingly impossible challenges.

Toward the end of this decade European understanding of the city's modernity began to change. Statistical reports and rumors about its surging trade and population continued to circulate abroad, as did news of its innovative approaches to new problems. These statistics and feats, however, were discrete; they could be quantified and described and then judged in relationship to milestones of progress elsewhere. Alert European observers began to suggest that Chicago's development was both more significant and less measurable, that its prophetic meaning was not necessarily material. This material evidence was undeniable, but the evidence was a consequence, not the cause. Even the commercial skyscrapers of the Loop, the new symbols of the city's progress, were consequences.

European humor about Chicago was a perceptive arrow pointing to the causes of the city's astounding development. The reactions of travelers to foreign places have always differed from those of the natives. Taking nothing for granted, visitors quickly identify what is new and then try to make sense of it from their comparative advantage. Madame Grandin understood this. Foreigners may notice small, amusing details that are completely imperceptible to the locals. When confronted by assumptions, practices, and results treated as normal by a local population but which may seem strange to them, visitors often resorted to humor, a semineutral ground providing a degree of protection against charges of ignorance or naiveté. They tend to reserve this humor for what seems most striking, inexplicable, disquieting, or revolutionary. This was true of their response to Chicago in the last decades of the century. The humor was not subtle, relying on exaggerations rather than irony, but it was surprisingly cohesive.

Here are a few examples. One cannot describe the city because all adjectives were invented before it appeared. Nor can a person write a reliable history of Chicago because the account will be obsolete when completed. This point was also made in a simulated French exchange: "When were you in Chicago?" "Last week." "Oh, well! Then you know nothing about it. The city has been entirely changed since then."[4] Several visitors cautioned that joking or exaggerating could be unwise; an absurd prediction might become a reality tomorrow. A British visitor observed that there were no old people in Chicago; residents did not have time to grow old. A British artist, Frederick Villiers, fabricated when he reported that one of the hotels, instantaneously erected to make money during the exposition, was gutted by fire while he was there. "At the time the firemen were carrying charcoal out of the rear," he reported, "the upholsterers were carrying in carpets at the front." And John Kendall maintained that "it takes two people to examine a tall building in the Loop, one to look half way up and the other to finish the job."[5]

These comments are similar in two respects. First, they are tall tales. Travelers stretched to find language effective in describing this unconventional metropolis. Second, the yarns focused on one issue—Chicago's contemporary understanding and uses of time. If traveler humor is a valid indicator in pointing to what is fundamentally new, then Chicago's temporal innovations—commodification of time, emphasis on the present, demand for speed, shift from craft to quantity, and accelerated change—were central to its reputation as the "shock city" of the age.

When presuppositions differ, humor will differ. This explains why jokes about Chicago published in the newspapers of eastern and midwestern cities in the United States were unlike the humorous reactions of Europeans in these decades. Fired by lively urban rivalries, American humor was much more derisive, ridiculing Chicago's politics, crime, and boondock-like ways. American satirists focused on the city's alleged social and cultural deficiencies. Already familiar with a quicker pace and transient conditions in their own cities, they did not deride Chicago for its preoccupation with time and speed. The difference, however, was that Chicagoans had acted earlier and with greater bluntness and dramatic flair. It was in The Loop, not in central New York or Philadelphia or Boston, where Europeans realized the future would not be like the past.

Western culture was changing. Americans, and particularly citizens in Chicago, adjusted to its new temporal reality and appeared to be more comfortable with it than did Europeans. The jokes about city descriptions being outdated on publication and available adjectives being ineffective refer to the rapidity of cultural change in these years. The French economist Paul de Rousiers, who was highly influenced by Chicago, called the early 1890s "an age of quick transformations."[6] William James had pointed out in 1884 that the present becomes the past as soon as one tries to think about it. In rhythm with these insights, Chicagoans showed less respect for the past than did contemporaries abroad who held longer to the belief the past was a chest of wisdom, continuing to offer effective systems of resolution to the present. Americans were more skeptical, aware that the past often provided answers to questions no longer asked. They were more inclined to try the new instead of sticking with the old. The possibilities of the future excited them, and they took risks in the present to exploit them quickly. Acting quickly was often wasteful and destructive—projects were discontinued, lives were lost, street and sidewalk construction was constant—and negative results might have been avoided had leaders debated until guaranteed solutions could be developed. European visitors repeatedly tried to warn Chicagoans that haste really did make waste. Friedrich Dernburg, an editor for the *Berliner Tageblatt*, granted that Chicago is "a city full of splendid starts, a city of wonderful moments, but there is nothing that is finished, that produces coherence, no point that offers a full, a total satisfaction."[7] Furthermore, when these impatient, restless, optimistic Americans succeeded, they did not dote on their successes or try to protect them from the prying eyes of rivals. In an age of "quick transformations," the duration of every victory was short.

The natives also seemed to be in a perpetual hurry. That is why they had no time to grow old. Scores of visitors described the hectic streets of The Loop, especially in the evening when the huge office buildings and stores closed. Some responded angrily. Oxford-trained journalist George Washington Steevens wrote, "The truth is that nobody in this rushing, struggling tumult has any time to look after what we have long ago come to think the bare decencies of civilization."[8] For decades, Europeans had noticed the ways in which Chicagoans tried to save time. Travelers in the 1870s described signs in windows advertising "quick lunch" and "chops in a minute." Accustomed to this habit by the time of the exposition, foreign visitors would have considered the tale about carpets being installed before the embers cooled both absurd and typical.

Chicagoans who moved smartly on the street and even at lunch also applied ingenuity in saving personal time to industry. The largest-scale demonstration of this occurred at the Union Stock Yard, where the number of hogs slaughtered and packed weekly in 1892 averaged fifteen thousand a day. The stockyards were probably the most remembered "must see" stop on a Chicago trip. Although revolted by the sights, sounds, and smells of The Yards, observers eventually acknowledged that they were witnessing mechanized and systematized procedures that were transforming American industry and causing increasing alarm in Europe. The earliest realizations that Chicago was intentionally commodifying time, although that phrase was not used, appeared in this literature around 1890. As was so often true in these years, the city became a clarifier of new procedures, regardless of where they originated, whether in the United States or in Europe. As a city without a history, and thus less influenced by precedent when responding to the accelerating demands of its rich region, Chicago's responses tended to be direct and undiluted by art or grace. The stockyards and the contained Loop, the city's hyperactive and over-scaled central business district, helped many Europeans understand meanings and implications they may have missed elsewhere. Initially described as the "lightning city," then as the "city of perpetual haste," Chicago around 1890 was celebrated for increasing productivity by saving time. According to Madame Grandin, the phrase "'time is money' rings in every ear." Its early attempts to commodify time may have been the most influential "gift" Chicago gave to the twentieth century.

The tall office buildings of The Loop, many twice the height of similar architecture in London, Paris, and Berlin, became an internationally recognized symbol of Chicago in the early 1890s. Their twelve, fourteen, even twenty-one stories seemed to complement the scale and ambitions of the city. Similarly, their dramatic increase in height over two decades reflected Chicago's sudden appearance. No other local product revealed so clearly the relation between time and profits. Finally, the buildings became symbols for European observers because they knew them well, having examined them inside and out on their daily walks in The Loop.

For skyscrapers to be profitable, they had to be erected quickly. The high cost of property in the tight Loop required that a parcel of land produce rents as soon as possible. To make this happen, architects and engineers, challenging tradition, hung exterior walls on skeletons of metal instead of requiring load-bearing outer walls that took longer to construct. They also privileged simplicity over art. Consequently, large buildings in Europe often took a decade to complete, whereas those in Chicago at the time of the exposition were finished in two years. This news circulated abroad through architectural journals. Shortly after the outer walls of four floors of the Ashland Block (1891) had been completed in thirteen days, reports about it reappeared in Vienna, Berlin, Paris, and London.[9] Commodifying time led to a transformation of architecture; speed became a primary factor. The sympathetic *Chicago Tribune* called it a feat "on which would hang a vaster deal of comment and sober speculation by the greatest builders of the world than any other similar event ever known."[10]

The increasing economic importance of time could also be noticed inside the new buildings. Observers explained that designers had planned for typewriters, telephones, elevators, and other labor-saving devices, unlike counterparts abroad who were more inclined to honor the grand tradition of architecture by resisting mechanical "gadgets." Those who worked in the new environment adjusted to the clock. Jacques Hermant, a French architect and delegate to the exposition, noted the absence of courting in business deals, obligatory meetings over wine in order to know better the individual with whom one hoped to sign a contract.[11] His colleague Adolphe Bocage provided further evidence. "Now a visitor arrives; the boss greets him by pushing his hat back, and quickly, before the visitor has thought to take off his coat and sit down, a business deal is concluded," Bocage reported. "A handshake, 'All right,' are all that is needed for a contract. No trifling rules of politeness, nothing which is not strictly business." One businessman, according to Bocage, hung a sign behind his chair stating, "I have read all the newspapers this morning; I have a barometer and thermometer at home; let's talk business, and not waste time."[12]

I have stressed Chicago's sudden appearance and economic growth, its prodigious engineering feats, its destruction and rebuilding in the 1870s, and the transforming effect of its temporal priorities on The Loop and industrial production because they shaped the city's international reputation in these years. Europeans thought Chicago had become a unique and important urban phenomenon, and their statements about its significance were often expansive. British consul James Hayes Sadler called it the most prosperous city in the world. Speaking for the building professions, the *Wiener*

Bauindustrie Zeitung reported that when the United States was mentioned, everyone thought of Chicago. Italian playwright and librettist Giuseppe Giacosa contended that anyone who ignored Chicago did not understand the nineteenth century for the city had become its "ultimate expression."[13] The prolific German travel writer Ernst von Hesse-Wartegg concluded, "I have lived long enough in America and have traveled the two halves of the New World for years. I can say unhesitatingly I consider Chicago the greatest wonder of America, the Urtypus of the distinctive American essence, the most American city of this huge land, much more so than New York or Boston or Philadelphia. It is perhaps the most powerful human creation of all time."[14] He labeled the city "das Museum der Neuzeit." Others offered similarly brief summations, identifying it as the "laboratory of the future," the "schoolroom of progress," and the "forefront of absolute newness."

Madame Grandin did not pay much attention to Chicago's feats, statistics, innovations, or constant change, the dominant themes of almost every other foreign observer. How could an observant person slight a profile judged astonishing by economists, scientists, architects and engineers, the press, educators, and even non-professionals? She didn't ignore these criteria entirely. She referred to the immense scale of the city and its instinct for quick processes, concluded "saving time" was an American obsession, and she complained about injuries and deaths caused by unrealistic deadlines. Her remarks about the stockyards, although brief, were perceptive—"models of organization." She did not discuss office buildings, but she thought department stores were impressive and convenient. These themes were, however, incidental to her portrait of Chicago.

What accounts for this? The length of a visit to a land affects the experience, as well as what is shared. Madame Grandin spent ten months in Chicago; other visitors and observers, including those who published reliable and informative accounts, rarely spent more than a few weeks. When time is short, travelers focus on material that is visible rather than on the subtleties behind it, on the surface not the texture. Conforming to this pattern, visitors to Chicago wrote about buildings, parks, efficient processes, and crowds on the streets. Even their approaches were similar. They usually described what they had observed and then enriched their descriptions with facts and impressions. Often they would compare what they had described to related subjects at home, sometimes making preferential judgments. If brief visits encouraged description, they seldom produced good analysis or reliable explanations of the historical stages of contemporary forms or conditions.

Almost all commentaries on Chicago in the early 1890s were written from the outside inward, the depth of the probe determined by various factors, in-

cluding the length of time in the city, the degree of curiosity, and the skills of
the observer. By contrast, Madame Grandin worked from the inside outward,
a route that often led to material that visitors on tighter schedules tended
to ignore. With respect to architecture, for example, she wrote not about
the office buildings of The Loop but the functional effectiveness of public
school design. She did so because some of her friends were teachers who
invited her to observe and share information about the French educational
system. Likewise, her growing familiarity with rooming houses meant she
was able to write informatively about domestic life and interior decoration.
Impressed by the social mobility available to American women—"certainly
one of the American virtues I appreciate the most"—she became curious
about the profession of nursing, and that interest led to comments about
nurses and the hospital environments in which they functioned.

Her understanding of her roles as traveler and writer is another reason
that her book is distinctive. I have not found another author in this literature
more conscious of her responsibility to readers or more faithful in trying to
meet expectations. While in Chicago she tried to honor her personal criteria
for being a responsible traveler. If she discovered something unusual, she
wrote about it, which explains many subjects not found in other commentaries, for example, shoe shine stands, cigar store Indians, popcorn carts,
boat dances, and political street parades. Although contemporary readers
of this excellent translation may find these sections less informative, they
nonetheless itemize peculiarities unfamiliar to Madame Grandin's audience. Fortunately, her sense of responsibility extended to subtler and more
complicated themes as well: the relations between mothers and children,
between students and teachers, and between husbands and wives. As her
curiosity and reflection about the exchanges of daily life intensified, her
"Chicago" became increasingly clear and also increasingly distant from the
"Chicagos" of hundreds of other observers.

Finally, Madame Grandin was a distinctive observer because her engagement with the city transformed her. I am not aware that this happened to
any other European who studied Chicago in the early 1890s, including those
who struggled to find language to express their shock. Numerous professionals became excited about specific attitudes or innovations they believed
would be valuable to their respective fields, but their lives were not fundamentally altered by them. Madame Grandin's was. Although her account
is packed with information not found in the writing of other contemporary
visitors and critics, it is ultimately a coming-of-age, or, more accurately, a
coming-to-realization, story. She looked beyond the amazing material city
and found transformative meaning in its daily moments. There she made
discoveries that affirmed her instincts and redirected her life.

A Parisienne's Adventures in Chicago: Discoveries and Consequences

Mary Beth Raycraft

"An old proverb calls Paris 'the Paradise of Women!' No, Paris is hell for women of spirit, the feminine paradise is America!"[1] So wrote Marie Lédier Grandin in her final chapter of *Impressions d'une parisienne à Chicago*. After spending ten months there, observing American life, she was not at all enthusiastic about returning to Paris. Having gained an appreciation for the freedom she experienced as a woman in America, Madame Grandin was hesitant to go back to France, where she felt that certain social constraints awaited. Madame Grandin's animated chronicle *Impressions d'une parisienne à Chicago* was published by the French publishing house Flammarion following her return to Paris during the summer of 1893.[2] This lively account reveals an unusual cross-cultural journey through fin de siècle Paris, Chicago, and New York.

Madame Grandin's trip to America and extended stay in Chicago were the results of her husband's collaboration on the Columbian Fountain project for the 1893 World's Columbian Exposition.[3] In late July of 1892, the Grandins boarded the French ocean liner *La Touraine* at the port of Le Havre, and six days later they arrived at the immigration service at Ellis Island. They spent several weeks with relatives in New York and then took a train to Chicago, where they would live from August 1892 until June 1893. While her husband spent his days in the sculpture workshops, Madame Grandin explored the city and recorded her observations. Her account of her visit, *Impressions d'une parisienne à Chicago*, is distinctive in two principal ways. First, Madame Grandin's curiosity and ability to get inside Chicago's social and domestic spaces result in a travel narrative that goes beyond the usual tourist reactions and provides a valuable resource for those interested in late-nineteenth-century Chicago history. In the space of fourteen chapters, she conveys everyday details of middle-class domestic life, describes behind-the-scenes preparation for the World's Columbian Exhibition, and reacts to the impressive and disappointing aspects of the city with precision and perception. Second, this is an exceptional book, given the effect that Madame Grandin's experiences in America had on her personal life, as embedded in the text is a more intimate story of self-discovery. Madame Grandin arrived in America with certain presuppositions about American life, yet her discovery of Chicago and confrontation with American values and behavior resulted in the redirection of her life. Although she did not focus extensively on her personal growth, the decisions she made following her stay in Chicago suggest that her trip had a life-changing impact. In order to fully appreciate the distinctiveness of her travel account, one must know something of her story.

Madame Grandin's Life before Chicago

Limited biographical information is available concerning the Grandins. Records from late-nineteenth-century Parisian salon exhibitions indicate that Léon Grandin (1856–1901) was a sculptor who had studied at the prestigious École des Beaux Arts.[4] After finishing his studies, he worked in the Montparnasse workshop of an American classmate, the sculptor Frederick MacMonnies. Beginning in the 1880s, Grandin regularly submitted his work to official Parisian salons. His 1886 submission was called "Portrait of Mme. G.," which makes one wonder if it was a bust of his wife.[5] Grandin also participated in the 1889 and 1900 Universal Expositions in Paris. Over the years, he and MacMonnies enjoyed a warm friendship and professional association.[6] Given their personal and professional relationship, it seems likely that Grandin socialized with American sculptors in Montparnasse and at the artist colony of Giverny, where MacMonnies and his wife, Mary, entertained fellow artists at their home.[7]

These few details are available concerning the career of Léon Grandin, but his wife's life before and after her trip to Chicago is harder to trace. Although several recent studies refer to her text as an important example of a French woman's impressions of late-nineteenth-century American life, limited information has been published concerning her biography.[8] A circuitous path of archival research resulted in the discovery of her marriage certificate, which opened a pathway for learning more about her. According to the marriage document, Marie Élise Léonie Lédier wed Léon Grandin on November 18, 1884, in Paris. The bride and groom gave their respective ages as twenty and twenty-eight. Before their marriage, both resided just a few blocks from one another in the Montparnasse neighborhood.[9] The marriage certificate also indicates that the bride was at the time employed as an *institutrice* (elementary school teacher), suggesting that she had attained a certain level of education.[10] Their marriage contract, drawn up four days before the wedding, reveals that Marie Lédier and Léon Grandin were both from middle-class backgrounds and brought similar financial contributions to the union. He contributed 6000 French francs' worth of clothing, furniture, and sculpture materials, and she brought 1500 francs' worth of personal clothing and jewelry, along with an additional dowry of 5000 francs provided by her parents.[11]

In addition to the information provided by the archival documents, certain aspects of Marie Grandin's personality and outlook on life can be gleaned from the pages of her travel account. The title of her chronicle, *Impressions d'une parisienne à Chicago*, communicates both the personal nature of the project and the author's status.[12] By identifying herself as a Parisian woman, Madame Grandin signals that her impressions will be shaped by her experiences in the civilized French capital. In describing the layout, neighborhoods, transportation, architecture, and cultural life of Chicago, Paris is her constant point of reference and comparison, and numerous references to it show easy familiarity with Parisian homes, theaters, streets, and parks as well as her strong attachment to the city. She alludes to her home city in a wistful manner and repeatedly emphasizes its unique status. When Parisian friends visited Chicago, for example, Madame Grandin went to great lengths to prepare a traditional French meal and comments, "All four of us had fun talking about our dear city and we chatted about many topics that are only of interest to Parisians."[13]

In her preface, "To the Reader," Madame Grandin clearly explains her reasons for undertaking the trip and for putting her experiences into writing.[14] As she introduces herself, she directs her remarks not only to Parisians but also to French citizens in general. Madame Grandin opens her preface by discussing the important educational value of travel and then directly criticizes her compatriots' tendency toward cultural superiority. Not only would venturing to other lands allow them to learn about other places, she maintains, but it would also open their eyes to their own weaknesses. By drawing attention to this attitude of superiority and then subsequently distancing herself from it, Madame Grandin presents herself as an open-minded traveler. Indeed, her inclination to entertain new ideas is apparent in both superficial and profound ways in her text. Unlike other European travelers who often cringed at the thought of American cuisine, for example, Madame Grandin eagerly tasted and appreciated new foods, among them a clam at a New York clambake, popcorn in the streets of Chicago, and American-style ice cream. She also considered, in a very careful way, differences between the social and political status of women in France and America.

After stressing the importance of open-mindedness, Madame Grandin puts forth her intention to communicate her impressions with honesty and exactitude. Her direct engagement with the reader in the Preface sets the stage for an effusive presentation of her observations. An energetic narrator with a flair for the dramatic, she expresses shock, surprise, and, at times, admiration for the people, places, and customs she encounters in America. Using a breezy, at times journalistic, style, she conveys images, thoughts, and impressions as quickly as they occur to her. Her sharp observational skills bring out her lively personality as well as the personalities of the many characters who play a role in her adventure. Moreover, her fine sense of humor, infused with a strong dose of sarcasm, allows her to sketch portraits and scenes that telegraph vivid impressions of American life. In short, Madame Grandin's account lives up to its title as well as the goals set out in the Preface as it presents the spontaneous and candid responses of a young Parisian woman to her confrontation with American culture.

Although she published under the name "Madame Léon Grandin," which signaled her married status, her travel narrative is very much dominated by the subject pronoun *je* (I) instead of *nous* (we). Other married women traveling with their husbands frequently recounted their adventures as a couple.[15] Marie Grandin, however, offers but a few meager details about Léon's appearance, habits, and preferences, such as his inability to sleep during the transatlantic crossing, his dismay with the attitude of American servants, and his dislike of boardinghouse food. In a suggestive comment presented in the very first chapter, she describes her feelings as she begins the voyage: "I had the illusion of crossing the ocean alone in search of the unknown."[16] The remark prefigures her relatively independent life in Chicago. While Léon Grandin was busy supervising the installation of the massive Columbian Fountain, Marie Grandin was free to circulate throughout the city. The fact that she was alone most of the day gave her a certain freedom of movement as well as the flexibility to pursue friendships and social activities. Not surprisingly, some of her most vividly recounted adventures were those that she experienced on her own, not in the company of her husband.

At the same time, however, Marie Grandin repeatedly identifies herself as a traditional Parisian bourgeois housewife. At numerous points in the text, she refers to herself and her husband as members of *la bonne bourgeoisie*, an indication substantiated by their marriage contract and dowry information. This label not only suggests their financial circumstance but also links her to the traditional image of the French bourgeois housewife known as the *maîtresse de maison* (mistress of the house). Marie Grandin expresses admiration for the French *maitresse de maison,* and allusions to her own domestic activities, including needlework, grocery shopping, and the preparation of elegant yet thrifty meals, suggest her identification with this model. Given that she was so imbued with French bourgeois traditions, she was exceptionally capable of commenting on American domestic habits. Throughout the narrative, she fervently puts forth the superiority of the French bourgeois housewife and presents herself as a woman who has thoroughly mastered the lessons of this tradition.

If no other clues existed, one would surmise that Marie Grandin's life as a sculptor's wife and teacher would have resumed in Montparnasse after her return from Chicago. A small, handwritten notation on her birth certificate, however, indicates that her story took an unexpected turn after she went back to France in June 1893. The brief note scribbled by the local mayor on the birth certificate not only reveals that her marriage to Léon Grandin faltered within a few years but also provides telling information about the new life story she constructed following her return from Chicago. To begin to understand the effect of her American experience, it is helpful to situate Madame Grandin's account in the context of other French travelers' narratives, particularly those written by women who visited Chicago in the late nineteenth and early twentieth centuries.

Nineteenth-Century French Travel Accounts

Throughout the nineteenth century, an increasingly large and diverse group of French travelers made their way to America.[17] The United States was a particularly attractive destination for French visitors. The early political alliance of the two nations during their respective revolutions sparked a sense of mutual respect and curiosity. In the late eighteenth century, numerous French writers produced books on political, social, and geographical aspects that revealed interest as well as skepticism toward America.[18] Nineteenth-century French visitors were interested in a wide range of topics, including the U.S. penal system, slavery, the situation of Native Americans, and religion. Among the most well-known nineteenth-century French travelers to America were the political and social anthropologist Alexis de Tocqueville, the gastronome Brillat-Savarin, the painter Edgar Degas, the composer Jacques Offenbach, the actress Sarah Bernhardt, and the novelist Paul Bourget. In addition to these more famous visitors, there were scores of other French men and women, including gold-rush enthusiasts, antislavery activists, teachers, naturalists, architects, and engineers.

Madame Grandin was one of many who offered impressions of America to a receptive readership during the nineteenth and early twentieth centuries. *"Voyageons!"*—her enthusiastic appeal to compatriots in the early pages of her account—conveyed the excitement surrounding travel in nineteenth-century France. She encouraged her fellow French citizens to join her in "running from north to south and east to west, accumulating useful documentation, recording the sights, and enriching our minds with new ideas concerning others and ourselves."[19] Many in her generation embraced her enthusiasm. A new faith in historical research encouraged travelers to share impressions, itineraries, images, maps, and charts documenting their adventures. Some used their travel accounts to put forth specific agendas, whereas others offered general observations on a wide range of topics. These travel narratives took a variety of forms, including essays, letters, journals, and fictionalized accounts. One of the most frequently cited early French travelers was François René de Chateaubriand. Following his visit to America in 1791, he wrote three fictional works in which the characters leave France and civilized society for the wilderness and natural grandeur of the New World.[20] His dramatic depictions of nature in America, including Niagara Falls, were eagerly devoured by French readers, including Madame Grandin, who praised his descriptive technique.[21]

Chateaubriand's fictional depiction of American life was in stark contrast to the scholarly analysis undertaken by early-nineteenth-century French writers. Alexis de Tocqueville, a young lawyer and royalist dissatisfied with the newly inaugurated July Monarchy of Louis-Philippe, distanced himself from the regime by spending nine months traveling in America in 1831 and 1832.[22] Along with his friend and colleague Gustave de Beaumont, he obtained a mission from the French government to study the American penal system. After submitting his report, he went on to publish his political observations and social analysis in the two-volume study *Democracy in America*, which appeared in two parts in 1835 and 1840.[23] Tocqueville examined American democracy in action and was one of the first French visitors to carefully observe and comment on the manners and morals of the young society.[24]

French travelers to America throughout the nineteenth century continued to elaborate on the topics that Tocqueville presented. Both male and female French observers brought up the subjects that they found most striking, namely issues of race, class, and gender.[25] The French noted the growing political tension surrounding the issue of slavery in the years preceding the Civil War.[26] They were also intrigued by the situation of Native Americans, who had long exerted an exotic fascination over Europeans.[27] In terms of social class, French as well as other European visitors were disappointed by American manners and complained bitterly about the impertinence of servants.[28] As French visitors observed domestic and social spheres, toured cities, and inspected cultural and educational institutions, they were sensitive to differences between French and American priorities, habits, and conventions.

A dramatic surge in the number of French accounts focusing on America occurred in the latter part of the nineteenth century and the early years of the twentieth century. Approximately five hundred books and articles, ranging from scholarly studies to travelogues, were published between 1870 and 1914.[29] Several factors contributed to the sharp rise in the number of French accounts. The stable diplomatic relationship between France and United States in the late nineteenth and early twentieth centuries favored transatlantic tourism and cultural exchange in both directions.[30] Steam power greatly facilitated both transatlantic crossings and rail travel, and the well-developed American railroad network allowed tourists to explore the East Coast cities of Boston, New York, Philadelphia, and Washington, D.C. Trains also linked the East Coast to the West via Chicago, and a growing number of travelers included midwestern and western cities on their itinerary. The world's fairs held in Philadelphia in 1876 and Chicago in 1893 drew many French visitors as both participants and observers and marked important moments for cultural exchange. French visitors came to see the "New World" and measure their cities, customs, and culture against the people and places they encountered.

Late-nineteenth-century French visitors were particularly interested in American politics. The United States had recently experienced a devastating war to end slavery and was beginning to grapple with the issue of integrating black Americans into society. France had definitively abolished slavery in 1848, and mid- and late-nineteenth-century travelers were interested in how Americans would attempt to resolve this difficult problem. Education and women's rights also caught their attention. In France, the passage of legislation in the 1880s—the Ferry laws—resulted in free, compulsory primary schooling for both girls and boys.[31] As they toured American schools and universities, French visitors often considered and commented on the changing education situation in France, particularly the impact of the Ferry laws.[32] In addition, the women's rights movement in America had sparked interest in France, and curious observers came to document the various types of American women—the miss, the flirt, the wife, and the mother—and their behavior.[33] In short, the commentary of French visitors on slavery, education, and the women's situation both responded to and engaged in the larger discussion of these issues in France at the time.

No single moment in the nineteenth century attracted more French visitors than the World's Columbian Exposition in Chicago in 1893. The publication of French accounts on America also peaked during that time.[34] Once the fair opened in May 1893, a steady stream of artists, writers, architects, engineers, and tourists made sure that a stop in Chicago was part of their itinerary. The attraction was twofold: visitors wanted to see Chicago and experience the exposition.

Several aspects of the city surprised the French visitors who arrived in Chicago in 1892 and 1893. Among them were its scale (five times the size of Paris); its activity, most of which was generated by business; its feverish pace; and its concentrated Loop, where there were huge crowds and towering buildings. Clearly, Chicago had recovered from its devastating fire of 1871. Following the fire, which destroyed the business district, the city center had been completely rebuilt using fireproof materials, essentially steel and brick construction. The reconstruction constituted almost a complete transformation that was particularly striking to Parisian visitors because their city had been heavily damaged and burned during the 1870–71 political uprising of the Paris Commune.[35] While Paris in the 1890s still showed vestiges of damage, Chicago seemed to have erased almost all traces of the fire. Furthermore, taller and taller buildings were constantly opening. Most of the city's celebrated nineteenth-century skyscrapers, The Rookery, Auditorium, and Masonic Temple, were completed between 1886 and 1894. Edmund Bruwaert, the French consul posted in Chicago in the early 1890s, went so far as to predict that "the most beautiful exhibition will be Chicago itself, its citizens, its business, its institutions, its progress."[36]

French visitors were also fascinated by the commercial significance of the city as evidenced by tall buildings, the concentration of business activity in The Loop, and the restlessness and vigor of the inhabitants. Some visitors, including the novelist Paul Bourget, felt that the Union Stock Yard, with its display of the latest innovations in meat processing, better conveyed a sense of American progress than did the fair.[37] Many French visitors also headed to Pullman City, just south of Jackson Park, to see an authentic company town. The visitors considered these industrial innovations, as well as the commercial energy of the city, as indicative of true American values and progress. Georges Sauvin, an enthusiastic French traveler who in 1893 went from coast to coast, discovering major American cities, concluded that Chicago was "the true American city" and the place where American genius finds greatest expression.[38]

Although many discovered evidence for their generalizations about the United States in the scale, rawness, and bustle of central Chicago, a few travelers detected American tendencies in the classical architecture and spatial organization of the exposition. The aristocratic Count de Soissons, for example, author of A *Parisian in America*, commented that "a person who was never in America could, by visiting the Columbian World's Fair, have an almost perfect idea of what this country is; what are its tendencies, aspirations, tastes, customs, polish and culture."[39] He detected the influence of seemingly paradoxical American values in the size, decoration, and commercial aspects of the fair. Soissons was impressed by the colossal expanse of the exhibition but disappointed in the architecture, noting that the buildings were nothing but "clever imitations or combinations of former styles."[40] He also criticized what he viewed as the overly commercial aspects of the displays and amusements, lamenting the American tendency to put profit before taste.[41]

Given that the Exposition Universelle in Paris in 1889 had been so successful, French visitors were eager to see how Chicago would respond. Both the scale and organization of the event were vastly different from that in Paris.[42] While the 1889 exposition in Paris was constructed in the middle of the city, Chicago's exposition was located miles from the city's center— The Loop. At the close of the fair, the buildings of Jackson Park were dismantled or destroyed by fire, with the exception of the Fine Arts Pavilion. The "White City" of Jackson Park, constructed from the ground up in the space of just two years, far surpassed the Paris fair in terms of size. French visitors described it as "colossal," gigantic," "dazzling," and "immense" and were taken aback by the ability of Americans to transform the landscape so quickly and extensively. More conservative French observers, including nonprofessional travelers, older visitors, and literary people, gushed that the White City seemed to be an urban fantasy, its crisp, neo-classical buildings set apart from everyday commercial life. Younger observers, especially those from business, architecture, and engineering, were more pragmatic and tended to be disappointed that the exposition had only updated history. Many of these critical observers suspected that Americans, concerned about being labeled materialists, wanted to demonstrate that they could also be cultured. Those who were disappointed often regretted that the exposition was stylistically retrograde rather than trying to make a new architectural-engineering-technological statement as Paris had done in the use of new materials—iron and steel—in 1889.

Although European critics did not find the architecture to be groundbreaking, several other aspects of the fair were noteworthy, including the manufacturing displays and the Woman's Building. In terms of the exposition as a milestone of progress, visitors seemed to acknowledge the manufactur-

ing power of the United States. The impressive exhibits in the manufacturing, mining, electricity, transportation, and machinery buildings emphasized
American innovation and development in those areas. Also, for the first time
in the history of the world's fair, there was a Woman's Building, which was
overseen by a board of "lady managers" representing all the American states
and participating foreign nations. Prominent women in Chicago, led by Bertha Palmer, wife of Chicago hotel magnate Potter Palmer, played a considerable role in the establishment of the Woman's Building.[43] Designed by the
architect Sophia Hayden, the Italian renaissance-style structure provided
exhibition space for works created wholly by women, including a mural by
the American painter Mary Cassatt entitled "Modern Woman."[44] The building also housed a library filled with books written by and about women and
served as the meeting place for the Congress of Women, where hundreds of
lectures and discussions were held during the fair, including presentations by
suffragists Julia Ward Howe, Susan B. Anthony, and Elizabeth Cady Stanton.[45]
For Madame Grandin, the Woman's Building was a particularly meaningful
and original contribution to the Columbian Exposition, and she enthusiastically praised both the exhibits and the schedule of lectures and activities.[46]

Although intrigued by certain buildings and displays, French visitors found
the expanse and large number of exhibits overwhelming. In contrast to the
symmetrical layout of the 1889 fair, many felt disoriented at the Chicago
Exposition because it seemed to sprawl in illogical and unexpected ways.[47]
In agreement with visitors from other European nations, French observers
tended to be more positive about the major buildings clustered around the
Central Basin than they were about the Midway Plaisance, where exotic attractions replaced the serious tone of the principal exhibitions. Leaving the
elegant and organized palaces of the exposition, they joined throngs who
moved from one curious display to another. Exotic entertainments, including
the "Streets of Cairo" with shops and a mosque, a magic booth manned by
the young Harry Houdini, and various bazaars and theaters including a North
African belly dancing show, lined the mile-long Midway Plaisance and gave
visitors a chance to indulge in different kinds of culture.[48] The newly invented
Ferris wheel made its debut and occupied a central location on the Midway
Plaisance, and most French visitors, including Madame Grandin, criticized
the monumental wheel as a failed attempt to upstage the Eiffel Tower of the
Paris 1889 exhibition.[49] Capable of holding two thousand passengers at a time,
the enormous structure was the centerpiece of the Midway Plaisance.

Chicago's reputation as a "wonder city," a place where one could discover
fragments of the future in the bustling present, was already acknowledged

in Europe by 1890. The exposition, then, was an added reason for French travelers to cross the Atlantic and then the vast spaces of the new continent to see a city that seemed to have more to do with the century to come than with the nineteenth. If these visitors expected the exposition to confirm the tall tales they had heard about the city, however, they were disappointed. The city center was all business, a product shaped by an accelerating demand over which its citizens had little control; they could only respond to the dynamic economic boom that transformed the Midwest in these years. The heart of the exposition, however, was an ideal expression—an ancient city in modern times. If Chicago's center seemed contemporary, vital, and raw, its exposition seemed to honor the past through architectural and spatial poetry. If French visitors were confused in their attempts to find the real America here, they had reason to be.

French Women Travelers' Accounts of Chicago

Before examining the Chicago that Madame Grandin discovered, a survey of the reactions of other French women who visited the city during the late nineteenth and early twentieth centuries will provide important context for her impressions. Reading their accounts highlights the particular aspects of America—specifically, Chicago—that attracted their attention. Nine French women travelers besides Madame Grandin who visited Chicago during the late nineteenth and early twentieth centuries also wrote informative commentaries about the city.[50] Their narratives cover the thirty-seven-year period between 1869 and 1906. For most of these women, Chicago was a brief stop on an extensive American tour, and their stay usually lasted less than three weeks. The accounts vary in length as well, from a few paragraphs to full-length book chapters. Given the fact that none of the women spent more than a few weeks in Chicago, it is not surprising that their generalizations, based on their particular experiences, speak to the necessity of summing up the city and its inhabitants based on brief encounters. The specific details that caught their eye accentuate the most striking aspects of the city and its inhabitants to French women of this generation.[51]

The women found Chicago to be distinctive from other American cities in several ways. They were astounded by its sprawling development, its impressive commercial and residential architecture, and its fast pace. Intrigued by the diversity of its inhabitants, they filled their accounts with descriptions of people they encountered, including African American shoe-shine boys, German immigrants, and various types of American women. Descriptions of the energy, youthfulness, and dynamism of Chicago abound, as the women presented a portrait of a lively city in which restless inhabitants seemed in constant motion.

In contrast to Madame Grandin, who was married when she lived in Chicago, most of the other French women traveled independently. Several had already achieved a certain professional status before their trip and arrived in America with a specific purpose. For all of these women, Chicago was a brief stop on an American tour that took them to numerous states and regions. Between 1869 and 1889, the writer and women's rights activist Olympe Audouard (1830–90), the inspector general for nursery school education Marie Loizillon (1820–1907), the actress Sarah Bernhardt (1844–1923), and Louise Bourbonnaud, a veteran traveler, all visited Chicago briefly. Among the many French women who attended the exposition in 1893, Marie Dugard (1862–1931) and Marie-Thérèse Blanc (1840–1907) published two of the more important reactions to the United States in the 1890s. Dugard was a high school teacher at the Lycée Molière in Paris and an official member of the French delegation to the fair. Blanc, an established journalist and novelist who published under the androgynous pen name Th. Bentzon, included Chicago on her American itinerary, which was devoted to an analysis of women's situations there. Around the turn of the century, accounts by Jeanne Goussard de Mayolle, Thérèse Batbedat, and Thérèse Vianzone were among the more significant publications by women. Goussard de Mayolle, accompanying her husband on a mining expedition to Colorado and New Mexico, made a brief stop in Chicago en route west. Batbedat, a translator and historian interested in Native Americans, stopped there on her way to a year-long stay in Seattle. In the early twentieth century, Vianzone, a lecturer sponsored by the Alliance Française who spent several months in Philadelphia, traveled to Chicago to present two lectures on French literature. Although their accounts are distinctive in terms of the timing, length, and purpose of visit, all these French women travelers expressed a degree of surprise at their first encounter with the city. Exactly what surprised them, and why, seemed related to the timing and purpose of their visit.

For Olympe Audouard, who described her impressions in À travers l'Amérique: North America, États-Unis: mœurs, usages, institutions, sectes religieuses (1871), the cross-country trip offered an opportunity to see American women firsthand.[52] A journalist and novelist, Audouard had been very active in the women's rights movement in France, and her immediate motivation for coming to the United States was to escape a difficult situation at home. In 1862, Emperor Napoleon III's imperial government objected to the political ideas she presented in her newly established literary/political journal *La Revue Cosmopolite*. She subsequently decided to go abroad, initially to Russia, Egypt, and Turkey, and, finally, to the United States, where she spent thirteen months traveling and observing society.[53] In all her travel accounts, Audouard explicitly used descriptions of the situation of women in other countries to criticize the laws governing marriage and divorce in France. In America, Audouard was especially interested in the burgeoning woman suffrage movement and in the educational and professional opportunities available to women.[54]

The population of the city was still small at the time of Audouard's visit in the late 1860s, but she was impressed by Chicago's commercial importance. By 1871, the city was served by more railroad lines than any other city in Europe or America and led in the volume of timber, grain, and livestock processed. She was also surprised by the possibilities for social mobility for those willing to work, including recently arrived German immigrants.[55] Admiring Chicago's railway system, commercial architecture, and factories, Audouard firmly stated that anyone interested in doing business or finding work should head straight to Chicago. Although Audouard did not explicitly describe women in Chicago, she did note that women occupied important positions at American universities, including a young woman professor who held a chair in Greek at an institution of higher learning in Chicago.[56]

While Audouard focused on the women's situation, Marie Loizillon, inspector general of nursery schools in France, toured the United States with the task of documenting what was happening in the field of education.[57] Her official mission in the early 1880s took her to nursery and elementary schools, high schools, colleges, and professional schools in Boston, New York, Philadelphia, Washington, D.C., Cincinnati, Chicago, and St. Louis. She subsequently wrote a report for the minister of public instruction that was published in 1883 under the title *L'éducation des enfants aux États-Unis*.[58] While the well-established Boston schools were judged superior to all others in many respects, Loizillon noted that Chicago schools were full of life and movement.[59] That characteristic, she explained, was related to Chicago's rapid growth and diverse population, which by the 1880s included representatives of all European nationalities.[60] Although Chicago's rapid growth during that time had prevented the construction of a sufficient number of schools to meet the demand of the population, Loizillon was impressed with the ability of the city to recruit competent teachers and provide services to students.[61]

Unlike Audouard and Loizillon, who were busy collecting information and statistics in cities across America, Sarah Bernhardt stopped in Chicago during her first American theatrical tour in January 1881 and presented a repertoire that included the French classics *Camille* and *Phèdre*. Bernhardt later published her impressions in her memoir *My Double Life*.[62] During her successful two-week run at McVicker's Theater, she stayed in a luxurious suite "filled with the rarest of flowers" at the Palmer House Hotel, where she was personally welcomed by Potter Palmer. Bernhardt claimed that she loved everything about Chicago, "its people, its lake and its enthusiastic audiences," and wrote that she "found these two weeks the most pleasant ones since we had arrived in America." In her free time, she explored the city and even visited Union Stock Yard, which she described as "a horrible yet magnificent spectacle!" As she wandered the city, Bernhardt was most struck by the "constant hustle and bustle of men." She also noticed an unusual characteristic of Chicago's women that would be echoed by later French women visitors: "they do not stroll down the street as they do in other cities, they walk quickly. They are also in a hurry, in a hurry to amuse themselves."[63]

Louise Bourbonnaud arrived in Chicago in 1888 in the middle of a rainstorm, and as a result she spent most of her time in the train station. An experienced world traveler and member of the French Geographical Society, Bourbonnaud stopped briefly in Chicago as part of her tour of North and South America. She spent just fourteen hours in the city, arriving in the morning from Niagara Falls and departing in the evening for San Francisco. In her account *Les Amériques*, the patriotic French widow devoted just a few paragraphs to the city.[64] Because Bourbonnaud arrived at one train station and left from another, she traversed the city in a carriage, and her comments were entirely based on what she saw while crossing the city and while waiting in the railway station. She expressed displeasure with the food at the station buffet as well as disgust with African American servers. Although Bourbonnaud described the city as "beautiful," the only aspects of Chicago that she specifically admired were its tall buildings and its refreshing beer.[65] Bourbonnaud remained very much a foreign outsider throughout her stay in the United States but relied on her authority as an experienced traveler to criticize American customs and proclaim the superiority of the French way of life.[66]

In contrast to the accounts of Audouard, Loizillon, Bernhardt, and Bourbonnaud, which are brief and communicate first impressions and snap judgments, Dugard and Blanc presented more subtle and detailed descriptions of Chicago because they each spent several weeks there during the World's Columbian Exposition. Dugard and Blanc, official visitors, arrived armed with letters of introduction that gave them an opportunity to meet and interact with prominent Chicagoans and visit cultural, social, and charitable institutions, including the Art Institute, Jane Addams's Hull House, women's clubs, and, of course, the Columbian Exposition.

Dugard's account of her visit to America, *La société américaine, mœurs et caractère, la famille, rôle de la femme, écoles et universités*, was published in 1896.[67] During the six months that she spent traveling across the country in 1893, her primary focus was education. In her twenty-five-page chapter "Chicago," Dugard used a journalistic style and organization, dating each entry and frequently conveying her reactions with fragmented sentences and exclamations. Dugard repeatedly emphasized the unexpected contradictions of the city. She saw dramatic contrasts everywhere she looked, including ones involving the weather, the streets, the hotels, the fair, and even the inhabitants. After her first day in the city, she was overwhelmed by the tumultuous crowds that rushed along the avenues and described the city as "something that is at once immense and unfinished." Even after a few days, she continued to emphasize the incongruous nature of what she saw in Chicago's streets and summed up her impressions by stating that "this city is strange."[68] Dugard stayed in a hotel overlooking Lake Michigan and, like many other travelers, used what she observed there as a basis for understanding American social life. She was most surprised by the contrast between elegantly dressed hotel guests and insolent servants who seemed to be preoccupied with everything except their work.[69] Echoing earlier British and European visitors to America, Dugard was taken aback by the absence of a true servant class. Her conversations with Americans, however, led her to discover that hotel employees were not necessarily uneducated; American college students, she learned, often accepted work in hotels and restaurants in order to finance their studies.[70]

As an official delegate, Dugard was invited to a number of social events, including a reception at the Art Institute and participated in what she called the "cosmopolitan whirlwind" of Chicago.[71] At the Congress for Secondary Education, which took place during the exposition at the new building on Michigan Avenue that would later become the Art Institute, Dugard attended meetings and gave a presentation on the value of artistic study at the high school level.[72] Although she was disappointed at the lack of rigor in the presentations at the congress, the large number of women participants and the important role that they played surprised and impressed her.[73] At the fairgrounds, Dugard appeared to be more interested in observing the crowds than the exhibits. Cataloging the different races and social types in the crowds, she was intrigued by the behavior of women of Chicago, noting that in spite of their sometimes poor taste in fashion they seemed to have the same energy and force as men. Although American women seemed to be behind the times in some superficial ways such as fashion and manners, she found them to be ahead in terms of educational opportunities and professional achievements.

Blanc arrived in Chicago in the fall of 1893, just in time to see the fair before it closed on October 31. A journalist, novelist, translator, and literary critic, she had published translations and reviews of American literature in the *Revue des Deux Mondes* for two decades and achieved recognition in French circles as a writer when she embarked on her first visit to America in 1893–94.[74] Blanc traveled in America for several months and published a series of five articles in the *Revue des Deux Mondes* between July 1894 and August 1895 under the title *"La condition de la femme aux États-Unis."* These articles were collected and published in book form in 1895 as *Notes de voyage: Les Américaines chez elles* and translated into English and published as *The Condition of Woman in the United States* in 1895.[75] In the preface to her account, Blanc justified her timely study by pointing out that at the time of her visit, woman suffrage was on the political agenda in several American states.[76] She also expressed a desire to correct the stereotypes concerning American women that had been put forward by certain male French writers.[77] Blanc's curiosity about the condition of American women drew her to settings in which women gathered, including the Woman's Building at the fair, and women's clubs and charitable organizations. Describing the Woman's Building, Blanc expressed disappointment with its architectural design and the quality of many exhibits but emphasized the importance of women's role and involvement at the fair.[78]

Although Blanc found the fair interesting on several levels, it was the city, its institutions, and economic and social energy, that most intrigued her: "I must confess that I saw nothing at the Chicago Exhibition so curious as Chicago itself."[79] Blanc had contacts that allowed her entry into two of Chicago's women's clubs, the Fortnightly, which was a literary club, and the Woman's Club, which had a philanthropic mission.[80] In her descriptions of the discussions and social rituals of these clubs, Blanc admired the members' enthusiasm for both cultural and charitable activities. She also toured Hull-House Settlement, an innovative civic project that had been established in September 1889 by the social activist Jane Addams.[81] Located in a former residence on South Halsted Street, Hull-House provided humanitarian and civic services to immigrants, and during her visit, Blanc met with a group of young working women and learned about programs and services offered to them. After speaking with numerous women leaders in Chicago, Blanc lauded their professional accomplishments, educational achievements, and energy in what at first glance appeared to be such a masculine domain. At the end of her chapter, Blanc concluded, "I have said that Chicago combines all sorts of contrasts; but nothing is more unexpected than the dominion of women in that great centre of vigorous manhood."[82]

Later accounts of visits to Chicago by French women echo the remarks of Dugard and Blanc regarding the unusual and dynamic nature of the city. Goussard de Mayolle stopped briefly in the city with her husband in the late 1890s. In her account *Une française chez les sauvages* (1897), she described her surprise at the immense sprawl of the city and compared it to a supernatural creature with gigantic arms.[83] Batbedat, a published translator, came to Chicago in October 1901 and was pleasantly surprised to find that the city was not nearly as filthy as she had anticipated. She was on her way west to Seattle to spend a year conducting research on Native American tribes.[84] Her travel account, *Impressions d'une parisienne sur la côte du Pacifique* (1902), included a chapter on Chicago, which she called "a magnificent city" with a kind of "noisy gaiety." Batbedat was especially impressed with "business buildings," including The Rookery and the Rand McNally Building. She also greatly admired The Auditorium, noting that it alone communicated the grandiose architecture of the city.[85] Lodging at the Auditorium Hotel, she appreciated its modern comforts, including an electric button that could be used to summon African American or Chinese servants.[86] Batbedat took advantage of her brief stay to visit a nursing school and enthusiastically spoke of the educational and professional opportunities available to American women.[87]

When Vianzone, a protégée of Blanc, arrived in Chicago during her American tour in March 1904, she immediately sensed that everything in the city was on a grand scale, including the weather, which welcomed her with thunder and lightning. In her account, *Impressions d'une française en Amérique* (1906), Vianzone called Chicago "an extraordinary city that deserves to be known."[88] During her stay, Vianzone presented two lectures on French literature, one at the Auditorium Building, where she was staying, and another at a university, presumably the University of Chicago. She also enjoyed shopping at the Marshall Field Department Store, which she found far superior to its Parisian counterparts.[89] Vianzone was struck by the hectic pace of the city and claimed that there were no strollers; both women and men seemed to literally run to their jobs.[90] In her final comparison, she described the city as an enormous child who had grown up too quickly.[91]

In these descriptions taken from French women travelers' accounts, Chicago emerges as a commercial center, a sprawling metropolis, and an overwhelming city of towering buildings and unfinished details where both men and women hustled through the streets. French women's perceptions of incongruous contrasts in the streets, crowds, and social settings suggest their attempts to make sense of life in this city that was so different from late-nineteenth and early-twentieth-century Paris. At the same time, their observations communicate the precise aspects that were most interesting to them, including a sense of what everyday life was like for American women. Admiring the fact that Chicago was a place where females had opportunity to study at universities and professional schools and could find work in offices, hospitals, and educational institutions, the visitors repeatedly emphasized the energy and progressive nature of its women.

Madame Grandin's Chicago

Madame Grandin resided in Chicago for ten months, an extended period that makes her perspective different from that of a tourist passing through Chicago for a short period. Although she discussed many of the same themes as other French women travelers, she presented a more complex view of the city and its inhabitants, uncovering details that few tourists noticed. She had a tendency to notice "small details imperceptible to native people."[92] Her commentary on certain issues, including gender relations and social and racial tensions, echoed the reactions of other French women travelers, but her approach was more subtle. She went beyond first impressions and quick generalizations to explore more complicated themes, including behavioral codes of gentility and respectability and relationships between husbands and wives, mothers and daughters, and teachers and students.

Although Madame Grandin visited many of the same places as other French travelers—hotels, department stores, the fair, and the stockyards—her lengthy residence and natural curiosity eventually led her to enter a number of salons, ballrooms, and schools, where she began to experience her own "Chicago" rather than that depicted in tourist guides for visitors to the Columbian Exposition. She often went behind the scenes, sometimes going so far as to push open doors. In some instances, thanks to her persistence, she saw a different Chicago from the one described by other French visitors. Writing about the fair, for example, she noted that "I literally watched the Exposition site come to life."[93] Her inquisitive nature made her hesitant to accept anything at face value, and she repeatedly made efforts to go beyond appearances and first impressions in order to learn the real story.

Unlike other French women travelers who chose to stay in hotels, the Grandins rented rooms in three boardinghouses on the south side of the city, an easy tram ride from the exposition grounds. Instead of limiting herself to "*la société élégante*," Madame Grandin explained that a boardinghouse offered the best opportunity to meet a wide range of people and gain true understanding of the intimate details of the American way of life: "Most of the other boarders were of modest means, some better off than others. I made a point of getting to know each one and learning all that I could from them about American life. I entered into the most intimate details of this American existence which is so different from ours and in this milieu I learned a thousand details about American life that I never would have, had I confined myself to elegant society."[94] In each boardinghouse, Madame Grandin carefully documented the familial and economic situation of inhabitants and described daily rituals, meals, and interactions among boarders. The varied group brought together under one roof supplied her with colorful although limited evidence of gender roles, social conventions, and traditions.

Mapping the neighborhoods and places in Chicago frequented by Madame Grandin is helpful in terms of visualizing her movements throughout the city (map 1). All of her lodgings were located within a fairly circumscribed area near Lake Michigan, south of The Loop and north of Jackson Park. The first boardinghouse, which had a view of Lake Michigan, was at 3700 South Ellis Avenue. In search of more comfortable accommodations and better food, the Grandins moved to another rooming house near Drexel Boulevard, which Madame Grandin compared to the elegant Avenue des Champs Elysées. Seeking more independence and privacy, the couple subsequently found lodging with kitchen privileges on 44th Street, near Wabash Avenue. Then, fatigued as a result of a near fatal gas accident, they followed the American example and spent the last part of their stay in the residential Everett Hotel at 3619 Lake Park Drive, where Madame Grandin was relieved of all household tasks and filled much of her time observing and socializing with the other tenants.

When she arrived in Chicago in August of 1892, a grueling heat wave was under way that would be followed by a severe winter and a rainy spring. Despite Chicago's weather, which European travelers often called extreme, Madame Grandin went for daily walks. One of her favorite spots was Lake Michigan, where throughout the seasons she watched its transformation during boating races, summer dances, and ice skating parties. Strolling along Drexel Boulevard or in Lincoln or Washington Park, she explored and admired the lush, green spaces of the city. Not content to restrict her research to certain neighborhoods, she made several excursions via train to Oak Woods Cemetery, Calumet Lake, Pullman City, and the Union Stock Yard, as well as to Milwaukee to witness the great fire of 1892.

Although she enjoyed strolling in the parks and on the boulevards, Madame Grandin was especially drawn to The Loop, the cultural and commercial center of Chicago (map 2). The throbbing heart of the city, approximately a square kilometer, was the focus of many of her expeditions—visits to The Athenaeum, the offices of the Woman's Building for the fair, the Chicago Public Library, and The Auditorium. An open tram car shuttled between The Loop and Jackson Park in twelve minutes, making it easy to go back and forth.[95]

The Athenaeum Building on Van Buren Street played an important role in Chicago's cultural scene, housing classrooms, offices, and studios as well as the growing collection of the Art Institute of Chicago. Madame Grandin frequented The Athenaeum regularly, visiting artists in their studios and attending lectures. In order to verify information about Chicago, she went to the public library, which was temporarily located on the fourth floor of City Hall at Lasalle and Washington streets. Her first meeting with Bertha Palmer, the driving force behind the Woman's Building at the fair, took place at the headquarters of the board of lady managers at Adams Street and Michigan Avenue.

The Auditorium Building, which attracted much attention during the fair for its stunning architecture and multifunction design, was also on her itinerary.[96] Not only did Madame Grandin admire The Auditorium from the outside but she also attended events within, joining, for example, distinguished foreign visitors at the exposition's inaugural ball in October 1892. The bustling commercial center of The Loop also offered shopping at the department stores of Marshall Field and Siegel and Company, whose complex architectural layouts impressed Madame Grandin. A stop at Gunther's Confectionery on State Street allowed her to indulge in the delicious American sweets that she found superior to Parisian confections and to chat with the colorful proprietor.

As she circulated throughout the city, Madame Grandin communicated the details of everyday life. She recounted her impressions in chronological order, and her approach was anecdotal. The digressive style of the narrative demonstrates her spontaneity as she attempted to comprehend and communicate aspects of American life as quickly as the details presented themselves. Peering into homes, classrooms, ballrooms, and club meetings, she commented on any aspect that caught her eye, including digressions on the habit of tobacco chewing and the use of the spittoon. This tendency is also evident on a stylistic level; she uses single-sentence paragraphs and prose peppered with semicolons, dashes, question marks, and exclamation points. The chapter titles echo this approach as well; each presents a long list of people, places, and situations encountered over the course of a specific period, with no attempt at thematic organization. Moreover, many of Madame Grandin's chapters end rather abruptly with no logical transition between them as she strings adventures together chronologically and leaves the reader to draw conclusions.

Madame Grandin uses several other stylistic techniques to engage readers, and in doing so she also renders the experience of everyday life more palpable. For example, she subtly encourages readers to become active companions on her strolls, shopping expeditions, and visits to the fair by using very systematic descriptions. When describing boardinghouses, schools, The Athenaeum, and the Woman's Building, she meticulously details floor plans and spatial arrangements, bringing readers into the text and connecting them intimately with the spaces of late-nineteenth-century Chicago. At times, her memory of events is so vivid that she switches to present tense, thus transporting readers into the immediacy of the moment. She also incorporates dialogue as a way of bringing certain scenes to life; by reenacting conversations with a diverse group of characters she allows readers to hear the voices of her acquaintances. Similarly, she often anticipates her French reader's response, prefacing an explanation with "Don't even imagine that in Chicago." In addition, the frequent use of questions in the text allows her to establish an ongoing dialog with the reader.

As Madame Grandin developed familiarity with her new city she became acquainted with an increasing number of Chicagoans. Instead of describing well-known public figures, she offers the first names or initials of the many men, women, and children she encountered. In this way, she is able to connect marital, familial, and social behavior with individuals, creating a more personalized association for the reader. She developed, for example, close friendships with three married couples and carefully described the interactions between these husbands and wives as well as the daily activities and domestic responsibilities of each. She also became acquainted with several teachers who allowed her to visit their classrooms and interact with their students in a way that foreign visitors rarely experienced. Her friendship with two female instructors at the Art Institute, Lydia Hess and Marie Gélon Cameron, enabled her to visit their studios and classes. After meeting and getting to know Bertha Palmer, she attended receptions at her elegant Lake Shore Drive mansion, known as "The Castle." Her friendship with a woman who was an electoral agent for the presidential campaign of Benjamin Harrison opened her eyes to American political debates of the time, including woman suffrage.[97] She went so far as to call her energetic, politically engaged friend "Mrs. H." "a woman of the future."[98]

Madame Grandin was frequently surprised at what she observed and readily admitted to occasional moments of shock or outrage over certain American behavior. Over time, however, these initial reactions were often reconsidered and modified as she came to a more subtle and profound understanding of American society and culture. Her willingness to comprehend more thoughtfully what she observed also reveals a sense of humanity in her contact with others, a quality not always apparent in other women travelers' texts.[99] Unwilling to rely exclusively upon observation, she discussed what she saw with her friends and acquaintances and even went to the Chicago Public Library to verify certain facts for her account. This tendency is particularly evident in her discussions of social mobility, racism, and gender relations. Madame Grandin's contact with domestic servants in various boardinghouses, for example, led her to investigate their wages and work conditions. She carefully documented their work agreements in order to better understand the conditions of their employment. Her impression of American servants changed as she began to comprehend the differences between class structure in the United States and in France and to appreciate the opportunities for social mobility that American society offered. She also had direct contact with African Americans on trains, in shops, and in the city. Initially, she referred to them as "the laziest and most abject race on earth."[100] She came to appreciate their spirituals and dances, however, and seemed to acknowledge their capacity for hard work.

The attempt to recalibrate first impressions is especially evident in her treatment of American women and gender relations. As she observed the everyday behavior of the middle-class women around her, Madame Grandin was at first surprised to find that Chicago homemakers, unlike their French counterparts, seemed to have little interest in dedicating much time or energy to the home. Instead of spending their days managing the affairs of the family, these women preferred to circulate about the city or attend social or cultural events. Her initial surprise became tinged with frustration as she wondered how American women could be so negligent of their domestic duties: "The solid, brave woman whom we so often see in France—hardworking, industrious, thrifty, proud of her little home and ready to assist her husband when needed by working outside of the home— this woman is a myth in America."[101]

Madame Grandin's reactions were marked by the cultural model of bourgeois life in late-nineteenth-century Paris, where middle-class households were managed by the well-organized *maîtresse de maison*.[102] This idealized wife and mother created a cozy, loving home for her husband that contrasted with the rough edges of the urban setting where he spent his day. Madame

Grandin was especially troubled by American mothers who were not concerned with transmitting household skills to the next generation. When an American high school teacher of her acquaintance invited her to meet with some of her young female students, Madame Grandin was impressed with their curiosity and energy, but she could not help but preach the bourgeois virtues of the French *maîtresse de maison*: running an efficient household, overseeing the children's education, making sure that everyone's socks were mended, and helping the servant prepare wholesome meals.[103]

Although Madame Grandin could be very critical of American homemakers, her attitude toward unmarried young women was open-minded and admiring. She was surprised by the fact that, unlike in Paris, young ladies in Chicago were free to socialize with young men away from the watchful eye of a chaperone. After observing both unmarried and married American couples, she concluded that the difference in this social custom was related to the fact that American men took their role as protector and provider very seriously. Moreover, from her perspective, it appeared that American men married for love, not money. In contrast, she openly criticized French men who, in her opinion, were far more interested in their fiancée's dowry than any other aspect of marriage. Madame Grandin's praise of American husbands provided her with a way of speaking out against French marital customs, specifically the dowry tradition and the division of household labor.

During her stay in Chicago, Madame Grandin visited several elementary and high schools, and her experiences there also helped shape her understanding of gender relations in America. Because she had worked as an elementary school teacher before coming to America, she brought a knowledgeable perspective to her descriptions of schools and curricula.[104] Not content to play the passive role of foreign visitor, she asked teachers precise questions about the lessons and peeked into bathrooms and lunchrooms. Madame Grandin was particularly struck by the natural interaction between pupils and teachers and impressed with the coeducational classes in elementary schools, where she noted that American boys were respectful and protective of girls, even at a very young age.

Madame Grandin's many visits to the Woman's Building at the fair reinforced her observations about the energy and independence of women in Chicago. She enthusiastically wrote, "The Woman's Building was without question one of the most interesting places of the entire site. I spent numerous days there, always fascinated and never bored as I always came upon an original or unusual display."[105] Dugard and Blanc participated in some of the formal events of the exposition, but Madame Grandin became part of a wider social network of women connected with the organization and execution of fair events. Her visits to the Woman's Building and her conversations with individual women involved in the project seemed to provide her with a place and framework for thinking about much of what she had noticed in Chicago in terms of education and gender relations.[106] Madame Grandin's initial criticism of American women's neglect of the home gradually gave way to a respect for their sense of independence and engagement in social, political and artistic life. No longer simply a foreign outsider observing the rituals of American culture, she started to become somewhat of an insider, developing a circle of friends, participating regularly in cultural activities, and frequenting favorite local establishments.

Whereas early in her stay Madame Grandin sharply criticized the physical and psychological detachment of Chicago women from their homes, as time progressed she became energized by their comings and goings throughout the city. In the latter part of her account, instead of focusing her attention on the differences between American and French life she began to describe her contentment in the Chicago setting. By the winter of 1893, the Grandins had moved into a boardinghouse in which they rented a private suite of rooms. Madame Grandin created, in her own words, *"un vrai chez moi"*—a true home of her own—for which she shopped, cooked, and cleaned.[107] In addition, her regular visits to classes at the Art Institute of Chicago, participation in the cultural activities of the Club Français, and the many social activities that took place against the backdrop of the World's Columbian Exposition suggest that she was indeed starting to feel "at home." She had even gained entrance into the highest cultural and social circles by becoming a habituée in the Gilded-Age salon of Bertha Palmer.[108]

After offering enthusiastic but measured praise for the city of Chicago, its inhabitants, the exhibition, and many different American establishments and institutions, Madame Grandin's tone shifts briefly yet decisively in her final chapter. Preparing for her return to France, she stood back and considered her American experience in the larger context of her life as a French woman and launched into the longest, most personal digression of the book. She is able to articulate the profound effect of the visit that had enabled her to see more clearly the frustrating situation of women in her home country:

> Dare I admit it? Even knowing that I was returning home and would see the dear friends and family from whom I had been separated from for more than a year, I felt profoundly sad at the prospect of leaving.
>
> I was leaving the place where I had lived freely, in terms of my thoughts and my actions. Some of these freedoms would not be tolerated on French soil where narrow prejudices, ridiculous etiquette and absurd conventions still

flourish. I was leaving the country where the laws, institutions, and morals fit so well with my natural sentiments, hopes, and inclinations.[109]

Although Madame Grandin condemned many aspects of life in Chicago as dangerous and destructive, she was strong enough to recognize and acknowledge her shifting values that were increasingly influenced by discovery of American life. Specifically, she was impressed by American women and the natural way in which they took their places next to men in their homes, workplaces, and classrooms.

Madame Grandin's travel narrative ended in July of 1893, when she and her husband boarded the American steamer *Le Paris* to return to France. As her ship left New York Harbor for Le Havre, she spotted the Statue of Liberty in the fog and dramatically declared, *"Je reviendrai!*—I will come back!"[110] This final declaration, atypical of travel accounts in that authors often eagerly anticipate homecoming, leads readers to wonder if she ever did return.

Madame Grandin's Life after Chicago

In the months following her return to France, Madame Grandin had numerous conversations with her good friend Marie Gélon Cameron, whom she had met at the Art Institute in Chicago.[111] These discussions are detailed in Marie Cameron's correspondence in the winter and spring of 1894. Edgar and Marie Cameron had left Chicago for Paris during the fall of 1893 in order to take painting classes at the Académie Julian. During the winter and spring of 1894, both the Camerons and the Grandins were living near Montparnasse.[112] Numerous references in Marie Cameron's letters reveal that the couples socialized regularly during the spring of 1894. In descriptions of Madame Grandin, Cameron repeatedly emphasized her friend's fascination with America and attempts to reintegrate into Parisian life. In a letter to her mother-in-law back in Chicago, Cameron described an evening with the Grandins: "We went to see the Grandins the other evening and enjoyed it very much. Grandin has become quite French again but Madame Grandin still keeps her American love. She has written a book *A Year of a Parisienne in Chicago* and is going to have it published."[113] In retrospect, Cameron's description of the Grandins seems to have prefigured a growing distance between the couple.

At the same time that Madame Grandin was getting settled in Paris, she was also anticipating the publication of her book. In several letters, Cameron enthusiastically described Madame Grandin's latest project, which was having her portrait painted by Edgar Cameron for entry into the 1894 Paris Salon.[114] Although "Portrait of the Author of *A Year of a Parisienne in Chicago*" was not accepted, Cameron reported that both she and Madame Grandin were very pleased with the work.[115]

In one of the last references to Madame Grandin, in a letter dated April 18, 1894, Cameron once again brought up her friend's feelings about America. Writing to her father-in-law, she observed that "Madame Grandin is changing in her ideas. She thinks now she can be satisfied in Paris but still she would be happy to go to America again."[116] Apparently, that sense of satisfaction was fleeting because at some point between spring 1894 and summer 1895 Madame Grandin decided to leave both her husband and her homeland. She embarked for a return trip to America in July of 1895 and arrived in New York on the steamer *Le Saint Louis* in the company of a young French man named Alexandre Ferrand. The ship's manifest indicates that they were married, although they would not wed until after Léon Grandin's death in 1901. Ferrand gave his age as twenty, and the age of "Mrs. Ferrand" was listed as twenty-three. In fact, according to her birth certificate she would have been thirty-two at the time. She was also expecting a child. In November 1895 she gave birth to a son in New York City, and in March 1898 she had a daughter.[117] Marie Grandin married the father of her children, Alexandre Ferrand, three months after Léon Grandin died, an event noted on the archival copy of her birth certificate.

During their early years in New York, the Ferrand family lived in Manhattan. New York City census documents indicate that Ferrand was employed as a furrier, while his "wife," Marie, was a housewife. The couple later moved to Staten Island, which in the early twentieth century was considered a tranquil refuge from the city.[118] Upon discovering her married name and her last address, it became possible to request a copy of Marie Ferrand's death certificate. She died on December 25, 1905, at the age of forty-one from acute nephritis. An excerpt from her obituary, printed in the *Staten Islander* on December 27, 1905, provides information about her family situation and activities at the time of her death:

> Madame Marie Ferrand, founder and president of the Staten Island branch of the Alliance française, and as near a philanthropist as a person could be without wealth, died at her home last Monday afternoon, Christmas day, after an illness that only lasted for twenty-four hours. Her untimely death is a great shock not only to her family but to those who loved her for her good deeds, for she was always active in doing something for the betterment of the community. She loved her work as president of the French Alliance and was also a member of the Woman's Club of Staten Island. As an accomplished pianist, she charmed

many an audience at charitable entertainments as well as private functions. . . . All who know Madame Ferrand have expressed their deep sorrow. It was only a very short time ago that she presided for the last time as it proved, at a meeting of the Alliance française and the members present were delighted with and remarked her charming grace as a presiding officer. Madame Ferrand had lived on Staten Island for several years. She came here from Manhattan. In France, before she came to New York she was well known in literary and artistic circles. She leaves a husband, Alexandre, and two children, a ten year old boy and a seven year old girl.

Although many details are lacking, the brief sketch in her obituary provides several pieces of information about her life in America. She had a devoted French husband; young children with American first names, Sandy and May; and an animated group of American and French friends. Her role in establishing and supporting the French Alliance of Staten Island showed her continued interest in sharing French culture with Americans. A number of unanswered questions remain, however, most notably why she left Léon Grandin for Alexandre Ferrand and decided to trade life in Paris for life in New York during the 1890s. What seems clear is that this open-minded young woman was attracted by the freedom from certain social constraints that life in America offered. This intercultural narrative that began as a chronicle of her time in Chicago ended with her transformation from outside observer to a fully engaged participant in American social and cultural life.

Madame Grandin's adventures as recounted in *Impressions d'une parisienne à Chicago* are complemented by her personal story that emerges from a trail of ship manifests, census records, and birth, death, and marriage certificates. It is the unfolding of these two concurrent stories—her impressions of Chicago and her passage toward self-discovery—that make Madame Grandin's book so exceptional among travel narratives. Her commentary on the city, its institutions, women, families, teachers, and students presents a nuanced account of life in late-nineteenth-century Chicago. At the same time, her curiosity about the city led her to discover a place where "the laws, institutions, and morals fit so well with my natural sentiments, hopes, and inclinations."[119]

A Note on the Translation

Madame Léon Grandin gives a precise description of the role and responsibility of the travel writer in her preface to *Impressions d'une parisienne à Chicago*: to share knowledge in an honest and exact manner with readers who are unable to travel. In keeping with this effort toward transparency, the sequence of words, sentences, paragraphs, and punctuation marks found in Madame Grandin's French text has been replicated to the extent possible. A few modifications, however, have been made in order to create a more readable text. Chapter titles have been added, and chapter subheadings have been condensed in order to more clearly indicate the topics covered. In some cases, sentences have been divided into two, or the order of words has been changed. A particular stylistic feature of this text is the author's use of brief statements or short paragraphs to communicate her spontaneous reactions to a situation. These interjections sometimes introduce a new idea or scene that is then more fully developed in the subsequent paragraph. At other points, the short sentence or paragraph functions as a kind of telegraphic, fragmented shorthand that Madame Grandin uses to convey her immediate impressions. Although these brief sentences and paragraphs might appear to break the flow of the text, they were preserved to accurately capture her thought process, reactions, and sentiments.

A PARISIENNE IN CHICAGO

Part 1

From Le Havre to Chicago

To the Reader

Ever since childhood, travel has seemed to me to be one of the greatest joys in life. What child has not lined up four chairs to create a train compartment and taken off in discovery of imaginary lands filled with marvelous phenomena! Now grown up, my passion for travel has endured but my mature outlook does not simply view it as just one of the liveliest pleasures that life has to offer. I also see travel one as one of the most effective means of education and instruction, superior to all other educational approaches in that students of all ages and abilities are able to benefit from it. Travel does not require the kind of serious study and abstract theories that often frustrate mediocre minds: it offers universal lessons and is accessible to the youngest of students. At each instant, a new piece of knowledge is gained, then another, and another. This information is accumulated, comparisons are made, and a sense of judgment develops almost unconsciously. Even in the most lethargic mind the thought process awakens and begins to function more easily and rapidly. Thought! The highest expression of life! Yet how few caught up in the slothful rhythm of daily life truly know how to think!

For French people, travel hardly seems necessary. We know that civilizations other than our own exist. But do we have the curiosity to learn about them and appreciate them? To what end? Our attitude seems to be colored by an idea that has dominated for centuries and that is shared by people who have little else in common:

We are the most intelligent, hard working, and overall superior people! The most beautiful, richest, and best-governed country is ours!

It is understood and agreed that this opinion is not to be discussed: in the eyes of French people it is one of the fundamental dogma of our religion of patriotism and to argue otherwise would be sacrilegious!

But no! It must be said that this chauvinistic illusion should not be one of the articles of patriotic fervor as patriotism understood in this way would be blindly ridiculous, narrow-minded and even egotistical. We should love our country in a higher and more intelligent way; we should judge ourselves in a more honest way, having the courage to judge our faults, our wrongdoings, even our weaknesses not so that we can impose them on others but so that we can correct them. By what means can this be accomplished? Travel to other places is exactly the remedy that can open our eyes so that we can see the wounds that we ignore or accept without thinking!

More than patriotic vanity, it is our nonchalance, our egotistical love of familiar surroundings that keeps us home on our native soil, next to the fireplace! Let us shake off our laziness! In this century of steam and electricity when it is so inexpensive and comfortable to cross continents and where the poet, eager for space and new suns no longer cries:

"Wings, wings, wings.

Like in the songs of Rucker."[1]

Let us travel! Let us run from north to south and from east to west, gathering useful information, cataloguing sights, and enriching our minds with new ideas and a fresh appreciation of others and of ourselves.

Travel! This word should be defined as "viewing with interest in order to remember in a happy and productive way!"

For those who are unable to travel due to daily responsibilities or material impossibilities, travelers should make it a point to share the spoils of their acquired knowledge with honesty and exactitude in the hope that it will prove useful and interesting to readers.

At Sea

Departure—Getting Settled Onboard—
Arrival in New York

How sad our departure is! In the somber homestead we leave behind tearful relatives. Separations frighten older people more than younger ones! Will those leaving ever return? This dreadful thought haunts the travelers as well and undermines their courage. In fact, they will truly need courage to accomplish even the shortest trip when their thoughts turn to the anguish and suffering they are about to impose upon those left behind.

Reason, however, must triumph over emotion; it must be recognized that our families' fears are rooted in part, in their old fashioned images of travel. They are of a generation for whom any trip constitutes a long and dangerous undertaking and are terrified by the idea that we are going to cross thousands of miles over land and water! It is a question of education and custom! Surely we will accept our children's departures more easily than our parents accept ours. Poor, fearful ones! You are behind the times and have our sympathy!

In spite of all bravura, emotion overwhelms and suffocates you during these endless goodbyes. My husband and I had just gotten settled in the carriage that would take us to the train station when my tears, which I had stoically held back during the goodbyes, began to flow.

Fortunately, the inevitable chaos of departure changed my train of thought; distracted by so much activity, my thoughts, though not gay, lost their sad intensity. I was in a much calmer state of mind by the time we disembarked from the train at the port of Le Havre, where we would begin our trip.

La Touraine, the newest transatlantic ship, is an enormous vessel [fig. 1]![1] In fact, it is more like a monument. Measuring 165 meters in length and 20 meters in width, the ship is equipped with two propellers, two engines, two chimneys, luxurious saloons, and electric lighting from one end to the other.

My curiosity was focused, however, on our cabin. Would we have enough fresh air? Would the bed be long enough to accommodate my height? These details might seem frivolous but to me they were very important.

I was quickly reassured. The attractive but tiny cabin featured a miniscule porthole that looked out over the ocean. Two wooden bunk beds topped with good mattresses and surrounded by curtains were firmly secured to the wall; a vanity, a sofa, and a clothes rack . . . that was all the furniture.[2]

I must add that there were some strange objects that surprised me: suspended above the beds were large fabric-covered squares tied together with cords. My husband pointed out that they were life preservers and the thought of a possible shipwreck made me nervous, much to my embarrassment.

This unpleasant feeling quickly passed.

I prepared for our first night aboard the anchored ship! I slipped into bed without giving too much thought to the life vests that hung above our heads similar to the sword of Damocles. With a turn of the button on our electric lamps, the cabin was plunged into darkness and we were ready to sleep.

But we were not even close to falling asleep as the chains that load baggage onto the ship were in desperate need of grease! The infernal noise made it impossible to sleep except for deep sleepers like myself.

My husband was unable to sleep and spent the night exploring the ship.[3] The next morning I learned that although second-class passengers like us had comfortable accommodations, the situation in third class was horrible! Men, women, and children all slept in the same area! Why had so much space been allotted to the reception rooms on the first floor? Wouldn't it be better to have smaller reception rooms in order to give a little more space to the poor emigrants?

Once all the preparations for departure were complete, a loud bell warned family members and friends to take their leave. Departure was imminent and everyone hurried toward the bridge. Sailors took their posts; some stood by the cap sterns while others maneuvered enormous cables or awaited orders from officers.

On the shore facing us, we could see a mass of family members, friends, and curious onlookers huddled in small groups.

At the signal, the ship made an abrupt movement; the cables were pulled up, the engines whistled, and we departed! And then quickly, too quickly, everything moved into the distance and faded into the horizon, with both the port and the houses melting into a gray tint. Soon the coastline was nothing but a thin line while all our hearts remained ashore.

The pilot, who had guided our exit from the port in a small boat accompanied by the friends of several well-known passengers, left us to return to Le Havre. This stop took just a few seconds. Handkerchiefs fluttered aboard both boats and then the imposing *La Touraine* and the small pilot boat began to move in opposite directions. After a few brief moments, the small boat disappeared exactly like the gray line of the French coast would soon vanish.

The tinkling of a bell called us to the dining room [fig. 2]. It was our first meal onboard the ship and I was surprised to find so many passengers there, although none of them looked very happy. Each passenger had heart and mind filled with preoccupations, so no one even attempted to be friendly. A somber meal, we conversed out of politeness since we were not yet ready to observe or study one another.

After lunch, it was time for a hygienic stroll on the bridge where I paced up and down for fifteen minutes. At the extreme front of the ship, where the space narrows to form the bow, there was just enough room for one person to lean against the angle of the boat; this quickly became my favorite spot on the ship.

At the rear of the ship, a large, uncovered area was reserved for second-class passengers. At that moment, almost all the passengers were outside trying to keep the coast of France in sight for as long as possible. I pulled up my chair and became lost in reverie while watching the horizon; the group of white seagulls escorting our ship accompanied their graceful flight with a rather discordant concert. Some of them perched on our large masts; others took off and flew from front to back, landing on the cords to rest. Most of them, however, followed the ship, occasionally skimming the pearly trace of the propeller's movement, which was so long that it seemed to attach our ship to land.

Once again, the ringing of a bell stirred me from my contemplative state! The bell called us once again to the dining room; on French ships one eats frequently and it is a kind of distraction for passengers like me who were fortunate not to be seasick.

Two-thirty in the afternoon! It was prune time; in other words this was the time of day when we were served a snack of consommé, prunes, and various pastries.

Several passengers whom we had seen at lunch did not appear in the dining room and even fewer came to dinner. Some were already sick and had taken to their beds, while others were on the bridge, bundled up and shivering in blankets, not daring to move. This sight made me fear seasickness but throughout the trip both my husband and I managed to avoid it and our stomachs functioned marvelously.

After the snack, I resumed my position at the ship's bow. Following a superb day, the sun began to set and slowly descended toward the water in a purple glow. Not a cloud in sight, the clear sky took on different hues in each direction: red in the west and ash gray in the east. The ocean was as calm as a lake and small waves gleamed like the scales of large fish. Finally, the sun disappeared completely and the radiant spectacle was over as the crescent-shaped moon rose in the sky and illuminated the night.

The indescribable spectacle of the sky created a sense of harmony and calm that penetrated and relaxed us. That July evening, after the sun had set, I remained at my post at the front of the ship. The wind was blowing and the accelerated pace of the ship made me dizzy with its loud noise. Alone, at the bow of the ship, I imagined that I was crossing the ocean by myself towards the unknown.

As I moved toward the rear section, I watched the ship's wake which stretched toward the horizon. Fireflies sparkled like quick and brilliant flashes of light against the surface of the water. Finally, at a rather late hour, I returned to my minuscule cabin.

We were no longer bothered by the same unpleasant problems that we had experienced the previous night but others annoyances took their place.

First of all, a disagreeable odor that I had detected the previous evening had become more pronounced.

Fortunately, the ocean was so calm that I was able to open our porthole and let in the ocean breeze. Another problem, however, had no simple remedy. The movement of the ship, which had been quite strong on the bridge due to the movement of the two propellers, became even more forceful in our cabin.

I was quickly able to adjust to the lull of the ship but my poor husband could not tolerate it and had a difficult time sleeping throughout the crossing.

Life onboard a ship is, by nature, very monotonous and even though the crossing from Le Havre to New York only takes about eight days passengers are always looking for ways to pass the time. The most popular pastime is observing the other passengers, deciding which ones to get to know, and which to avoid. During the second dinner of the crossing we met a gentleman who gave us some disturbing news regarding the cargo of our ship that left me cold.

He told us that there was a small cabin at the bow of the ship, near the very spot that I had found so enchanting. Although I had noticed this cabin on the previous day, it had never occurred to me to think about what it might contain.

According to this gentleman, the cabin had been transformed into a mortuary and contained two cadavers.

They were the bodies of two Americans, a young man and a young woman who were victims of a train accident in Switzerland. Their families were having the bodies shipped to America.

I admit that I would have preferred that the gentleman not share this information with us as it only depressed me and made me avoid my favorite spot at the bow of the ship.

The presence of the two coffins onboard, however, did not dampen spirits as I had imagined it would. From the second day on, conversation flowed more easily. The sight of another ship increased the passengers' excitement, especially those traveling in third class.

Although their accommodations were horrible, these poor passengers seemed to be the happiest people onboard. I attended one of their meals and found it to be very primitive and lacking in appetizing dishes. The sailors brought in large cauldrons of food, each of which contained ten rations. Each passenger then took a serving; the poorest families often had only one spoon so they sat around the pot and passed the spoon.

When the meal was over, the third-class passengers, most of whom were German and Italian, began to organize a dance. Their orchestra was made up of two accordions and as soon as the melody began, all of the first and second-class passengers hurried to the balcony that overlooked the third-class section.

It was a spectacle worth seeing. The excellent music, gleeful enthusiasm of the dancers, picturesque setting, and colorful costumes would have made even the most miserable person smile. Couples danced to the moving rhythms and occasionally a German man tried to invite a pretty Italian lady to waltz.

The German musicians presented selections from the admirable repertoire of their homeland. When they finally stopped playing due to fatigue, the voices of their compatriots stepped in to replace them.

The melodious voices of these men and women and their sense of harmony made this spontaneous concert one of the most delightful pleasures imaginable.

In their native language, they sang their national hymns with such conviction and patriotism that they impressed us all. These impoverished men and women, chased from their native land by misery, held their homeland in their hearts and sang of it with such love that it provoked in us the most intense emotion. The pleasure was, in the end, so complete that another concert was planned for the following evening.

This concert, given at the rear of the ship, was as successful as the first one. This time the opening song was "La Marseillaise" and without any concern for decorum, most of the spectators joined in the singing.

Ah! How that hymn, that sublime song seemed more beautiful and grand than usual! In spite of myself and without even realizing it, I was crying real tears. Perhaps this was exaggerated and ridiculous sentimentality, but let those who have never experienced such emotion throw the first stone at me.

The next day, a thick and icy fog which became increasingly dense every fifteen minutes soon made it impossible to see either the bow or the stern of our ship. Every five minutes a siren rang out, since we were approaching Newfoundland and had to steer clear of fishing boats. On the bridge, passengers were bundled up in their warmest clothing but shivered not only from the cold but also from a sense of melancholy. This dark, cold day ended with some sad news.

One of the ship's employees had died suddenly, the victim of some unnamed illness.

None of us had met this man, however, when I heard that in just a few hours his body would be thrown overboard, I was chilled by the news.

It seemed to me the height of horror and injustice. We already had two cadavers onboard that had made the entire trip with us. Why not put the body of this poor man who had worked on the ship for ten years in the same storage area?

But no! There was the serious question of who would pay for the cost of transporting the body. The widow and orphans of the man were not well off and would not be able to afford these costs. Even his ten years of devoted service, which had not been very well compensated, did not give him the right of free passage. So, into the sea!

Indignant, I decided to attend the poor man's funeral. My presence would substitute for that of his unfortunate family who did not yet know of his death. I would whisper the prayers that his widow and orphans would have otherwise done.

To spare the passengers the sad ceremony, the funeral was secretly scheduled for four o'clock in the morning.

I learned this information from our steward and asked him to please wake my husband and me at three-thirty in the morning so that we could attend the ceremony. We woke up and went down to the bridge where the service was about to take place.

A number of curious onlookers had already gathered and soon the funeral procession got underway. The captain was first, followed by the commissioner, the doctor, several officers, and finally the coffin which was carried by four sailors. The smoky flames of the sailors' resin torches provided the only light. The flames' red reflections created a sinister feeling in the cold, foggy night as the piercing sirens continued.

One detail immediately caught my attention: there were two holes on the top section of the coffin that would allow it to fill with water and sink.

A few ceremonious words were quickly spoken by the captain and then the doors of the balcony were opened. Before slipping the coffin through the doors, one of the propellers was halted to prevent the coffin from getting caught in the ship's wake.

The coffin was then placed on the slanted plank and as everyone gathered around, I dropped to my knees and said goodbye for his family. On command, the sailors lifted the torches and the plank, which groaned in a sinister manner, and was then lowered toward the ocean. The siren continued to sound its painful wail.

Red and smoky in the fog, the torches on the coffin resembled puddles of blood. The plank dropped and the coffin fell into the water, making the most gruesome sound I have ever heard. The coffin disappeared almost immediately and a few seconds later, the sea became rough again. Soon everything was once again calm and all that could be heard was the plaintive cry of the siren.

Chilled to the ears, my teeth chattering, and filled with fear, I hastily returned to our cabin following the ceremony.

Throwing myself upon the bed, I nervously cried warm tears and eventually fell asleep. Upon waking, I learned that another momentous event had occurred during the night: a baby girl had been born on the ship.

The eternal contrast of things: joy mixed with sadness, misery next to abundance, life side by side with death.

This happy event distracted us from our sad thoughts; even the sky brightened and we were then able to see the fishing boats on both sides of our ship.

Everyone onboard was talking about the baby.

"It is very likely that the child will be named after the ship as was the case on the *Champagne* where a similar event occurred," I was told by a little boy whom I had befriended.

In fact, when the birth certificate was drawn up by the captain, the newborn baby was named *"Touraine"* after our ship. Although this unusual name probably would have been difficult for a young lady in Parisian salon circles, it was sure to create a sensation on American soil.

Naturally, I was very eager to see the new passenger and her mother, whom I pitied for finding herself in such a place for such a circumstance. While I was on my way to see the baby, the father appeared on the bridge with the child in his arms.

Poor child! She was not very pretty but did have robust arms and legs and a clear desire to live even though she had arrived earlier than her mother had anticipated, no doubt due to the ship's movement.

"But sir, aren't you afraid that the baby will be cold out here?" I asked the father, who looked very awkward holding the infant.

"The cold, Madame? Oh, the children of the poor are not afraid of it as they are fortunately very strong. This is my sixth child and not one of them has ever been sick for a minute," he replied.

"So are you going to America to make your fortune?" I asked.

"Yes," he replied. "In France I was unable to earn enough money to feed my family and my wife cannot work as she is busy taking care of the children. When I have work, I earn three francs per day but I do not always have work. That's why I left but it weighs on me."

Two big tears welled up in his eyes.

Everyone was quite taken with the child and wished her luck and prosperity. To make the road ahead easier for her, someone came up with the idea of collecting money for a little dowry. The idea was greeted with enthusiasm and everyone contributed what they could. The sum was so generous that when the captain presented it to the family, the father was very moved and hesitated to accept it. That evening, everyone was in a joyful mood, glowing with the pleasure that had been bestowed on the poor family and playing music and games.

The next day, however, a sense of boredom ruled once again as we were all very eager to see land. Fortunately, the heavens favored us and another incident both broke the monotony of the trip and accelerated our progress across the Atlantic.

At dawn, another ship had begun racing with ours. We had passed it during the night and it was trying to regain its lead position. Greetings as well as aerial signals had been exchanged, which were the mode of conversation for each captain. This ship, which was as large and beautiful as ours, was a German vessel named the *Bismarck*.

It had left Hamburg three days before our departure and was supposed to arrive in New York one day ahead of us. Large bets had been placed in America and Germany on this race between these two ships.[4]

Once apprised of the situation, we were all feverish with excitement. All lorgnettes were glued on the *Bismarck* which was falling farther and farther behind and a veritable burst of enthusiasm broke out onboard once it became clear that the German ship could not pass us. Even the ladies clapped their hands and I noticed that even the Americans shared in our joy. In fact, everyone was pleased with this event. The most surprising aspect of the adventure was that we had actually encountered our adversary on the high seas, which was such an extraordinary coincidence that no one left the bridge.

The weather and the sea were superb that day, with the ocean as blue as the sky. Seaweed trailed behind our ship and flying fish came and stretched out on the ocean's surface to sun their backs.

But suddenly, toward nightfall, thick clouds moved in and the temperature dropped. Lightning was visible on the horizon, the air was heavy, and once the storm broke, it began to rain.

We were only a few hours from port. All of a sudden the rain stopped and lights were lit onboard. Then, in the darkness in front of us other lights glowed. These came from lighthouses and at first appeared dim like hanging lanterns and then gradually became brighter.

It was the port!

At the rear of the ship, a sailor calculated the depth. An order was given and the anchor was thrown overboard. The ship, which was slightly inclined to the side, came to a halt.

We had arrived.

Not at the port but at the hygienic service.[5]

Since the crew and the passengers were in good health, we did not have to be quarantined but simply examined by a doctor.[6]

We had to wait until the next morning so there was nothing to do but go to sleep. This last night onboard proved to be the best of the trip.

Upon waking, a sparkling, magical setting stretched out before us.

The shore was edged with houses shaded with luxurious foliage; in the immense ocean bay, all kinds of boats were swirling in every direction; and on the coast overlooking the ocean stood the colossal Statue of Liberty, by the sculptor Bartholdi.

Disappointment, however, concerning this statue.

Despite its gigantic proportions, in the great expanse of the setting it appeared to be of ordinary size and was not much more impressive than the smaller version at the tip of the little island on the Seine in Paris.[7] The harbor is so vast that, in order to make this statue stand out, it would be necessary to place it on a mountain.

Once the visit to the doctor was over the ship got underway to its final destination.

Within one hour we would arrive in New York after a trip of just six days, fifteen hours and ten minutes that covered a distance of 18,000 leagues.

Our ship rapidly crossed the distance that separated us from the point of debarkation, maneuvering around the other vessels which surprised me with some of their unique features.

First, the whistle was unlike the strident sound that one hears in French harbors. Instead, it was a prolonged vibration of two harmonious notes.

My eyes were even more astonished than my ears at the many different types of boats! Among the different crafts were ferry boats, which I would never have imagined, equipped with large wheels that transported horses, carriages, and even train compartments.

As we impatiently watched this spectacle from the bridge, we shook hands with the other passengers and said goodbye with the familiarity of old friends. We even planned a reunion with our fellow passengers for the following week.

We finally reached the point of debarkation, a large building that resembled that of Le Havre.

There we were to be met by my husband's relatives. Since my husband had not seen them since he was a child, I wondered how we would ever recognize one another.

In France, this would have been impossible given the confusion that reigns at the point of debarkation. In New York, however, it was very easy to find our relatives thanks to the orderly way in which the port is organized.

In the waiting area, the walls are divided into large squares and marked with letters of the alphabet. Our luggage was unloaded at the spot that corresponded with our first initial, making it very easy to locate. [8]

Under the capital letter "G" we found both our luggage and our family members. Recent photographs helped us to recognize one another. We quickly introduced ourselves and established a certain familiarity with these charming relatives who would host us until we moved on to Chicago.

Familiar with the usual procedures, they helped us with the customs formalities and then put our luggage on the "American Express" which would transport it to their home. All that remained for us to do was to head there ourselves.

New York

First Impressions—The City's Neighborhoods—
Life in Morissania

When I think back on my initial glimpse of New York my head fills once again with the cacophony of infernal noises and fantastic apparitions that flooded it at that first moment.

In front of me, at the dock exit, lay an ugly narrow street crowded with tall, unattractive red brick houses that seemed to go on forever. Utility poles lined the street and their thick framework of telegraph cables made it appear even more narrow. No sky! A wide railroad viaduct ran parallel to the street. From above, came the noise of steam-powered trains. From below, rose the tumultuous racket of vibrations, shouts, and streetcar and carriage bells, to which people on the sidewalks seemed completely oblivious. The sidewalk scene did not resemble in the least that of Paris, where workers and elegant society ladies rub elbows. Here everyone looked much the same: tall, thin, well dressed, shaven, and in a hurry.

We boarded a streetcar that went under the viaduct and the vibration was terrible for my ears. In addition, the horses guiding our carriage were wearing collars with bells and the employee in charge of collecting the money wore a counter on his chest. Each time he registered a new passenger, it would make a most disagreeable sound.

The street car was filled with male passengers and at first glance, it would be difficult to guess their true age. They all appeared to be young men, since none of them had a beard or mustache.

While impeccably dressed, they did not seem to be as stuffy as the British who are so stiff in their collars.

Upon exiting the street car, we climbed the stairs to a steel bridge to wait for our train. We did not have to wait long as trains pass every three minutes.

Train cars are comfortable and well laid-out with small platforms between them such that passengers can circulate from one end of the train to the other. Inside, the seats are arranged with their backs to the windows. In the center of the car, the seats face one another creating a kind of small salon.

Peering through the windows, I was able to look into the houses that line the train tracks. What a pleasure it must be for the inhabitants of these buildings to have train passengers peeking into their homes every three minutes! Moreover, heavy black smoke and grease penetrate the apartments each time the windows are opened, not to mention the constant noise. Is it possible that someone will want to introduce such a mode of transportation in Paris? I certainly do not contest the practicality of the "Elevated" but I would never use the term "attractive" to describe it. I am certain that its most zealous supporters in France have never seen it.[1]

We exited the train to make one more connection, and an hour and a half later, we finally arrived at our relatives' home.[2]

Ah! Standing in front of it, I already begin to make my peace with New York.

Their property is located on a wide street lined with tall trees. The neighborhood is quiet and lush, with lovely homes set in shade-filled yards, similar to the Parisian neighborhoods near the Bois de Boulogne.[3]

We stop in front of a wooden fence that surrounds an English-style garden. As we enter, two white goats frolic while a superb cow grazes peacefully.

A hammock swings between two trees, and beyond, is the large, graceful, true American house, constructed of painted wood and shaded by tall trees. Beautiful green plants decorate the steps, while climbing roses and vines encircle the porch columns.

Someone has seen us arrive and the door opens. A charming confusion ensues with cousins big and small rushing to greet us with welcoming kisses. These relatives were new acquaintances yet, by the following day, we would be as close as lifelong friends.

Our relatives live very comfortably but are by no means millionaires. Some work as businessmen or have a professional career while others manage a factory or a store. They are the equivalent of our solid bourgeoisie in France.

But what a difference between their lifestyle and that in France! Their existence is so much more intelligently conceived!

Instead of the pretentious yet stingy luxury of our bourgeois homes, everything here is given over to comfort and fantasy. The contrast is evident in the appearance of the house as well as in the carefully selected furnishings, from the vast bed and the large armchair to the arrangement of the bathroom. Unlike the narrow bathrooms in Parisian apartments where one can barely turn around, our relatives' bathroom was spacious and bright. Well-equipped, it contained a large sink with hot and cold faucets, a bathtub, and all of the latest hygiene inventions.

The living areas were also superior to ours in terms of both their dimensions and decoration. Americans do not share the French concern with parallel arrangements or matching sets of furniture. In truth, however, the real American living room is not located inside the house, as the front stoop is where people spend delightful evenings when the weather is pleasant.

During the two days following our arrival, we spent time resting as our charming family helped us recover from the fatigue of the trip. My cousins then volunteered to show me around the city of New York and I took advantage of their kind offer!

The intellectual capital of America, New York is neither the largest nor the most beautiful city in the United States. Chicago surpasses New York on both counts, though it is not especially attractive. Except for a few impressive thoroughfares like Broadway and Fifth Avenue, all of the streets are narrow. Because the buildings are very tall, the streets are dark and lacking in air and sunlight. The army of utility poles, telegraph wires, and large iron bridges of the Elevated all make the scene unattractive.

Constructed on the island of Manhattan, the city is not very wide but stretches lengthwise to such an extent that I believe that it would be impossible to walk from one end to the other in a day.[4] The symmetrical arrangement of streets allows people to circulate much more easily than in Paris. Avenues run the length of the island and the numbered streets run crosswise. The house numbers always start at one side of the island and two elevated railroad lines go up and down the main avenues.

New York is divided into neighborhoods; there is the Italian quarter, the French quarter, etc. Some of them are not very interesting while others are quite unusual, namely the Jewish quarter and Chinatown.

The Jewish quarter is one of the most populous and dirtiest areas of the city.[5] Although the Jewish religion dominates, the inhabitants of this neighborhood come from all over the world.

Some of the families date back to the establishment of the city. Contrary to the custom, the Jewish residents in this area are not wealthy.

Miserable and sordid, they make their money from all sorts of lowly businesses including the buying and selling of used clothing and black market activities. This hodgepodge of activity contributes to the unpleasant look of the area. Piles of rags and junk are everywhere and occasionally a child or a young woman emerges from the top of the pile, resembling the biblical figure Rachel.

The Jewish race is scorned and Americans speak of the Jews with un-imaginable disdain when they say "He's a Jew!"

Very different, Chinatown.[6]

As clean as a bowl of Chinese porcelain. The long, yellow faces and Asian dress of the inhabitants give one the impression of being in Peking.

Isolated in their calm routine, in the middle of the hustle and bustle of American life, the Chinese behave as if they were in China. Stubborn and determined to protect their customs, they are petrified in their culture and refuse any assimilation.

The fabric, utensil, and shoe businesses are exclusively Chinese in this neighborhood. Chinese restaurants feature small plates and chopsticks.

There are even Chinese priests and judges who reverse the judgments of American courts in accordance of the laws of the Celestial Empire.

Due to racial antagonism, one race being so different from the other, Americans detest the Chinese.[7] This hate and scorn is silently returned by the Chinese whose only reason for going to America is to get rich.

For the most part, the Chinese are in the laundry profession. Although they earn American money, they never spend it in American businesses. In-stead, they save their money. As soon as they have enough to buy a bamboo shack and a rice paddy, they escape like thieves with their treasure. Even the unfortunate ones who die in America return to China for burial. Special ships transport the bodies back to their homeland.

From time to time, Americans try to put a stop to this Asian invasion by deporting them in large numbers. However, in spite of all of the official decrees, the Chinese continue to prosper in New York and their number is not decreasing.

Another unusual neighborhood is the Bowery, the oldest section of New York.

Located at one end of the island, it is inhabited by a population of ques-tionable character. One could not venture there in the evening without risking disagreeable adventure.

Theaters, concerts, and balls abound in this neighborhood but they are frequented by unsavory types.[8]

The oldest church in New York, which is surrounded by a cemetery, is also in the Bowery.[9]

The cemetery, located in the middle of such a crowded area, surprised me. I have since noticed a similar situation in other American cities. This practice shows an admirable American trait as their respect for the dead counterbalances their love of real estate speculation. Although the land could command high prices, the city recoils at the idea of chasing sleeping ancestors from the place they inhabit.

Surrounding almost the entire city, the riverbanks of New York, with their immense stretch, present a tumultuous scene.

A clutter of boats and a forest of masts and sails obscure the view of the ocean. From docks to steamers to tall buildings, the New York riverbanks resemble the market neighborhood in Paris known as "Les Halles."[10] The constant hustle and bustle together with piles of merchandise arriving from all over the globe: sacks of coffee, bales of cotton being stacked by men of all races but mostly Negroes, all bring to mind the Parisian marketplace. The neighborhood never sleeps nor do the bars, adding drunken tumult to the noisy work rhythm.

But the riverbanks are not the only heterogeneous place in New York. In streets and walkways, people of all races stroll past one another, including a large number of dark-skinned women. What I found particularly amusing was the unanimous preference of these ladies for white dresses. Both older and younger women wear them and they are very flattering to pretty women, but make women with yellow or black skin look all the more unattractive.

Another interesting aspect of women's dress is the white apron that many ladies wear at home and sometimes even out in the city. Made of fine cotton and decorated with lace or embroidery, the aprons are attractive when worn with a hat and gloves. At first, I thought that these women were housemaids or nursemaids, but the great number of women wearing aprons makes me think that this is a fashion of middle-class women in general.[11]

This is one of those small details that is imperceptible to the native people, but which the foreigner notices with great amusement. Another example is the sign used on tobacco shops which invariably consists of a life-sized statue of an Indian in his feather costume or a female Indian wearing very little. Molded of papier-mâché, one of the figure's hands extends a pack of cigarettes while the other hand points to the shop's entrance.

Shoeshine stands are as numerous as tobacco shops in New York.

The shoe shiner is a true businessman in New York and must certainly make a fortune in a short amount of time.

His stand is not modest and primitive like those in Paris. At each street corner, there is a raised platform set with a row of comfortable armchairs.

The client sits down and reads the newspaper while the shoe shiner kneels at his feet and polishes his boots to a glossy shine. For this service, Americans pay five cents, often several times a day. In addition to these finer establishments, shoeshine boys are found in every street. They carry a wooden box filled with brushes and polish and charge less for their service.

It is true that the comfortable chair is missing!

The peninsula of Manhattan has expanded in a way with Jersey City to the west and Brooklyn to the east. A large number of businessmen have their private residence in Jersey City, Brooklyn, or Morissania which is a charming neighborhood on the Hudson River.

Ferry boats carry passengers from Jersey City to New York every five minutes, along with their horses, carriages, and railroad cars. This type of transportation, however, is inconvenient in winter when ice on the river sometimes interrupts boat service. The idea of creating an underwater tunnel between Jersey City and New York is being discussed.[12]

Brooklyn is connected to Manhattan via a large, suspended bridge. The Brooklyn Bridge is a marvel of genius and audacity that only Americans could design and execute.[13] With a single thrust, the bridge covers a span of nine hundred meters in width and its curved design allows even the tallest ships to pass under its unique and majestic arch. The bridge also supports a two track railroad viaduct where trains pass. Standing before this daring construction, which seems to be man's challenge to nature, even the most ignorant person experiences a profound sense of admiration.

In terms of New York monuments, there is little to say. Although their dimensions are vast and they are executed in a playful architectural style, they are not, overall, very interesting artistically. Art, in general, is not the natural tendency of this nation. New Yorkers proudly display their tallest buildings as we vaunt our most marvelous cathedrals.

These tall buildings, some of which have fifteen stories, belong for the most part to newspapers like *The World, The Tribune,* and *The Times.*

All of them are constructed using the same model. Three or four elevators manned by black attendants run from bottom to top and back again, at a dizzying speed. Each floor houses financial, legal, medical, and dental offices!

Throughout the day, a flurry of activity takes place but in the evening they are deserted except for the night watchmen. These establishments are devoted exclusively to business so there is no residential housing.

One of the prettiest spots in New York is Central Park, an enormous park with avenues lined with tall trees, superb flower gardens, and a terrace where you can listen to live music.

Many horse-drawn carriages as well as smaller carriages similar to our cabriolet cross the park.[14]

The Metropolitan Museum of Art is located on the grounds of Central Park. Not very impressive. Admittedly, there are rare laces, Bohemian crystal, Chinese porcelain, and precious antiquities; but in terms of the fine arts of painting and sculpture, few items are of interest. It is true that the museum was only recently established.[15] In a short amount of time, however, I have no doubt that Americans could acquire artistic masterpieces from every era.

It will be a while, however, before this museum rivals certain private collections such as that of the enormously wealthy banker Vanderbilt. He has assembled a collection for his personal pleasure and that of his friends. Once a year he opens his marvelous gallery to the public for the entry fee of fifty cents per person. Yes, fifty cents is the fee set by this millionaire, the total sum of which probably enables him to purchase another masterpiece that he would otherwise be unable to afford. All irony aside, the idea of charging less fortunate people an admission fee is something that we would find distasteful in France.

The Museum of Natural History, which I prefer to the Metropolitan Museum, is also located in Central Park.

More than fine arts, Americans instinctually appreciate works of nature. No expense has been spared in assembling the most varied and unusual examples.

One of the prettiest collections is that of precious stones, some of which have been extracted from American soil, then collected and lovingly displayed.

In the gardens of Central Park and elsewhere in the city, statues, which seem to grow in number each day, have been erected in honor of great American men.

Many of them are the work of European sculptors but others, including some of the better ones, are done by American sculptors who have studied in Paris.[16]

These sculptors are American by nationality but their artistic education is French as it is in Paris that they study, live, and create works destined for America. Some of the sculptors return to their native country but the majority of them stay in Paris and go back home for occasional visits, happily coming back to their Parisian ateliers.

To accuse them of patriotic indifference would not be accurate in their case. This voluntary exile is simply the result of the lack of artistic resources in America; no specialized institutions for the advanced study of art, no museums with documentary material; art or at least the facilities for artistic development are still in their infancy here.[17]

Not only do Americans appreciate our sculpture and painting, but they are also very admiring of French theatrical works which are often performed here by well-known French actors.

Although American plays exist, they are always more or less modeled on or borrowed from our productions.

During our visit, it was not the season of the big touring shows so we attended an American play. I much preferred to see this sample of national literature than to see Sarah Bernhardt or Coquelin again in a play by Sardou.[18]

The popular play at the time was *A Trip to Chinatown*.[19] This production had nothing in common with the comic opera of François Bazin! It was a droll vaudeville comedy in the style of Hennequin or Bisson and although the plot was not very interesting, the production was quite daring.[20]

We went with some of our family members, several of whom are quite religious. The other boxes were filled with young girls accompanied by their parents and friends. In America, where people are so careful with their facial expressions, I was very surprised to see young and old ladies, prudes and respectable women, all smiling without hesitation at even the most bawdy moments.

One particular scene would have been scandalous in Paris.

It was a love scene between two young people!

In France, such scenes are generally accompanied by passionate kisses on stage. But in New York, in order to give themselves over to tenderness, the lovers went behind a screen. The spectators could not see anything but could hear everything, which seemed much more shocking than any explicit dialogue.

It is true that the young ladies who attend with their friends are acquainted with the harmless familiarities of the "flirt" and are not shocked by these scenes.[21]

Another American spectacle that I enjoyed even more was the pantomime presented at the Casino.[22]

This huge establishment is not found in the center of New York City but rather near Jersey City which is located on a peninsula surrounded by rocks and accessible by ferry boat.

The immense grounds of the Casino house restaurants, theaters, concert and dance halls, and one of the largest hippodromes in the world. Here in this vast space used exclusively for pantomimes, I saw three thousand actors come to life.

In the rectangular theater, spectators were seated in tiered benches that surrounded the stage on three sides.

The show was called *The Fall of Babylon* and it made an indelible impression on me.

Neither the most imaginative of our fairy tales nor the most graceful of our ballets would withstand comparison with this spectacle. Legions of men and women moved in perfect order; the ballerinas wore light and graceful costumes which playfully reflected the electric lighting and created a sort of rainbow with the star ballerina in the center performing a strange and bizarre dance similar in style to that which Loie Fuller brought to Paris; chariots crossed the stage at a gallop and a final fire engulfed Babylon; the sumptuous city was brought to life along with its people, the splendor of its orgies, and the tumult of its collapse.[23]

The denouement was as unexpected as it was imaginative. For a reason that I never understood, a group of American Indians chasing a herd of buffalo suddenly appeared in the midst of the red flames of Bengal, coming from all directions of fiery Babylon! In this era of extreme symbolism, I believe that there was a secret connection between America, the Syrian city of Babylon, buffalo, and the Redskins but I am not sure exactly how to interpret this.[24]

Another place of amusement is Madison Concert, a pleasant architectural monument with elegant columns supporting its galleries.[25] The building is three stories tall and occupies an entire block in the most beautiful neighborhood of the city.

P. T. Barnum and Wild Bill Cody have presented shows on the ground floor. A theater occupies the second floor and above it is a kind of terrace topped with an observatory tower where I attended a concert.

In terms of the concert program, there is not much to say as they performed songs, balancing acts, and short plays, similar to performances in the *cafés-concerts* on the Champs-Elysées in Paris, before the same kind of mixed audience.[26]

But the terrace was charming, filled with shrubs and scented flowers; the air so pure at this altitude; the summer sky filled with sparkling stars! A fairylike panorama of the city could be seen from the top of the observatory, with the lights of New York City, the Brooklyn Bridge and the majestic ocean on the horizon!

All of the shows begin around seven in the evening and finish no later than eleven, probably due to the distances that spectators have to travel to get there and back. We seldom arrived home before one in the morning.

Methods of transportation are not lacking in New York City. First of all, there is the Elevated which I must say functions perfectly. Every ten streets there is a station with an "up" staircase and a "down" staircase. No congestion, no waiting, thanks to the frequency and regularity of the trains which are filled with passengers. The trains carry as many passengers as they can. Some passengers have seats while others stand, as the goal is to arrive home as soon as possible.

Although there are many places of amusement in New York, there are just as many charitable institutions. These charities are not run by the city but are private initiatives.

A large number of homes, for example, house poor people for as long as it is necessary for them to find employment. Institutions that educate the children of poor families have also been established.

One of the charitable institutions that I visited was the Juvenile Asylum.[27] I cannot say enough good things about this home that takes in several thousand students from immigrant families. Here, order, cleanliness, and decency reign and the neat appearance of the children shows that the care is worthy of praise. The most important compliment, however, is that although the home is run by the Episcopal Church, there is absolute freedom of thought. Unlike what goes on in other countries, the charity does not impose its faith on those who receive its help.

Although the pupils are not obligated to stay for any length of time, they usually remain until they have completed their studies. They are not asked to leave except for very serious reasons but are free to leave at will, when their families ask for them. The teachers treat the pupils with kindness and respect.

They have a difficult task, since the students come from all over Europe and have varied educational backgrounds and personalities.

From what I have heard, the result of this education is very satisfactory. After living and studying here students become good and honest Americans, ready to enter the business world.

These little excursions around the city did not prevent me from savoring all the sweetness of American life with our loving family in Morissania, whose charm could not have been greater and of which we were now a part. I was so happy and comfortable that the days went by too quickly.

From early morning, the house was filled with the happy sounds of children. We would often organize a horseback riding outing, followed by a lazy afternoon nap in the hammock. We would also do archery and even play football, a sport that I did not really enjoy. In the evening, all of the cousins would come home from work and we would gather around a big table and have a feast. After dinner, we would sit on the stoop and organize little concerts. We would sing old French songs, accompanied by a violin, a mandolin, and a banjo. It was a joy for us to spend long hours in the fragrant garden, bathed in blue moonlight, sparkling with the glow of fireflies.

Eventually, however, we had to leave for Chicago as we had to arrive there by a certain date. For one of our last evenings in New York, our cousins organized an Indian feast.

All morning long, cousins big and small gathered seaweed. They then arranged stones in a spot in the yard and started a fire on top of them. Once the stones were hot, a bed of seaweed was placed on them, followed by a layer of clams. What delicious clams! I am not sure if they are available in France since I have never seen them before. This shellfish is about the size of a medium oyster but the shape is more like a cockle. The taste is that of oysters and mussels but with a particularly delicate flavor. In New York, clams are featured in chowder, omelets, and clam cakes. They are delicious in all of these dishes but not as tasty as they were that evening at the clam bake.

The clams were covered with seaweed and then topped with lobster, another layer of seaweed, chicken, more seaweed, and finally hot stones.

The mixture cooked for several hours while we took many pictures of the house and of our hosts. Finally, everything was ready and perfectly cooked. We sat on the grass as this meal had been prepared in the style of savages and had to be enjoyed in the same way. Ah! The chicken was excellent, more delicious than any I have ever tasted. The lobsters and clams would have impressed even the most finicky of gourmets! What a curious sight we must have been, grouped around the pile of smoking seaweed! What fun! I can still hear laughter when I think of that evening!

From New York to Chicago

Banks of the Hudson—Buffalo—Niagara Falls

We took the Michigan Central Railroad line to Chicago, making a stop in Niagara Falls [fig. 3].[1] Our spacious compartment, called the "Palace Car," was not at all similar to our train cars in France.

With high ceilings, wide rooms, a pleasant decor, and fresh air thanks to the large windows, these salonlike compartments of American railway cars are equipped with armchairs that allow passengers to pivot as they please, similar to those on ships.

A marvelous trip, it was the sort of excursion of which one dreams, across the delightful pleasures of a magical landscape.

We began our trip along the banks of the Hudson River, an adorable valley surrounded by tall mountains on both sides. These mountains are not a continuous chain of peaks but irregular in size with deep gorges running between them.

Occasionally, we would suddenly dip down into one of these gorges and catch a glimpse of a pretty village or a mountain, covered with a green, impenetrable forest. In other areas, the mountains were rocky, formed of violet colored rocks, reddish boulders, and yellow and red stones, their golden, amethyst, and ruby tones reflected in the river.

The landscape changed as we crossed gray valleys, swamps, and finally, forests.

We were approaching the city of Buffalo, named for the wild buffalo that roam in these plains and woods.

Since there would be a twenty-five minute stop, we planned to eat dinner and hurried toward the buffet.

Small tables had been set and fans resembling large black butterflies circulated the air above them. Four tall Negroes surrounded each table with large fans. As we took our places, they began to fan us with their refreshing instruments.

Why did they not use the fans to cool down the food? Everything was so hot that we could not eat it for fear of burning our palate and esophagus!

The train was ready to leave again before we even had a chance to swallow a bite of food. The price: four dollars, the equivalent of twenty French francs, for nothing![2] It is true that we had nothing to complain about in terms of the fanning.

We went back to our seats and rested until we reached Niagara where we were going to spend the night in a hotel.

At least we were going to sleep in a hotel which I preferred to the promiscuity of sleeping cars.

We slept until we arrived in Niagara at one o' clock in the morning, an hour behind schedule.

So there we were, in the middle of the night, looking for a place to stay. In the middle of the night but not in the middle of darkness as the city was more brilliantly illuminated at night than during the day. In America, shops do not close their shutters at night. The gas or electric lights remain on, and night watchmen patrol.

It was easy for us to find hotels, but the first two we checked claimed that all of the rooms were taken! Perhaps they were wary of the fact that we had no luggage as we had left everything in the baggage compartment of the train in order to be more comfortable. Finally, the third hotel that we tried opened its doors to us!

We had arrived, without knowing, at the Hotel of the Falls. Since the hotel was located so close to the falls, we paid an exorbitant price. If only we could have gotten some sleep for our money! However, since we had the advantage of staying so close to the falls, its frightening noise kept us awake for two hours. We were all the more unnerved as we did not know exactly where we were and what was causing the noise.

In the morning, we went to visit the falls and I will not even attempt to describe this crushing spectacle.

It would require the pen of a writer such as Chateaubriand to evoke this terrifying marvel, this unique cataclysm among all of the phenomena of creation.[3] But there is one profanation, one sacrilegious element that I want to point out which is the setting created for this prodigious chaos.

A pretentious and ridiculous English-style garden surrounds the falls on the American side. An English garden! Boxwood bordered plat bands, shrubs, and rustic bridges stand in the face of rocks that seem to have been gathered by the hands of Titans. From these rocks comes a thunderous noise and a threatening mountain of water under which one threatens to be engulfed!

Across from the "Rock of the Ages" and the "Wind Caves," it is possible to rent wet suits designed to protect visitors from splashes while going under the immense arc of water! Isn't this dishonoring the sublime, the grandiose aspect of this nature before which one feels reduced to nothing!

A long suspension bridge thrown over the river connects the American and Canadian sides. Although the bridge spoils the landscape, it offers a splendid view of the area. After paying a fee, visitors can go up on the bridge and see the "iron horse" of the American falls. A spray of water rises up and foam boils furiously, forming holes in the mass of waves which later become more transparent and peaceful.

More than simply enraptured by these powerful manifestations of nature, I was struck with fright before their sublime character, I found the rapids to be especially admirable. These thousands of currents turn in all directions with a continuous breaking of waves. Here and there, the crest of a rock pierces the foam and the whole thunderous mass of water resonates until you feel that you will go deaf from the noise. This vision of the falls remains in my memory as a scene of unrivaled beauty.

From the Canadian side, we climbed Victoria Tower and took in a panoramic view of the Canadian rapids (less tumultuous and not as beautiful in my opinion as the American rapids) and the green oasis of three sister islands that sits in the middle of the river. Beyond the falls, the river continues on its calm, playful route.

Our brief stopover came to an end too quickly and we got back into our train compartment; a sleeping car this time, as for better or worse we had to spend the night there.

Leaving Niagara, we had to cross the plains. Since it was not yet sunset, we were able to enjoy the landscape. The plains are a kind of desert made up not of sand but of greenery, a glaucous sea extending to infinity. No trees, just grass moving in waves as the wind blows! Sometimes the grass is tall and other times it resembles a lawn. In some areas, swamplike grass grows and in others, the grass is dry. All regions of the plains, however, are inhabited by large cows, sheep, and pigs. We saw many groups of black pigs that would run away as the train approached. The cattle seemed to be grazing in specific sections, according to the type of vegetation. In the swamp-like areas, few animals grazed. There were no train stations, only stops for cattle companies. Beams were placed on the ground so that boarding passengers could cross the swamp and reach the train.

Night began to fall and the passengers arranged their beds. It is torture for me to spend the night in these sleeping cars; men's and women's bunks are right up against one another with only a simple curtain protecting passengers from indiscreet glances.

Travelers of both sexes made themselves at home and changed into their nightclothes. They did not hesitate to slip into bed wearing only the minimum of clothing.

I, who am not a prude, was truly scandalized by such a lack of modesty and I refrained from following their example. Fully dressed, I threw myself onto the bed; my husband was facing me and he did the same. I was so tired that I fell asleep, rocked by the rhythmic sounds of my companions' breathing.

A bump in the middle of the night awakened me abruptly. Then nothing! Instead of the vibration of the train, there was only a calm and quiet that scared me so that I jumped out of the bed and hurried out of the compartment.

"Look!" said my husband, who I saw standing in front of me. "We are on a boat!"

It was true. We were gliding on a beautiful lake and the moon had cast its blue light on the deep water. My husband, who had watched the entire maneuver, explained it to me.

Upon arrival in Detroit, the train had stopped at the edge of Lake Huron, near a waiting ferry boat. A third of the train and the engine boarded the boat. Next, the second third of the train was placed parallel to the first section. Finally, the third section was loaded in a similar way and the ferry boat crossed Lake Huron, full steam ahead.

A superb night, a splendid view and a deliciously sweet sense of calm!

After getting off the train, I explored the ferry boat. Thirty minutes later, we arrived on shore and a similar maneuver brought us back to the rails.

The rest of the night passed without incident. The next day when I awakened, we were riding along another lake so vast that it resembled an ocean: Lake Michigan.

We were finally approaching Chicago, as Lake Michigan borders the southern and eastern sides of the city. The northern and western sides of the city are edged by a polluted river, whose water drains into the limpid water of Lake Michigan.[4] This opening serves as a port and as a channel and many ships come via the lake to do business in the immense city.

We entered Chicago from the south side. The train crossed a long stretch of the city before reaching its destination.[5] My eyes widened at the sight of buildings even taller than those in New York.

We crossed the exhibition area which was in the early stages of construction.[6]

Every now and then, the train cut through a street filled with carriages and pedestrians. With no barriers to protect them, they all simply moved back as the train approached; the railroad tracks are as unprotected as those of the streetcars and the locomotive's bell is the only warning that alerts people to get out of the way.

Surprisingly, they do not have more accidents than we do in France, where it seems that we are always watching out for one another.

Here, it is the country of "take care of yourself and I will take care of myself" and this egotistical refrain has positive results.

At the end of the line, all passengers disembark from the train and step directly into the street instead of being stuck like sheep behind a locked door, awaiting permission to exit. The lack of formalities and the small number of employees reduce the process to its most simple form, which serves everyone well.

Part 2

Chicago

Boardinghouse Life

Looking for "Home"—American Domesticity—
Local Customs

We found ourselves on State Street.[1] The very appearance of this street took me aback and gave me my first inkling of the immense sprawl and grand scale of this city where, apparently, everything could be found. Over the course of our stay, this idea was never dispelled.

It would be difficult to imagine the impressive width of this thoroughfare as well as the originality and height of the houses that line it. The whimsical architecture of the homes borders on delirium. No two houses are alike; there is a mix of many different styles representing all historic periods; some of the houses resemble fortresses with crenulated towers, others are flanked by turrets, and still others seem to defy the laws of balance, leaning to the right or to the left like the leaning tower of Pisa.

In terms of elevation, New York is surpassed by one hundred arms' length. On State Street, the Masonic Temple rises to twenty stories and nearby there are many other buildings that reach seventeen or eighteen stories.

Through the help of friends and by mail, we had arranged in advance to stay with an honorable American family. As soon as we arrived at the train station, we set about looking for our "home," a task that was neither comfortable nor pleasant. It was early August and the Fahrenheit thermometer, which is the only one used in America, measured between 100 and 110 degrees.[2] Chicago's sprawl is five times greater than that of Paris and the only information we had concerning our lodgings was the address on Ellis Avenue, which is located on the south side of the city. [3]

In order to get more detailed directions, we approached a policeman. A Herculean figure, he was dressed in a flamboyant uniform worthy of a comic opera: black trousers, a black waistcoat with a yellow leather belt, a white metal star decorating his chest similar to that of the Legion of Honor, and a gray felt cap like that worn by German policemen except that it was not pointed.[4] He carried a ribbon wrapped club, which served as both a weapon and a sign of authority, and instantly brought to mind the battles between Guignol and the police commissioner in Parisian puppet shows.[5]

Although his dress was certainly inferior to that of our boot-clad police officers who are the envy of Europe, his polite manner far surpassed that of his French counterparts. After having searched his numerous pockets and exhumed a street index, he finally informed us that Ellis Avenue was on the south side of the city which, of course, we already knew.

It is an American habit to use the points of a compass to indicate the route and even the location of a house.

Armed with this precious piece of information, we decided to find a streetcar going in that direction. We simply waited on the sidewalk as waiting stations, numbered tickets, and above all, the important person who distributes them, are all unknown to Americans.

The simple funiculars are similar to the Belleville funicular with the difference being that they function perfectly.[6] They use neither horses nor engines and stop wherever there are passengers waiting to board, except in the middle of intersections. Of course, like everything that is American, the streetcars change their appearance with the seasons. During the summer, they are open so that air can circulate but have curtains that can be drawn to protect against the sun, rain, or dust.

About thirty minutes later, we got off the tram at a street near our lodgings, our search facilitated by the nearby exposition site.

Once again, we asked for directions and easily found Ellis Avenue which is a very long street with at least five thousand numbered dwellings.

We were looking for number 3700! Fortunately, we discovered that we were not very far away. The houses lining the street were as original as those I had seen on State Street. Made of wood for the most part, each house had a small plot of grass in the front framed by white stones, similar to those that surround graves in Paris cemeteries. If only they had a little iron railing, the sad picture would be complete. We finally arrived in front of the home we had been trying to find.

A very pretty house, it stood on the corner of Ellis Avenue and one of the cross streets.[7] The usual small funereal plots of grass were in front but at least some pretty vines hid the foundation stones and entwined the posts of the porch, which had seven or eight steps, as is customary.

We were welcomed by a servant and as we entered, the room brought to mind my stay in New York.

In Paris, we have long abandoned the custom of lining up furniture against the wall like a row of onions and instead, try to create a kind of charming, artistic disorder. Such a difference between our rooms and the free flowing

American whimsy! Their rooms, it is true, are better suited to this kind of decoration as they do not have the same limitations as ours in terms of the monotonous regularity of construction.[8]

The ceilings are very high and the rooms are spacious, as big as those of our painters' and sculptors' workshops. Similarly, they have a staircase which is a sort of gallery that leads to the second floor. In this immense hall, which was decorated with original wall hangings and an eclectic choice of furnishings, the overall effect was unexpectedly charming.

The rustling of a dress in the upper hallway interrupted our inspection. We looked up to see the graceful and elegant shadow of our hostess descending the staircase, her slender frame wrapped in a pink cotton batiste dress! But in contrast to this graceful, youthful figure, what a face! It was that of a fifty year old spinster. Her cold angular features and ugly dark eyes, which were the color of coal, were framed with white hair, coquettishly arranged in a twist.

In a sharp and affected voice in keeping with her unfriendly gestures, Miss Flack began by telling us that the guests who boarded at the house that she ran with her mother, were of the highest respectability.

A slight disappointment: we thought that we would be accepted as pensioners with a family and here we found ourselves in a boardinghouse of distinction which was going to cost us dearly in every respect.[9]

We tried to reserve judgment for the moment, as nothing that she had said was that disagreeable. What we wanted most was to see our room, freshen up after our trip, and have lunch as our stomachs were growling.

At the mention of lunch, Miss Flack appeared very surprised and told us that the midday meal had already been served. She went on to say that the first responsibility of guests was to learn the customs of the house.

Seeing, however, that we had just arrived and were not familiar with the rigid rules of the establishment, our charming hostess decided that she would make an exception. She asked a servant to prepare the meal and in the meantime, took us to our room.

The large room was located in one of the turrets and had an adjoining water closet and a bathroom complete with sink and bathtub.

The main room was quite spacious and served as both a sitting room and a bedroom. It resembled a bedroom in that it contained a very elegant bureau for our clothes and an armoire with an enormous mirror. The absence of a bed, however, gave it more the appearance of a sitting room.

Where the devil could the bed be? We could find no trace of it, neither in the main room nor in the bathroom.

At that moment, however, we were not in need of a bed so we quickly freshened up and proceeded downstairs for lunch in the dining room.

Miss Flack and our lunch were waiting for us. The lunch was elegantly set out on a dazzling tablecloth and served on beautifully decorated porcelain dishes. But on these dishes, oh! such miserably thin slices of ham, so thin, so thin that I could have devoured them all myself. But there were two of us! And we did not want to appear to be gluttons. I was hoping at least that something more substantial would be served after the ham, but much to our disappointment, a second platter emerged from the kitchen holding only very meager slices of cake. All of this was accompanied by fine tap water. Upon leaving the table I was just a little more hungry than I had been when I started, my appetite increasing as I ate.

In spite of this disappointment, I reserved judgment. I reasoned that since Miss Flack had not anticipated our arrival, nothing else was available in the kitchen except for this less than satisfying snack. A substantial dinner would make up for the stinginess of this first meal.

Imposing silence upon my stomach, I spent the rest of this first day unpacking our suitcases and putting away our clothes. It was while I was hanging them up that I discovered the bed.

It was in the armoire, the large armoire whose size had taken me by surprise! The mirror actually formed the base of the bed and two feet located at each end supported it. Once we unfolded it, we discovered a box spring topped with a thin mattress.

This is the "folding bed," which is very popular in America, as it allows a sitting room to be easily transformed into a bedroom [fig. 4].[10]

In every one of our lodgings, I immediately tried to find a favorite retreat. On the ship it had been a spot at the very front of the bow and at my cousin's home in New York it was the rocking chair on the porch. Here at Miss Flack's, it was the turret that had views of the street and the lake. I spent much time simply admiring the beautiful lake, so enormous that it resembled an ocean. The dinner bell awakened me from my reverie.

Miss Flack presided over the meal, of course, and introduced us to the other guests.

There were just a few boarders: a Canadian gentleman who, to our great delight, spoke French as well as we did, his wife, a charming lady who unfortunately did not know one word of French, and an older American bachelor who seemed to adore Miss Flack. That was it except for Miss Flack's mother who was also present but did not really count, as her daughter overshadowed her completely, which by the way, is an American custom.

In contrast to European families, older relatives in America seem to occupy a secondary position even in their own homes; respect is not understood in the same way on both sides of the Atlantic.

Dinner was supposed to carry off any illusions that I had nourished, or rather, that had nourished me until that hour. Just like lunch, it was served in a very elegant manner but it was also very skimpy. The slices of meat were so thin that they were practically transparent and Miss Flack's dark eyes became inflamed with a dreadful anger whenever anyone accepted her offer for a second helping.

My husband and I exchanged desperate glances. Would we starve to death in this overpriced boardinghouse? Mr. Pitcher, the Canadian gentleman whom we quickly befriended, shared our misery concerning the menu but warned us that we were likely to find the same sort of food or worse in other boardinghouses.

I later verified this myself and found that the small portions are due to two factors: American women's dislike of domestic chores and the high cost of servants.

Maids are commonly paid between five and six dollars per week which is equivalent to twenty or thirty French francs.[11] Two maids barely suffice even in a modest home as the one who cooks would never agree to perform any other task and the opposite is true for the one who serves. At eight o'clock in the evening, they go out or invite friends to their rooms and the employer has no right to object. They are free on Sunday after two in the afternoon so, if a hostess is serving Sunday dinner, she must find a way to make do without them.

To be served in such conditions requires practically a fortune, so many choose to live in a boardinghouse or a hotel in order to avoid these difficulties.

On the verge of starvation, we wondered if we would also die from lack of sleep. I worried about this as we climbed into our folding bed. The mattress was so thin that the springs poked us and needless to say, I was in a very bad mood the next morning.

I woke up early as breakfast was served at seven o'clock. Although we would have preferred to sleep later, we had no choice but to get up.

The previous evening we had left our shoes outside the door thinking that they would be polished and returned promptly. Mistake! The shoes had not been touched. My husband, believing that they had been forgotten, rang for a servant. As soon as the maid arrived my husband showed her the shoes and gave her a reproachful look. She opened her eyes wide and seemed very shocked. To our surprise, she dropped the shoes and ran downstairs.

Just a few minutes later, Miss Flack came to tell us that it was not customary in America for servants to polish their masters' shoes. She added that she was upset by this incident, not because of our inconvenience but because she was afraid that the maid might resign! We almost thought that she would go so far as to ask us to apologize![12]

This would have only seemed natural in this country where it is necessary to use niceties when speaking to servants so that they are not offended.

As for our shoes, my husband, like all the men here, had to find a shoe-shine stand while I had to brush my own clothing and boots.

The next day, I began visiting people whom I had contacted in advance. This first day in Chicago was a series of surprises, almost all of them amusing.

The heat is unbearable in August; American women, like us, wear very lightweight dresses in white or pastel colors. Men simply remove their jackets and carry them over their arm. They calmly stroll about without vests but instead wear wide sashes, similar to the ones that were recently introduced several summers ago in Paris. Almost all men wear top hats.

Though the top hat is an odd accessory, I was even more amused by the large straw hats worn by horses! Damp sponges are placed under these hats, just like under the stovetop hats favored by men, to protect both horses and men from sunstroke. Men sometimes replace the sponge with a large cabbage leaf.

All of the horses sport these protective hats, but I saw one who wore an even more complicated outfit that included blue trousers, a blue sheath covering his neck and back, and of course, a large hat that tied under his neck! The sight was so funny that I could not help but burst out laughing, much to the shock of my fellow passengers and the coachman. They explained to me that the horse probably had sores and that the clothes protected him from insects and mosquitoes.

If the animals are protected in this way, it goes without saying that the coachmen are not directly exposed to the heat of the sun; all of the carriages are equipped with large white umbrellas that are attached to the back of their seats.

Despite all these precautions, heat stroke frequently occurs in horses. The animals remain in the street until a special car comes to collect them.

Another summer scourge is the large number of insects, so fierce that all windows and doors are fitted with metal screens to prevent these pests from entering the house. Although these screens give homes the appearance of a meat locker, this is certainly preferable to an insect invasion. When you see a pretty young lady behind one of these screens, it is easy to imagine that it is Rosine cloistered away by her jealous Bartholo.[13]

One of the most repulsive habits seen in American streets is the tendency not to use a handkerchief.

The first time I saw a gentleman engaged in picking his nose, I experienced such indignation and disgust that I almost scolded him. I have since tried not to notice this very common practice.

This deplorable problem is probably due to the fact that laundry services are so expensive. The handkerchiefs that I have seen are soiled and the undergarments of even the most respectable people do not appear to be very clean.

Unfortunately, this lack of cleanliness is not Americans' only shortcoming. Another habit is just as bad.

For sometime, I had noticed that there was a small porcelain vase in every sitting room but I had no idea as to its use. I had also remarked, with disgust, that men were chewing tobacco and spitting it out in trams and train cars. I had assumed that this habit was confined to the lower classes and was sorry to see that there were so many ill-bred people. In the elegant salon of Miss Flack, however, I saw a gentleman of utmost respectability take out a pouch and put some tobacco in his mouth, something that in France would cause one to blush!

This vice is indeed very widespread and is shared by people of all social classes; even some women chew a gum that has an unbearable odor all day long, while others, who are not satisfied by the gum, chew tobacco.

The compensation for these faults, I must declare, is the superiority of American men over French men in terms of their respect and kindness for women of all ages and social classes.

In the streetcars, a man never allows a woman to stand without immediately offering her his seat. This polite gesture is so natural that the lady surprises everyone when she thanks him. Similarly, if a man sees a woman in the street, even a female servant, struggling with a bulky or heavy parcel he offers to help her.

My first days in Chicago passed quickly. At Miss Flack's, the temperance regime did not let up, but I did have the opportunity to get to know the other guests, particularly Mrs. Pitcher, the Canadian gentleman's wife.

She was a likable young woman, very sweet and adorable. Since her husband was busy all day long so she did not go out very much. Most of her time was spent in her room reading or sewing all sorts of things for Mr. Pitcher. Her companion was a red bird, known as a cardinal.

Although we think very highly of our sparrows, I do not think that their small brains could be as well organized as that of this cardinal. Trained by his mistress, he quickly became comfortable with me and surprised me with his behavior. He would sit on Mrs. Pitcher's shoulder and give her little pecks until she gave him a kiss. Very playful, he would take snaps from a fur piece but would put them back as soon as Mrs. Pitcher scolded him, seemingly understanding everything that he was told.

He adored his mistress and would gaze at her for long periods of time, chirping gaily. When eating a tasty morsel, he would hasten to share it with his mistress by placing a tiny crumb between her lips. Occasionally, he would catch a fly that had managed to get inside and would try to share this delicate prey with his mistress.

September brought cooler weather and the evenings were very pleasant. This was the best time of year to stroll around the lake or to take a ride on one of the pretty boats. Nothing is more pleasant than to take a boat around Lake Michigan on Saturday evening.[14]

It is customary to begin the period of Sunday relaxation on Saturday evening. The austerity of Sunday and the rigidity of religious practices prohibits any profane distraction so young people attend dances on Saturday evenings, often on board one of the cruise ships.

Beginning at four in the afternoon on Saturday, all of the shops close and young people abandon jobs and chores and hurry to enjoy the evening. American morals allow young ladies and men complete freedom of action and appearance so everywhere there are happy couples and laughing groups of young people that fill the parks, walkways, and boats of Lake Michigan.

These boats are taller and longer than those that cruise the Seine. A reasonably good orchestra is set up on the bridge of the ship and the rest of the space is transformed into a dance floor.

Chairs are placed around the dance floor for those who do not wish to dance. As the boat moves away from shore, the orchestra strikes the first sparkling note and couples head to the dance floor to twirl gracefully.

People in America dance very well and the men do not balk at dancing the way French men do. All of the young people take dancing lessons and young men find this pastime very enjoyable, not a painful chore. The dress is always proper, even in mixed dances like those on the lake boats. During this public dance, no activity occurs that would scandalize even the most proper of English ladies as people come for no other reason than to dance.

The cruises generally last about two hours; it is a short excursion across the width of the lake which seems more like an ocean. Apart from the fact that it has fresh water, Lake Michigan is similar to an ocean in terms of its beauty and expanse. (Saint Joseph, which is across from Chicago on the narrowest part of the lake, is eight hours away, a longer crossing than that between Dieppe and New Haven.) Terrible storms sometimes arise very suddenly and each autumn the tally of victims is recorded. Lake cruises are suspended during the seasons with bad weather.

Another excursion that Chicago residents happily take is a tour of the five Great Lakes: Michigan, Superior, Huron, Erie, and Ontario.

The round trip cruise takes three weeks and nothing is more marvelous than the sight of the rich foliage and metal deposits on the banks of each lake. The picturesque scenery also includes the homes of vanquished American Indians. North of Saint Paul, there is an Indian community of these poor aborigines who live according to their old customs. The members are under surveillance by authorities and, even though their prison is larger than a cell, they have neither independence nor liberty.

It is unimaginable to think of the invasion of this country by a foreign race that took everything from the native inhabitants who were unable to defend their territory and who succumbed under the number and force of the enemy. They are reduced to a kind of enslavement in their own country.

It is easy to understand their rebellions and the atrocities they have committed. However, their race is not the worst. In terms of intelligence and character, Indians are far above the Negroes, who in my opinion, constitute the most abject and stupid race. They are low creatures, vile and rampant, who through their faults became American citizens.[15] Indians, who are much more capable of being civilized and who maintain their pride, are surrounded like wild animals.[16]

Kindness and forbearance would have more easily tamed them. Americans, who are so fond of independence, should have understood how much the Indians valued their own independence and should have treated them as brothers, who although still ignorant and barbaric, are able to learn and develop, instead of as cattle.

The Indian is blessed with brilliant qualities; he is courageous, artistic, industrious, and learns very quickly. The civilization of this uncivilized race would have been a noble and profitable thing for the prosperity of this country.

At that time, preparations for the World's Columbian Exposition were well underway and all of the buildings were to be completed in time for the four-hundredth anniversary of the discovery of America. This section of Chicago was buzzing with activity; workers toiled endlessly as a city seemed to rise up out of the ground.

Grandiose palaces arose almost magically; canals lined with parapets, embankments, and gardens were constructed and connected all of the different sections of the fair.[17] In the workshops, decorative sculptures were created. The monumental fountain to the glory of America, whose parts had all just arrived from France, was being erected and already looked imposing.[18]

In the haste to finish, however, sufficient precautions were not taken. In America, saving time is more important than saving lives. As each day passed, the number of victims of this enormous undertaking increased. Funeral cars frequented the workshops, coming to pick up the wounded and the dead. I trembled when I thought of the many workers who climbed and balanced like monkeys on the fragile scaffolding. Huge buildings miraculously emerged from the ground. I promised myself that I would not set foot in them when they were crowded for fear of a collapse. Unfortunately, my fears were justified.[19]

Because the exposition site was near the lake, almost all of the buildings were constructed on pilings; entire trees had been used for this purpose. Their mutilated trunks continued to live in the moist soil and even sprouted young branches. As a result, the Liberal Arts Pavilion appeared to be sitting atop a forest.

Free to pass my time as I wished, I spent most of it at the exposition site, watching it come to life and watching its crowds of workers.

In the morning, they arrived with white metal lunch pails which they immediately placed in the shade under the pile of clothes they had just discarded. Workers never wore their work clothes to the job site. Instead they left them in the workshops or factories each evening and put them on again in the morning. Since there was neither a cafeteria nor drinks for sale, the workers had to bring their own meals and beverages. The only drinks available came from water fountains, which were located on every site, and provided ice cold water.

If a worker wanted to bring a few bottles of beer, it was necessary to fill out a number of forms and to obtain many different authorizations. This rule was not created by the builders, but was due to the fact that the exposition was being erected on lands belonging to the temperance regime.

This land once formed the small city of Hyde Park, whose inhabitants were members of the temperance movement and prohibited all fermented drinks in their territory.[20]

As Chicago expanded, it encompassed Hyde Park as well as other small towns, but all of the annexed areas retained their rights and customs. In preparation for the opening of the exposition, it was necessary to enact new regulations in order to lift the ban on alcoholic beverages.

The temperance regime is respected in America.[21] During a three or four day train trip, it is sometimes not possible to purchase wine or any drink other than water for periods of twenty-four hours or longer while crossing part of the temperance zone.

In France, such a law would cause an outcry. I, however, am far from condemning this practice, as alcoholism plagues all large cities and can never be battled energetically enough.

Water is the beverage of choice for most Americans and no one is the worse for it.

Although Miss Flack's boardinghouse was not in a temperance area, we were still subjected to the most rigorous fasts. The quantity of food was so insufficient that we often felt weak and faint.

We could no longer tolerate this strict diet at any price and set out to find a better housing situation.[22] But where could we go? All of these establishments were similar and according to people who had stayed at several, some were much worse than ours in certain respects.

What to do? Although it seemed difficult, I longed for us to have our own place. Fortunately, an incident occurred that helped us make our decision.

It was a Sunday and God knows the sadness of that day!

All of the shops are closed and there is no place to spend time except in church. To make matters worse, meals on Sunday are scheduled in the most foolish way. Since the servants have the afternoon off for their own convenience, lunch is served at one o'clock. This meal is the only food provided until the next morning. This was especially difficult at Miss Flack's!

Every Sunday, she served a roast chicken that was so dry that it resembled painted cardboard. Picking what appeared to be meat from the bones was such a tedious task that no one had any desire for a second helping. Moreover, Miss Flack's gracious offer of "more meat?" was always accompanied by such an awful glare that it cut one's acceptance like a whip.

The roast chicken was invariably served with a legion of small side dishes that my husband called "bird baths." These small dishes contained baked potatoes, two or three slices of cucumber, raw tomatoes, under-ripe melon, and other condiments of this type. The only agreeable item on the menu was ice cream, but that was hardly enough to sustain us.

On that particular Sunday, at six in the evening, a cold supper was served that consisted of a slice of cake and a few berries!

We could not tolerate the situation any longer! In our indignation, I immediately announced to our hostess that we would leave the boardinghouse at the end of the month.

Where would we go? Fortunately, I found temporary lodging for us and later found a long term solution in the boardinghouse of a young widow.

She had furnished rooms available and offered to rent us a room and give us use of her kitchen and dining room. She undertook all of the other domestic chores which would have been very disagreeable to me without a maid. This was not exactly the arrangement that I had envisioned but the young woman seemed so friendly that we accepted.

It was easy to move and at the end of the month we left Miss Flack's boardinghouse without any regrets.

New Lodgings

Fellow Boarders—Triumph of French Cuisine—
Attempted Burglary

Once out of the boardinghouse of the rapacious landlady, I was initially pleased with the change in residence.

Our new house was much less elegant than Miss Flack's, as was the neighborhood.

Located on a lively, commercial street, the house was directly across from a school.

The house was about ten years old and had a proper, yet simple design. It had neither turrets nor exterior ornamentation, and its only distinguishing feature was a front staircase. This stoop is one of the unique features of Chicago architecture. In the evening, people sit outside to enjoy fresh air and to watch the street activity, just as they do in our French provinces. Two patches of grass flanked the stoop and dahlias and chrysanthemums sprouted here and there, much prettier in their charming disorder than they would be in a proper arrangement.

Our spacious ground floor room faced the street. Originally, it must have served as a front sitting room as every American home has two sitting rooms, a front parlor and a back parlor.

A very comfortable room, it was furnished with one of those beautiful rugs that are typical of American comfort. Thick, plush, and made of soft wool fibers, these sumptuous rugs are nothing like our thin, miserable rugs at home. There were a few other pieces of furniture including a folding bed that, unlike the one at Miss Flack's, had a real mattress, a wooden chest, a large standing mirror with paper flowers glued to its frame, and an unusual Japanese screen. Two tables, one of which was made of a very pretty marble, were covered with linen tablecloths, embroidered with bright silk flowers. Completing the decor were a sofa and several rocking chairs that were padded with brightly colored, silk embroidered cushions. Here and there, vibrant pieces of silky fabric were strewn over the furniture or held in place by a vase or knickknack.

This decorative profusion, with rooms filled with knickknacks, pieces of fabric, and paper flowers, has been in style in America for about twenty years. Although the arrangements are not always tasteful—especially the paper flowers which I would eliminate—they are quite charming and the colorful fabrics create a feeling of gaiety and comfort.

Another American luxury, costly even for the middle class, is the white curtains that cover windows. Only in very wealthy homes does one see drapery made of tapestry or other fabrics.

Several more rooms were located on the ground floor and the layout of the second and third floors was similar. The attic was divided into a number of small rooms and all of the rooms, except for Mrs. A.'s quarters, were occupied by other guests.

Most of the other boarders were of modest means, some better off than others.[1] I made a point of getting to know them and learning all that I could from them about American life. I initiated myself into the intimate details of this American existence which is so different from ours. In this heterogeneous setting, I learned a thousand details about American life that I never would have found out had I confined myself to elegant society.

Perhaps that is why I do not regret my stay at Mrs. A.'s home.

This excellent woman was about thirty years old and had been a widow for four years. She had two daughters, Eva, who was eight and Alice, who was five.

Her immediate and warm kindness toward me was rooted in the fact that I was French. This was exceptional, as in general, French people are not loved in Chicago where the majority of the population is of German descent.[2] Mrs. A.'s father was French. Since she was orphaned at a very young age, she had never had the opportunity to study French. Her greatest regret was that she was unable to read the beautiful French books that her father had left her. She expressed a childlike delight when I promised to teach her to speak and read French.

While her husband was still alive, she, like most other American women, led a life of incredible idleness. She was not even responsible for the upkeep of the home since the family lived in a boardinghouse in order to have fewer chores.

When her husband died accidentally, she obviously had to change her ways.

The boardinghouse rent brought her a sizable income. She was also very skilled at making inexpensive clothing for herself and her daughters. All of her feminine qualities, however, were undermined by an unbelievable disorder in the house. There was always tremendous clutter, a mess of all kinds of things!

Her personality was quite whimsical and she loved to sing. The very sweet and poetic national hymn, "My Country Tis of Thee," was her favorite song and she would often sing it to her two daughters while they sat on her lap. That is how I learned the song.

Mrs. A. adored her daughters but she brought them up in a way that at first stupefied me, turning upside down all my ideas about education. She never scolded them, and this seeming indifference unnerved my French sensibility.

One day Eva, the older of the two girls, left for school at nine in the morning as usual but did not come home for lunch. I thought that the mother, like any French mother, would be worried and would run looking for her daughter. I, myself, was very distraught with feverish anxiety and would have given anything to know where the girl was. But Mrs. A. did not move. It was not until the clock struck four and her daughter was still not home, that she went to the school only to learn that the girl had not attended that day. Mrs. A. then returned home and calmly took up her chores. I was more worried than she was and gently questioned her about friends or relatives the girl might have visited. "She will come back," Mrs. A. told me in a calm voice, "she has money in her pocket."

At approximately seven in the evening, the little girl came home looking sheepish. I was sure that she would be welcomed with a severe reprimand. Not at all!

"Where were you?" her mother simply asked. "You had me worried!"

Worried! I had not noticed that she had been in the least preoccupied, but knowing her sincerity I did not doubt her word. Eva sensed her mother's concern and burst into tears.

Throwing herself into her mother's arms, she told us that she had spent the whole day at Washington Park with her friends.

Mrs. A. accepted this explanation and did not scold Eva further regarding playing hooky. I was sure that she would do it again but would tell her mother the next time to spare her any worry.

The idea of forbidding the child from playing hooky did not even cross Mrs. A.'s mind. Americans do not believe that parents have the right to impose their will upon children.

Their philosophy is to allow children to learn directly from experience.[3] They argue that no child ever learned from simply listening to other people

recount their experience. These principles are logical but we would be in-
capable of applying them in France.

How many times did I rush to help Alice after she fell down while Mrs. A.
remained seated! Her mother adored her but never moved even though the
little girl rarely cried after falling except if she had really injured herself.

Her mother, of course, comforted her but only with these stern words: 'I
warned you Alice. I told you that you would hurt yourself. I hope that this
time you have learned your lesson."

Alice would cry all the louder and then would kiss her mother and continue with her life lessons.

This Jean-Jacques style approach is the foundation of American education.[4] Like any system, it has negative aspects but I believe that the positive
elements outweigh the negative. Although the mother's instinct for tenderness might suffer, children learn how to handle situations by themselves.
They are rarely afraid, yet though they are not fearful of cats or dogs, they
never tease these animals. They know that animals have claws and teeth to
defend themselves so if they pull the cat's tail and are scratched, they know
that it is their own fault. In addition, I was struck by how docile domestic animals are in America. This is undoubtedly due to the fact that both
adults and children treat them well. The birds are so friendly that it would
be very easy to grab them but I have never seen a child try to chase them
or hit them with rocks like French children are so fond of doing. American
children have been told that birds are precious animals that must be taken
care of and protected, and since no one ever lies to them, they believe it
and act accordingly.

If a child is not lied to, he will never lie. And why would he lie since he
has such freedom of action?

This candor is often lacking in French children who lie for fear of being
punished. I would like them to be as honest as American children but their
honesty depends upon us.

In all respects, childhood in America is much happier than in France.
Free from all constraints, children live their own lives and not those of their
parents. In America, one never sees a four or five year old boy dressed in
elegant clothes with his hands forced into tight gloves, accompanying his
mother on her visits.[5] He is never required to sit still on his chair and listen
to a boring conversation.

Even before I came to America I found this French custom ridiculous
and always had some toys available when children came to visit. This often
displeased the mothers who were eager to show how well behaved their

children were and how capable they were of staying in one place for hours, as immobile and as mute as statues.

American children do visit their friends, not those of their parents. It is not unusual to see a small child alone in the street on his way to visit a friend.

In fact, it is completely acceptable for children to be in the street unaccompanied by adults. Rich and poor children alike play on the sidewalk and unlike in France, no one assumes that they are poor, uneducated, or abandoned.

Left alone with neither parents nor servants watching them, they are fully capable of protecting themselves from cold and hot or from having their feet crushed under those of horses. They take perfect care of themselves because their parents instill in them the necessity of doing so early on. In France, we are so intent on thinking for our children and warning them of possible harm that we neglect to develop these important qualities in them.

This kind of education is completely contrary to ours in both the physical and moral sense; no constraint is placed on the development of the mind or the body, as the child is free from its earliest days in swaddling clothes. American children are not spoiled in the same way that our children are. Here, parents neither punish their children nor joke with them. Children laugh together but adults seldom laugh with them. When the father speaks, his words are always taken seriously.

American parents offer but do not impose their advice and consequently, it is more likely to be followed.

Parents are respected but not in the blind way that is common in France. Before a child even knows what his responsibilities are to his family, he knows what their responsibility is to him. He knows that his parents must support him and that the law prohibits them from striking him, under penalty of imprisonment.

But American children also know that parents have the right to give up unruly children and this weighs heavily upon their little minds.

Every little American boy has two dreams: to become president of the United States and to earn a large fortune, which is a less ambitious and more attainable goal.

The love of money is one of the first instincts apparent in American children. This thirst for wealth, which we would hate to see in our own children, leads American children to imagine all sorts of ingenious ways to earn and save money.

When a child reaches an age at which his parents judge him to be mature, he is given a monthly personal allowance. This is a way of teaching the child to both manage and save money. It is common, for example, to see young boys walking barefoot with their shoes over their shoulders, trying to preserve them for as long as possible since they have to purchase them with their allowance.

I have seen other young boys who spend their entire vacation selling newspapers. With a large bundle under their arm, they jump with surprising agility onto the street car, moving from one compartment to the next, selling papers.

Any profit that they make is theirs to keep. Almost all children have savings that they are free to spend as they wish.

Across from our room, two young ladies shared the back parlor. They were not related in any way but were two friends who worked in the packaging department of a laundry business and lived together to split the cost of lodging.

In Chicago, there are several of these large laundries. They resemble huge beautifully equipped factories and everything—washing, drying and ironing—is done by machine.[6]

In terms of whiteness and brightness, the result is superb! From an economic standpoint, however, it is a different story! It is certainly preferable, however, to having laundry done by hand. The Chinese dominate the hand laundry industry and have a nasty habit of spitting on laundry to dampen it.[7]

These large laundries each have three or four branches in the city. They have numerous horses and carriages for delivery and many depots in bakeries, stationary stores, and other establishments. Since commercial rents are so high in Chicago, it is common for several businesses to use the same address for very different services.

One of these places was very close to Mrs. A.'s house and served as a bakery, a milk store, a telegraph office, and a laundry depot.

The people who use these laundry services are generally working men and women who leave home early in the morning and have no one to do their laundry for them. Concierges, who willingly do laundry in France, are nonexistent here.[8] These kind, working-class neighbors could not exist in this country where the attitude is "every man for himself." The laundry customers wrap and tie their clothing in paper and include their name, address, and a detailed list of the contents. If the laundry is not appropriately packaged and tied, it is not accepted.

Many women, like my young neighbors, hold jobs in the packaging department and earn the reasonable salary of one dollar per day.[9]

A couple lived on the second floor in the room just above ours. Mr. H., an inspector for the water company, was a strapping fellow of about thirty-five. He had a mustache and a scar on his face that he had valiantly received in the last war.[10]

An officer in the volunteer army, he was as happy as a child to participate in the festivities of the Centenary, looking superb in uniform on horseback. He was the best man in the world, a very pleasant conversationalist, extremely polite, and adoring of his wife in a way that is unknown among French men.[11]

Mrs. H. deserved this attention as she was a charming woman who was at least ten years younger than her husband.

Short and a little stout—which is rare for young American women—her face expressed such energy that without her female attributes, one would have mistaken her for a young man. She was also quite masculine in terms of her personality and intellectual capacities, and was one of the most respected and influential electoral representatives.

At that time, the presidential elections were coming up.

A zealous friend and admirer of Benjamin Harrison, Mrs. H. struggled furiously against the increasingly numerous supporters of Grover Cleveland.[12] She attended many meetings and was a brilliant orator, giving long speeches that were both lively and captivating. Her husband, the most loyal and fervent of her listeners, enthusiastically showed me the beautiful bouquets of flowers presented to his wife after each meeting. He flattered himself with the idea that they were glorious trophies and a prelude to definitive triumph.

But what a tiring and feverish life that poor woman led. Her entire day was spent sending telegrams, making telephone calls, writing speeches, and doing research to refute expected arguments and interjections.

Her tremendous physical and mental energy amazed me. I could only compare her enthusiasm and energy in the fight for Harrison with the skepticism, laziness, and cowardice of the majority of French politicians, who, during the legislative elections, put forth their interests instead of those of others.

Mrs. H., unlike some of our campaigners, never resorted to scandal or rumor to advance her candidate. She always spoke in a dignified manner and everyone respectfully listened to her.

By the time the elections came, I had lost contact with her. I am sure that the defeat of Harrison was difficult for her but it would not have been the end of her career. She is one of those people who is energized by defeat and in my opinion, a woman of the future.

A lady and her daughter lived on the same floor as Mr. and Mrs. H. The woman had been abandoned by her husband, a situation which is quite rare in America. This poor lady had once occupied a brilliant social position but was now reduced to earning a living for herself and her daughter. Very sad and in frail health due to fact that she had to work, the unhappy woman had all of my sympathy. I would have liked to have helped her and her adorable eight year old daughter who seemed to share her mother's chagrin at their situation. The mother worked as an employee somewhere in the city and spent the entire day at work. Little Edwige went to school and as soon as she arrived home she did her chores or read her magazine. In America, there are many excellent publications for children, most of which are published and directed by women.

Edwige did not play very much and the lighthearted behavior of our hostess's daughters seemed to bore her. One sensed in this child the annoyance of someone whose social milieu had changed and who felt superior to the other children. I wanted to take care of her and distract her. She had studied piano and enjoyed coming to our room to play mine.[13] Unfortunately, as soon as the other girls knew that she was in our room, they would quickly come in and I would have to ask them all to leave in order to avoid total chaos. Sometimes I would take them for a walk on Drexel Boulevard, a delightful street that resembles our Champs Elysées [fig. 5].[14]

We were often accompanied by Gyp, a charming little black dog who was Mrs. A's favorite. I sometimes spoke French to this intelligent animal. The dog's impatience and anger with this incomprehensible language was very funny to see, as was his delirious joy when I finally spoke to him in English.

Almost all of the boarders were agreeable and interesting, except for a young man who lived in one of the rooms on the top floor.

He was taking courses at the Protestant seminary and was preparing to become a pastor. In the winter, instead of studying in his room, he would sit in Mrs. A's warm dining room. I have no idea how he managed to study there with the constant coming and going of delivery people, neighbors, and children.

A strange appearance for a future pastor! He was very ugly with rough, angular features and small eyes that never met anyone's gaze. He always seemed annoyed or uncomfortable, two expressions that are quite rare in America.

In fact, he was not an American but a German who had come to Chicago when he was very young. He detested me and I cordially returned his sentiment. We seldom spoke to one another and when we did it was a strange kind of exchange.

His hatred for France was clear even in his most innocent remarks.

"All French people are devils," he told me in English with his coarse German accent. "Their impiety will cause them to disappear from Europe, crushed by the pious nation of Germany, as they are the scandal of the universe."

Ah! If only I were a man I would have stuffed those hateful and stupid words down his throat! Instead, I joked with him and congratulated him on the charitable feelings his religion inspired in him.

As I mentioned earlier, I was able to prepare our meals in the hostess's kitchen.

Since I was preparing the meals myself, I also had to do the grocery shopping, an activity that I did not enjoy at all but that I had bravely decided to undertake.

I always took my dictionary with me to the shops, and the few times that I forgot it, I was immediately exposed as a foreigner. Once for example, I asked for "mind" of veal instead of brains. Fortunately, the butcher was very agreeable and simply chuckled at my ignorance.

Markets in Chicago are unlike those in France in that you can purchase everything under one roof.

Across from Mrs. A.'s house there was a grocery store that was rather pompously named "Empire Grocery." Fruit, vegetables, bread, fish, meat and other staples were sold there, with each product displayed in a separate area. The entire market was very clean and the meat counter was kept dark in order to keep flies away.

In another butcher shop, the same precautions were not taken. I requested a quarter of beef and the butcher took it out of an enormous meat locker.

Upon arriving home, I unwrapped the meat from the package and found that my steak was literally covered on all sides with crushed flies. In the short amount of time that it took for the butcher to cut, weigh, and prepare the meat, the flies had stuck to it!

Groceries in Chicago, particularly meat, are about half the price of what they cost in Paris. A filet of beef of excellent quality costs seventy-five centimes per pound which is the equivalent of approximately 450 grams. Leg of lamb and veal are sold for between sixty and seventy centimes per pound.

Fish is delicious and quite inexpensive. Coffee costs one franc and twenty-five centimes, sugar is thirty centimes, and tea is priced between one and one franc fifty centimes per pound. Products imported from Europe are also very reasonably priced except for certain special items.[15]

In terms of wine, it is better to avoid it. Californian wine sells for five francs per gallon which is equivalent to about four liters. It has a very unpleasant taste and is too alcoholic. In order to get French wine of even mediocre quality, you have to pay two dollars per bottle.

The most popular beverages are water and milk. However, Chicago brews a large quantity of excellent beer that is sold throughout America. Milwaukee, which is located fifty miles from Chicago, is an even greater producer of beer.

The large number of people of German descent explains the excellent quality of this beverage which is truly delicious. Beer is sold at a very reasonable price and is consumed in great quantities by the most cosmopolitan inhabitants of American cities.

In America, as elsewhere, the French have a reputation as excellent cooks and connoisseurs of fine food.[16] For this reason, each time that I stepped into the kitchen to prepare our meals I was immediately surrounded by curious spectators. I will never forget their surprise one day while I was making *pot au feu*, a traditional French beef stew.

This mixture of water, meat and vegetables seemed strange to them and their surprise reached its peak when, using a sugar cube and a spoon, I made the caramel that would color my broth! In America, veal stock is often used but it is colorless and bland. The only soups that are consumed are made from concentrate but no one knows how to make them. The pleasant aroma of the stew impressed the ladies and when the broth was ready, I offered them a taste. They unanimously declared it to be delicious and decided that Mrs. A. would prepare a *pot au feu* the next day, under my supervision. To show their appreciation, they named the dish "Mistress Grandin's Soup" and the recipe circulated around the neighborhood.

This attention was flattering at first, but soon became annoying. All of my dishes were soon being tasted by these ladies without my permission, and the situation became intolerable. I decided that it was time to move.

One night, during the last weeks of our stay at Mrs. A.'s, a burglar broke into the house. He attempted to enter the house through a ground floor window in our hostess's bedroom.

Fortunately, she was not asleep and thanks to the moonlight she spotted the burglar just as he was trying to raise the window.

Frightened, she screamed for help. As soon as he heard her scream, the burglar prudently left. By the time the men in the house arrived in Mrs. A.'s room, the burglar was already far away.

I asked if any of the men were armed but this idea seemed surprising to them.

"Why should we be armed?"

"But in order to shoot this horrible rascal."

This notion scandalized these people. Since the burglar was clearly after money and did not intend to kill anyone, they did not believe that they had the right to shoot him. The possibility of capturing the burglar and turning him over to the authorities did not seem very useful to them as they explained that he could be out on bail the next day.

I was forced to concede that we had acted for the best by obliging him to leave. No one was even going to try to bother him in his retreat.

The following morning we noticed that the burglar had taken some of the laundry from the clothes line, including shirts, socks and undershirts. He had left the women's and children's clothing which would have been useless to him, a delicate turn of behavior that we appreciated.

This lax attitude toward burglars is not uncommon in Chicago. As a result, criminals are becoming more daring each day, capable of holding their own with classic Italian bandits.

Around the same time of this incident we heard that another crime took place in the Wabash boardinghouse which was close to our lodgings.

One evening, while all of the guests were having dinner in the dining room, a band of ten masked individuals broke into the house. They had a revolver and took all of the ladies' jewelry. Then, in a blink of an eye, they went to the upper floors and stole everything of value that they could find.

Not one of them was arrested!

An even bolder bandit had committed similar robberies in Chicago and other northern cities. Riding a feisty horse and armed with a revolver, he stopped carriages and stole from women. It took a whole regiment of policemen on horseback several days to capture him.

From time to time there are even instances where trains are hijacked and pillaged.

Chapter Six

World's Columbian Exposition: Dedication Ceremonies

Visit to a School—Ball at the Auditorium—
Celebratory Parades

On October 10, 1892, the city of Chicago began donning her finery for the Dedication Ceremonies of the Fourth Centenary. Houses and streets displayed multicolored flags and banners featuring the portrait of Christopher Columbus. From all points in America, large crowds of citizens arrived to attend the dedication ceremony of the exposition.

I do not know why so many people criticized this exposition. Americans could rightly be proud as it was one of the marvels of the century. The amount of money, energy, and enthusiasm that went into the planning of this event is beyond estimation. Its location on the banks of Lake Michigan alone would transport you with admiration. It is impossible to describe Americans' enthusiasm upon seeing the site, the exterior sections of which were almost complete. The festivities went beyond simple pride and joy. Children were the most excited of all and many had spent their savings on decorations for their homes and schools. It seemed that every child was waving a small American flag, which were sold in packages of twelve.

On special occasions, such as celebrations or trips, it is customary for Americans to send friends a flag. Even as a foreigner, I received a beautiful silk American flag with seventeen stars, each representing a state. The flag was a gift from Miss H., a distinguished young painter who had studied in France and whose family had welcomed me in Chicago. This gesture gave me great pleasure.

On October 21st, the city awoke with great enthusiasm and was greeted with radiant sunshine. Flags and banners fluttered everywhere while tricolored awnings stretched over the streets. The glorious sky was sprinkled with stars, just like the flags. I attended a Presbyterian Church service with Miss H.'s family, which was one of the many religious celebrations taking place in the city that day.

The pastor's sermon was full of patriotism and honored the memory of Christopher Columbus. The sacred hymns were very moving, especially "My Country Tis of Thee," which is both a religious and patriotic song. This hymn, whose words are so beautiful and whose melody exhales an infinite charm, almost brought me to tears. My complex emotional reaction was linked in part to my thoughts of France, whose flag shares the same colors.

The unveiling of the new statue of Christopher Columbus was to take place that day as well. The work of an American sculptor, the statue had been erected in a small park in the center of the city.[1] Instead of attending that ceremony, I chose to go to a celebration that was being held in the public school across from our lodgings.[2]

Nothing is easier than getting permission to visit an American school as one simply makes a request to the director.[3] Often, the head of the school is even willing to give a tour of the classrooms.

On that special day, the school was opened to all visitors. From the ground floor to the fourth floor, the building was decorated with flags and wall hangings. The main entrance displayed a drawing of a large ship created by the pupils to commemorate the voyage that brought Columbus to America.

At one o'clock in the afternoon, all the boys and girls gathered with their flags in hand. A crowd of parents and friends entered at two o'clock, all holding flags.

The classroom doors were then opened and pupils were in their usual seats with an American flag fluttering above each blond or brown-haired child. The teachers stood behind them, holding bundles of flags. In a sort of vestibule which could be seen from all classrooms, a bust of Columbus stood on a pedestal decorated with American flags.

Each class took its turn parading in front of the hero's bust, singing and waving their flags. A boy of about twelve years old came forward and stood next to the bust. At once timid and proud, he wore a badge that I think he had received for good behavior. He presented a speech in honor of Columbus, traced the history of the discovery of America, and expressed the appreciation of all Americans to Columbus, this great and brave man to whom they owe their glorious country.

Upon finishing his speech, he began to sing the national anthem and was joined by everyone else. He then placed his flag at the foot of the bust and everyone else quickly followed suit, filing past the statue and adding their flags to the pile. The ceremony was moving in its simplicity. One could sense in both the children and the adults a mixture of enthusiasm and solemnity, as they expressed their deep love for this country, a land of intelligence, science, and liberty. As we left, the teachers gave each of us a large silk ribbon bearing the image of the American flag and a medallion representing the arrival of Columbus in America inscribed with the words "National Public School, Columbus Day Celebration, October 21, 1492–1892."

That evening, we were invited to a sumptuous ball at The Auditorium given by officials of the city of Chicago and of the exposition for American and foreign representatives [fig. 6].[4]

The Auditorium is one of the largest buildings in Chicago.[5] The entryway faces Michigan Avenue, a spectacular street which is bordered by the lake on one side and by homes on the other. An immense cube entirely constructed of a purple hued American stone, the building is topped by an enormous square tower.

This impressive structure houses a theater that is also used for parties and receptions, the largest hotel in the city, and several different businesses including a French language institute.

The theater is considered by Americans to be the rival of the Paris Opera.[6] To be honest, the grand scale of this theater makes such a comparison impossible. Moreover, the lavish interior decor of the Paris Opera is completing lacking here. This American theater is quite simple and sparse, in keeping with the sober appearance of the building's exterior. The entry is not at all majestic as it is just a few steps up from the sidewalk and the door is crushed by the heaviness of the building.

Inside, the theater had the sumptuous appearance of an official gala, whether in Chicago or Paris.[7] Lush flowers, green plants, and velvet wall hangings decorated the long marble staircases; bright lights shimmered in the mirrors and in the polished gold decor; military uniforms decorated with shiny medals and colorful ribbons stood out against black tuxedoes pinned with boutonnieres, and the ladies' ravishing gowns were literally blinding with their sparkling constellations of precious stones and diamonds.[8]

Royal princesses would not be able to compete with the magnificence of these millionaires' wives. On their bare shoulders, in their curled tresses, in the cleavage of their dresses, and even their satin shoes were covered with jewels that made it seem that Golconde was stirring.[9]

The loges were draped with garlands of roses and lilacs and on the parquet floor below, couples waltzed and did the Boston with charming grace.[10] I was struck by how different the ambiance was from our stiff, formal balls in France. As I have already said, Americans truly enjoy dancing and this gave a sense of true pleasure to the party which is not the case with French balls.

Buffet tables were scattered around the room but there was none of the disorder that occurs at these events in France. The supper was excellent, served on small tables, which is the most agreeable method. At the exit, the valet service was well organized.[11]

Almost all of the guests had come in private carriages as owning a carriage in Chicago is truly indispensable for those who can afford it. Although taxicabs are plentiful, they are not considered acceptable transportation for a lady going to a ball. It is necessary to rent a carriage and the price varies according to the distance traveled.[12] The exact fare is up to the driver but one pays between twenty and twenty-five francs for round trip fare to the theater, which is quite expensive.[13] Cabs are spacious enough for four people.

In spite of their high prices, these cabs are always in demand. It is perfectly acceptable for a young lady to go to the theater or out for the evening in the company of a young man. But this privilege requires the young man to pick up and bring the young lady home in a carriage. He also must offer her flowers for her dress, along with the requisite bouquet which she keeps with her throughout the evening. One can only imagine how popular the cabs are! In terms of flowers, young ladies use them in overabundance. Unlike the French custom of pinning a small bunch of flowers to the shoulder or chest, American ladies prefer to keep the stems and leaves on so that the bouquet often covers the entire front of the gown.

This custom of allowing young girls to go out with young men without a chaperone would seem very strange, improper and even dangerous in France.[14] Any fears, however, are largely unfounded. While dangerous incidents occur from time to time, they are clearly the exception.

A young American man views himself as the young lady's protector and behaves much like our chivalrous knights of the past. Devout and devoted to their ladies, they honor rather than abuse the trust placed in them.[15] Unfortunately, this species has disappeared in France. Even if a young man in America is very much in love with a young lady, he will never say anything that could offend her. This camaraderie between boys and girls begins when they are very young.

From the time they take a seat in the classroom, American boys are taught that their role is to protect little girls. They are very proud of this duty which they uphold throughout life.

In fact, one article of American law concerns the protection of women.[16] The fact that this protection is officially stated is evidence of the moral superiority of American men over their European counterparts. The American man's profound sense of dignity leads him to protect everyone and everything around him.

He does not admit that he has an obligation to a weaker and less gifted creature than himself; rather it is his wife who depends on him for everything. As a young man, his first goal is to earn enough money to marry the woman he loves and then provide a comfortable and happy life for her and their children.

Once married, he works incessantly to improve the situation of his growing family. He takes care of all business difficulties but never brings the bustle of business into the home where his wife enjoys sweet comfort.

His choice of a wife is motivated by love, not money. How different from French men whose only concern is the dowry!

"I am going into business and I need to make a good marriage in order to pay for my establishment! My studies will pull me from obscurity, I have artistic talent that will make my name and will allow me to marry an heiress." The dowry is used to purchase a business, to pay lawyer's fees, or to cover debts incurred during their wild single years.[17] One never hears a French man say "my fortune will allow me to marry a penniless woman!"

Although working-class marriages in America are similar to those in France in that there is no dowry involved, I observed one major difference. Once the couple marries, the man no longer allows his wife to work. Only in exceptional cases of great need does the husband permit his wife to work, as any financial contribution by her is considered insulting to him.

Help from the wife, in the form of either money or work, is considered a moral failure, practically an infamy.

Adoration and respect for women here is not like in France, where it is just one of those pretty theories put forth but hardly applied; simply pompous words that belie actions. In America, actions are corroborated by words.

Any infraction of the laws designed to protect women is punished with the most rigorous penalties. The American man finds them such as they involve a financial payment.

If a man fathers children, he is responsible for their upbringing even if he does not marry the mother. According to the law, he is required to pay whether he is single or married.

This is a matter for reflection. If the American man is not naturally superior to his European brother, he will certainly become so by reason and by force. He will become increasingly intelligent and moral while others will become less so.

On the day following the ball, the celebration continued with military and civil parades across the city.

At exactly two o'clock in the afternoon, officials took their places in carriages for the procession from The Auditorium. The Vice President, standing in for President Harrison who was at his ailing wife's bedside, state representatives, and other important officials were applauded by the crowd and led the parade.

For several days, Chicago had witnessed the arrival of an innumerable mass of soldiers with representatives, if not from every state, then at least from every regiment. These groups of soldiers preceded and followed the official carriages that were decorated with state flags and the American flag.

The parade continued for four hours. In the midst of enthusiastic applause and hurrahs, clanging cymbals, and lively march rhythms played by military bands, the parade passed by with uniforms of every color: blue, white, green, red. Foot soldiers, cavaliers, and artillery men each paraded in turn through clouds of dust kicked up by horses and by the wheels of caissons and cannons.

Although the soldiers' uniforms were more or less similar to those of the French army in terms of cut and color, the caps were very different. Almost all of them were beautifully embellished with feathers that were long and soft, like those of the Italian infantry.

The gloves were also different from ours: yellow instead of white with wrist bands.

If the lowly soldiers' caps were accented with feathers, what can one say about the feathers on the generals' headdresses? The French styles were completely dull in comparison.

Although all the participants were warmly applauded, the American Indians received the most enthusiastic greeting.

Wearing dark blue outfits that brought to mind those of our hunters, they walked in a stiff, yet calm manner. Their tall stature, long, severe faces, and dark, sparkling eyes gave them an imposing presence.

In spite of the frenetic applause, their expression remained unchanged. I would have liked to have seen a glimmer, even of anger, in their eyes. This indifference is more tragic than hate as it represents the apathy of the last vestiges of a race.

The American army came next in the parade. In honor of Columbus, the Spanish and Italian delegations were given the second position. The German delegation, which was the largest of all, followed. Groups of schoolchildren, and carriages bearing the symbols of letters, sciences, and arts completed the procession as it moved through the streets of Chicago and stopped at the principal city monuments.

The following day at ten-thirty in the morning, the parade formed once again for the dedication ceremony of the exposition [fig. 7].

The Liberal Arts Pavilion was chosen as the dedication site due to its spacious dimensions.

Constructed entirely of iron, it was the largest building of the exposition with its total surface measuring four thousand square meters.

Government representatives and foreign dignitaries took their places on a dais in the center of the pavilion. Behind them sat five thousand vocalists representing choral groups from all over the United States. Although 150,000 guests had been invited, even more people forced their way in and filled the building to the rafters.

The national anthem opened the ceremony and was followed by a prayer led by a pastor. Many speeches were then presented. All were quite similar as they always are in these circumstances, expressing pride and joy in the success of the exposition, praise for the United States, and thanks to all who had helped with this tremendous project.

The Vice President spoke first and was followed by a number of other more or less brilliant speakers including Mrs. Potter Palmer, whose speech had a remarkable eloquence and was a great triumph.[18]

Mrs. Palmer was the founder and organizer of the Women's Exhibition in Chicago. It is thanks to her and her tireless persistence that women's work had been granted a special place in the exposition. Mrs. Palmer's name is very well known in Paris where during her last visit she charmed and impressed everyone with her business sense and diplomacy.[19] Admired and adored in America, she uses her immense fortune in intelligent ways. As a woman, she is most interested and devoted to women's causes. She is involved in projects designed to improve women's lives as well as to develop their scientific, literary, and artistic education.

In her energetic and vibrant speech before the mostly male assembly, she proclaimed the equality of men and women in the domain of work. She also demanded equal appreciation for women's work and asked that an all female committee be formed so that women's work could be evaluated by women, just as men's work is evaluated by men.

After the speeches and songs, the Protestant bishop and archbishop each blessed the exposition and concluded with a final prayer.

Following the ceremony, we all scattered around the "White City," which is the name that Chicagoans have conferred upon the site.

As we headed toward the exit, we passed a group of four generals dressed in parade uniforms, decorated with feathers and medals. They were talking with great animation and I stopped for a few seconds to observe them. I was particularly struck by a tall, distinguished man in the group when suddenly the object of my admiration turned in my direction. Alas! Standing right next to me, he pressed his index finger on his nostril and quickly blew out some mucus that must have been bothering him.

Frozen in my tracks, I stifled a cry of indignation, the naiveté of which even amused me.

Oh! Such a handsome general!

The general, unaware of my reaction to his gesture, then took out an elegant handkerchief and proceeded to wipe his nose. Ah! But too late! Much too late!

It took the view of the lake, so limpidly blue and so superb in its immensity, to help me recover from the shock of this incident. In order to harmonize with the grandeur of the lake, it was necessary to create vast palaces as large as those on the lake shore. Although some of the smaller buildings that were to be annexed to larger ones had not yet been completed, the overall effect was harmonious. The lines and facades of the large buildings were not masked or cut by the secondary structures. In their unfinished form, certain buildings had a severe, sober kind of beauty that they would later lose when decorated with ornaments in poor taste. Others would benefit from decoration, but their appearance at that point was admirable.

It was in these empty buildings that almost all of the military detachments were housed and there they received numerous visits.

The American soldier is not at all like our French soldiers who are obliged to perform military service. Unlike their French counterparts, Americans join the army because of their love for it, not out of a sense of obligation. They live a comfortable life, earn a good salary, and are permitted to marry and live with their families. Fortunately for them and for the prosperity of their country, they are rarely mobilized for war. They are called into service, however, during American Indian revolts.

The crowd was especially attracted by the encampment of Indian soldiers.[20]

Even though many visitors were staring at them, the Indians remained as impassive as they had been during the parade. The cold impassibility evident on some of the faces was dreadful. Few of them speak English; they speak their own language among themselves but learn the language of their conquerors quite easily. A military career appeals to them for a number of reasons including the impressive uniforms, the opportunity to use arms, and the generous amount of leisure time that soldiers enjoy. Indians are, by nature, both brave and lazy and they respond well to the sense of authority that comes from being in the army. The number of Indians admitted, however, is limited as it would obviously be dangerous to allow large numbers of them to become soldiers.

They respond well to instruction and as soon as they establish themselves in one of the territories granted to them, a school is opened for all who are interested in attending.

Many pastors assume the role of educating these primitive creatures and have very good results.

They live among the Indians and their families and are loved and respected.

But there is a curse of this civilization that takes over more rapidly than the good works: it is alcohol! Americans, who make a great effort to combat alcoholism, seem to encourage alcohol consumption among the Indians, perhaps as a way of more quickly exterminating this ethnic group.

This race, which was so glorious and powerful before its conquest, gets smaller each day and is near complete extinction.[21] Shouldn't Americans make an effort to preserve some of the native children of this rich land?

That evening, following the dedication, Chicago was illuminated with fireworks bursting out all over the city. The fireworks over the lake were the most spectacular as their reflection on the huge sheet of water seemed to spread out to the extreme edges of the earth.

Throughout the day, trams, trains, and boats transported an enormous number of visitors to the Exhibition site.[22] When the fireworks were over, great commotion ensued as everyone departed at once.

The trams were so congested with people that they could not move forward but fortunately, some thoughtful passengers disembarked so that the trams could proceed. The boats were so overloaded that I never would have consented to board, as it seemed that they were about to sink under the weight of so many passengers. So many people jammed onto the trains that it was impossible to sit down and difficult to breathe. When we came to our stop, we had difficulty making our way through the mass of people.

No one complained though, as everyone felt that the most important priority was to get home safely. The trains continued to run until they had accommodated all the passengers and many of the tickets were not even punched.

In Chicago, train tickets are not sold at the station but instead can be bought in ticket offices or in most stores.

They can be purchased in quantities of twenty-five, fifty, or one hundred, with the price per ticket decreasing with the number of tickets purchased. This system is much more practical than ours, where a photograph and other ridiculous formalities are necessary to obtain a train pass.

The ticket is punched each time a passenger boards the train. That particular night was exceptional as there were so many passengers on-board the train that it was impossible for the conductor to punch all the tickets. In a spirit of generosity, the railroad company offered a free ride to those passengers lucky enough not to have their tickets punched.

Those who do not have tickets pay the conductor directly and receive a small paper receipt. The paper stubs indicate the number of tickets purchased onboard. Since it is much more expensive to buy tickets on the train, most passengers purchase them beforehand.

Chapter Seven

The Milwaukee Fire
Presidential Campaign—City in Flames—
Funeral Customs

Every thing came to an end, as the torches were extinguished and the festive music faded. After three days of celebration, the city returned to its
usual routine. The three day holiday was unusual in this place where there
is so much activity.

The exposition festivities had brought two of our Parisian friends to Chicago and we very much wanted to entertain them at our place so that it
could be like old times in France. Even though it was a very small party,
numerous obstacles arose.

I had first looked into the possibility of having a hotel caterer prepare a
meal that would be served at our home. Apparently, this is not very commonly
done in Chicago and was deemed to be very inconvenient. The price would
have been exorbitant and the only menu options available were American
boiled vegetables served without a trace of butter, which did not interest
me, and roasted meats, in fact very well roasted meats.

After thinking it over, I decided to prepare the meal myself. This plan was
not going to be easy since I did not have adequate cooking equipment for
the preparation of the dishes that I wanted to make. My hostess' kitchen
tools consisted of a few, very simple utensils. Even so, I was able to make
do with her primitive saucepans, my industriousness making up for the im-
perfection of the tools. An additional problem was that I could not imagine
serving the meal in our hostess' dining room.

All of the boarders in the house would have come in to watch the spectacle of four French people enjoying a nice meal. I avoided this situation
by setting up a table in our bedroom. Mrs. A. lent me the table, as well as
a nice tablecloth, and I rented all of the dishes and the silverware. When
the table was set, I was very satisfied with the result.

My curious neighbors did find a way to sneak into our room to admire all of the preparations. They were particularly surprised to see me placing a rose in the glass at each place setting.

In terms of the dinner, I must say that it was a great success. A delicious consommé was followed by a superb lake fish served with a white sauce, which was a triumph for me! Filet of beef followed, served with a sauce made with whiskey instead of Madeira. Everyone seemed to agree that the whiskey was a welcome substitution. For a vegetable, we had California peas with butter followed by a salad and roast chicken! I served fruit and a variety of pastries and sweets for dessert. I did not have to worry about making the pastries as they are readily available in abundance in America and no other place makes more exquisite sweets.[1]

Many French cooks will laugh when I say that the ingredient that I had the hardest time finding was parsley! I needed some for the fish and this fragrant herb is not easy to find in Chicago. Mrs. A. and her friends could not believe that I was spending so many cents on this green herb that was simply going to garnish the fish.

They also could not comprehend why it was necessary to spend so much time keeping an eye on the sauces. They all swore that they would never have the patience to undertake such a recipe and attributed this dedication to the demanding palate of the French.

These special recipes were even enjoyed by the resident religious student whom I had taken to calling "Monsieur le Pasteur." He tasted all of the sauces and seemed to particularly like the one flavored with whiskey. This, of course, did not stop him from speaking out against the moral corruption of France. According to him, our nation was so infested with vice that it would end up in the depths of hell.

This saintly outburst only made me smile. I guessed that Mr. Pastor was criticizing my cooking just like the fox in the fable.[2]

Since I did not have anyone to assist me in serving the dinner, our landlady, Mrs. A. graciously offered to help. I believe that she was motivated as much by curiosity as by a desire to help. Her stupefied expression at the different aspects of the meal amused us all.

During certain moments of this dinner with our friends from Paris, I really felt that we were at home. All four of us had fun talking about our dear city and we chatted about many topics that are only of interest to Parisians. All of a sudden, we heard a deafening noise of drums and trumpets that interrupted our conversation and drew us to the window.

A kind of outlandish procession was passing by, made up of a crowd of men carrying tri-colored umbrellas. They were preceded by a group holding resin torches. An unpleasant music accompanied this parade that resembled a Mardi Gras celebration.

The large umbrellas seemed to me to have no purpose on a day when the whether was superb. Not at all! The umbrellas displayed the colors of the Republican Party and its presidential candidate Benjamin Harrison. Behind the long line of umbrellas was an enormous banner bearing the slogan "Vote for Harrison." Finally, more torch-bearing men brought up the end of the parade.

After this carnival-like battalion had passed, we sat down again and had just resumed our conversation when a new clanging began; it was a marching band accompanied by a second parade that, like the first group, was preceded and followed by torch bearers. But this group was composed for the most part of distinguished gentlemen dressed in red jackets and top hats. These men were democrats and supporters of Grover Cleveland. Booing whistles came from the windows of our boardinghouse, as Mrs. H.'s eloquence had converted everyone into a Harrison supporter. In response to this hostile declaration, we were given a cacophonous serenade in which the discordance and unevenness of the instruments matched the enthusiasm. We felt most sorry for all the foreigners in town who were completely indifferent to both Cleveland and Harrison.

Our ears shattered by the noise, we left our post at the window. But every evening leading up to the election we witnessed more of these political demonstrations. There were slight variations in the costumes or rather the disguises of the participants, but invariably the Democrats wore red and the Republicans favored red, white, and blue.

As the election approached, gatherings became noisier and the discussions between the two parties became increasingly heated. There was even an exchange of gunfire between them but that did not stop the daily hubbub from continuing.

Policemen simply observe political demonstrations and do not intervene except in the case of a dangerous exchange. As long as propagandists stick with noisy, inoffensive demonstrations, they are free to demonstrate as they like. Our police force should take this attitude of calm and indifference as an example, as there were few serious brawls given the number of demonstrators.

One evening, around the same point in time, my husband returned from the grounds of the exposition and informed me that the city of Milwaukee was in flames.[3] We immediately decided to head to Milwaukee. A city in flames is a horrible spectacle that one does not see every day, even in America.[4] According to my husband, Chicagoans were just as curious as I was to see the catastrophe. Although Milwaukee was four hours away via express train, a crowd of people was already headed there from Chicago.

Once we made the decision to go, there was only one problem to resolve. I had roasted an enormous chicken the night before that we had not had a chance to eat. I certainly did not want to abandon it to the voracity of the reverent young pastor or any of the other boarders.

Taking the chicken with us seemed to me the most practical solution. I also took some bread and fruit and packed everything in one of those small baskets that you can buy from fruit sellers. These baskets are made of bamboo and have a graceful form. You see them on the arms of the most elegant women, filled with golden grapes or delicious peaches.

With our provisions in hand, we left at seven o'clock in the morning for Milwaukee and naturally, during the trip, no one spoke of anything other than the catastrophe. After two days, the city was still in flames and the fire was increasing in intensity.

Well before our arrival in Milwaukee, we saw compact clouds of smoke coming from the horizon. As we approached, these clouds of smoke were broken up by flames that seemed to touch the sky. Once we got off the train, the temperature immediately seemed to rise even though the fire was not in a neighborhood close to the station.

Located north of Chicago, Milwaukee is similarly situated on the banks of the lake and on a river. A prosperous city, Milwaukee's riches come from two industries: the production of beer and lumber. Milwaukee gracefully rises on the side of a hill and is coquettishly pretty and clean, two rare qualities in an American city. The train station, located on the lake shore and surrounded by a flower garden, is a true monument. The graceful architecture of the station is complemented by the gray stone used in its construction, and by the flower garden surrounding it. The streets going up the hill are wide and well constructed, and have electric tramways. They reach a dizzying speed when they descend and an occasional blue spark flashes if the iron arms come into contact with the live wire.

From the sumptuous appearance of the homes, we realized that we were in the wealthy, residential area of the city. The fire, in fact, was on the other side of the river in the most highly populated part of the city, an area where factories were located.

At that moment, we had nothing to fear in this aristocratic corner of the city. Fortunately, the wind was blowing in the opposite direction and the river was acting like a barrier, making it impossible for the fire to cross over to this neighborhood. Even so, I was very surprised that daily life seemed to be proceeding as usual. Whether the inhabitants were indifferent or simply resigned, they went about their business without seeming to worry about the fire that was devouring the other half of the city. Was it possible to avoid thinking about the fire under the red sky and its reflection of the flames?

On the other side of the river, we saw an unforgettable spectacle of horror and beauty that resembled hell in all its splendor. The sky looked like a backdrop for an incandescent tableau as gigantic plumes of flames reached toward the sky. Burning wood flew through the air as a result of explosions of dynamite and sparks soon ignited surrounding buildings. As we advanced in this direction, the heat and stench became intolerable. A mass of people surrounded the fiery furnace without concern for their own safety. The fire had already consumed fifteen blocks of houses which was approximately one hundred buildings and equivalent to the area of four *arrondissements* in Paris.[5] The wind, up to that point, had prevented the spread of the fire to the other side of the city but that could always change. Even the width of the river would not have sufficed to prevent the spread of flames.

In spite of this horror, the crowd remained calm. Spectators as well as people chased from their homes gathered, but not one moan of anguish was heard.

I witnessed none of the tearful scenes that I had expected, such as people crying over the fate of their families and friends and lamenting the loss of possessions. There was none of the horror and sadness that we usually see in this situation. A perfect calm characterized these spectators as they watched houses burn without attempting to save furniture or precious belongings.

I was astonished by their apparent indifference but soon learned the reasons behind the calm demeanor of the onlookers. First, the number of victims was relatively small: fifty-five people had perished which was a very small number for an American catastrophe. Secondly, the fire had not yet reached any houses.

In terms of mementos—those precious objects that we keep with such devotion and whose destruction is so painful to us—Americans are far less sentimental than we are in this regard. They do not attach the same importance to these items. With their health and money intact, they are stoic in the face of catastrophe.

Unable to nourish itself with these upsetting emotions, my stomach began to make demands. Since we had been so eager to arrive at the scene of the disaster, we had not eaten since six o'clock in the morning. I suddenly remembered that we had brought along our bamboo basket filled with food.

We walked away from the smoke and heat of the fire and identified a charming spot for our meal.

High above the river bank, we found a shady park where we were all alone.[6]

It was a most agreeable spot for a picnic and we had everything we needed to make us comfortable. My husband went down a path and found a clearing filled with picnic tables. These were, without a doubt, used for picnics which are often organized during nice weather. I would have been happy to sit on the grass but since the ground was cold and wet, the bench was much appreciated. We quickly set our lunch out on white paper plates and if the wind had not been so strong as to threaten to carry off our chicken, it would have been a most agreeable meal. Branches of enormous chestnut trees stretched overhead while tall pine trees majestically accentuated the somber grace of the landscape. The river ran smoothly with its harmonious hum and the birds, frightened by the glow of the fire, took refuge in the treetops. Some were crying out in distress while others were singing their usual songs with insouciance and pecking about our feet in search of breadcrumbs. As I relaxed in this beautiful setting, I scolded myself for enjoying this pleasure while the fire continued to rage, claiming perhaps more victims. The wind became stronger and I was cold, so we abandoned the remainder of our picnic to the birds and headed back towards the fire.

The blaze continued to intensify and large lumberyards, which had been preserved up to that point, seemed to worry the firefighters.

American firefighters are a very unusual group! In both small towns and large cities, fire brigades are made up of groups of volunteers. Larger cities offer some payment but for the most part, firefighters are brave people who have other jobs in the community. They are very striking due to their strapping size and distinctive uniform: a rubber raincoat designed to protect them from water. However, the coat is so bulky that they have a hard time getting around. Their head is protected by a helmet made of black rubber with a broad border. Dressed in this way, one cannot expect them to have the agility and boldness of our French firefighters. They do not climb onto burning beams to save people or personal items. Instead, they are content to maneuver very powerful water pumps and blow up abandoned houses with dynamite.

The quickness with which these fires develop and take hold is such that once the safety of the surrounding area has been secured, there is not much to do other than watch the flames.

Neither firemen nor policemen prohibited people from walking in the fire area.

The streets in American cities are very wide, with sidewalks made of wood. As the fire burned the sidewalks, it appeared to be coming from underground. A section of this neighborhood was inhabited by factory workers, which explained the agglomeration of small wooden houses next to large stone and iron factories. These fragile houses naturally burned like matchsticks, but the fire also devoured much more solid buildings. The merchandise depot of one of the rail companies was completely destroyed, leaving only its twisted iron framework. The merchandise contained within the depot continued to burn and turned into a glowing mountain of unrecognizable goods.

A windmill across from the train depot collapsed on one side while a wall eight stories high miraculously remained intact. On the other side of this barrier, piles of grain were on fire. A locomotive factory had practically disappeared in flames, leaving smoking ashes and a few blackened machines that no longer seemed to be made of copper and steel but rather of wood and cardboard. A chemical manufacturing plant had collapsed and its crumbling walls now resembled antique ruins. The burning chemicals and their red, blue, and yellow glass containers gave off acrid fumes. From one minute to the next, new outbreaks of fire took hold, tossing sparks and flames into the sky. A former cigar factory was reduced to a few flaming packages of tobacco.

One of the busiest commercial streets had been devoured by fire but only on one side. On the other side, business continued as usual, with busy, animated stores facing the ruins of their neighbors. Only the facades of these multistoried businesses remained and they were held in place solely by their foundations.

These ruins were the result of dynamite explosions undertaken as a preventive measure to limit the fire. As the fire continued, it left nothing in its wake but hot, smoky ashes and an acrid odor that penetrated our clothing for several days. The heat coming from the ground burned our feet.

Wherever wooden houses had stood, only their skeletons remained. They were reduced to piles of ashes with a few household items visible in the rubble, such as stoves, kitchen utensils, or sewing machines.

As we walked freely through the devastation I found one aspect scandalous. Once a block of houses had been destroyed and the flames extinguished, a crowd of people would hurry toward the burning ashes to pillage the remaining items. They would cart off whatever suited them: a fireplace screen, a machine that could be repaired, usable kitchen equipment. This was done in front of a policeman who did nothing to stop the odious pillaging. This smoky ruin resembled a huge pile of trash invaded by an army of garbage pickers. It is true that some were simply looking for a souvenir of the catastrophe. I even picked up a fragment of fine ironwork. This was the exception, however, as most were searching for gold or melted coins.

I shared my indignation at this kind of behavior with a policeman. He explained that the looters would be disappointed. Since most currency is made of paper, the chance of finding melted coins was remote. Only in the case of a burning bank would the police prohibit looting.

Just seconds after this conversation, I saw an individual discover a set of five or six silver spoons! This looting continued for five or six days as looters freely went through the ruins hoping to find an intact object that had not been touched by fire. They went about their digging, crying out when they discovered something that had been spared.

This situation, I admit, encouraged me to pull a childish prank. I was still carrying my empty picnic basket on my arm. Surreptitiously, I placed it among the ruins and watched to see what would happen. Five minutes later, I had the satisfaction of watching someone "discover" and then triumphantly claim it. Little did they know that it had been brought there from Chicago by a Parisienne.

As the hours passed and darkness descended, the sight of the fire became all the more terrifying and impressive. Flames took on all colors of the spectrum and burned-out ruins looked otherworldly. From time to time we heard the lugubrious sound of buildings collapsing. Ashes, which looked dull in the day light, glowed red in the shadows. Piles of coal that were probably the stockpiles of residents slowly burned. Some flames were green, probably due to a fusion of burning metals. This enormous furnace was surrounded by a suffocating halo of heavy smoke.

Impressed yet terrified by this spectacle, I found myself unable to move. I was trembling, not from cold, as the heat was asphyxiating, but due to nerves.

In any case, we had to think about finding something to eat. Our morning picnic had long passed and it was not going to be easy to find a restaurant. As soon as the fire had broken out, measures had been taken to assure housing for those left homeless. All of the hotels were full due to the number of people who had come to see the fire. Although the city was not in high spirits, people did not seem to be sad but rather very animated. As I have said, there were few victims relative to the heavy population in the section of the city that had been destroyed. In terms of material losses, most companies were protected with insurance. Unlike in France, American companies are well-insured so they are guaranteed substantial reimbursement for any losses.

We had to walk for more than an hour to find a place to eat, but had the good fortune to come upon a German tavern where we enjoyed an excellent meal for a reasonable price. The tavern was clean and pleasant and red-and-white-checked tablecloths gave it a rustic air. We dined on delicious German sausages, washed down with delicious, frothy beer!

Having recovered our energy, we continued to watch the fire. So absorbed were we in watching the flames that we missed the last train to Chicago. Dining in Milwaukee had been a problem so we were wondering how we would ever find a place to stay under the circumstances. We were dead tired as we went from hotel to hotel looking for lodging. Alas! There was not one room available, not even a mattress that we could put over a table! Would we have to spend the entire night wandering the streets?

Streetcars run all night in America so my husband mentioned the possibility of spending the night in one of these vehicles. We could take it from one end of the line to the other. Before settling on this option, we decided to make one last effort to find a hotel room for the night. I was so exhausted that my husband settled me in the waiting room of the train station and went off alone in search of a room. I have no idea how long he was gone but he did find us a room. I do not know how I managed to get to the hotel but late the next morning I awakened in the hotel bed.

The fire was still blazing but people had emptied their houses so the devouring flames had only empty dwellings in their path. The wind had calmed down as well so it was just the heart of the fire that needed to be tamed.

We took the train back to Chicago but the memory of this horrible catastrophe would stay with me for a very long time.

Upon our return, I learned why the fire victims had been so calm and my admiration for them diminished somewhat. In case of a fire, the victim is relieved of all of his debts. Apparently, fires are sometimes deliberately set so that people can clear debts with their creditors.

The warm temperatures that had allowed us to have an October picnic did not last. Each day, the temperature dropped, flowers and leaves fell to the ground, and stoves were lit in all of the houses.

In our boardinghouse, Mister future minister, who was practical and always cold, had managed to get the job of fire stoker. In exchange, he received a reduction in rent and was able to swap his cold attic room for a small room located near the stove. At night, he had to recharge the heater with fuel and without fail, he awakened at midnight and at three in the morning to do his job. This horrid German man carried out his duty but made no effort to be quiet and woke us up every night with his terrible clatter. He must have roasted in that small room as our room was so hot at times that we had to get up to get some air.

Fortunately, the windows in America are much more practical than those in France. They are constructed of two separate panes, one set above the other, which slide up and down in a frame. This system allows one to get as much air as desired.

On November 1, All Soul's Day, the weather was ghastly. The sky was filled with thick gray clouds and a torrential rain fell. In Chicago, November 1 is not a holiday as the Protestant religion does not recognize the dead with any special kind of ceremony. With the miserable weather, I felt very sad on that somber holiday and was thinking about both the people I had left behind in France as well as the dead.

I very much wanted to visit a cemetery in memory of the friends that I had lost. Instead of leaving flowers on my friends' tombs in France, I could leave some flowers on the grave of someone here in Chicago.

Despite the frightful weather, I jumped on a streetcar and went to the cemetery south of the city.[7] The deserted nature of the place surprised me and even the rain could not explain the lack of visitors. Crossing a muddy path, I entered the door and started down the main passageway when I heard a voice call out: "Your number?"

My number! Taken aback, I asked the guard to clarify his question.

"Which of your relatives are buried in this cemetery?" he asked.

"None of them! I am a foreigner and it is a custom in my country to go to the cemetery on November 1 to pay respects to the dead."

It was the guard's turn to show his surprise. He then politely but firmly told me that since none of my family members were buried in the cemetery I would not be allowed to enter! Tears welled up in my eyes at the thought that I would not be able to leave a bouquet on one of the graves. I was about to leave when a woman who had overheard our conversation spoke to me.

"Are you French, Madame? Me, too! I understand the sentiment that has brought you here. If you wish, we can both go to the grave of my husband."

I thanked her effusively and followed her to the grave. Cemeteries are always sad and somber places but American cemeteries are even more so than ours in France. The dead here seem so isolated and forgotten by the living. There were neither funerary monuments nor wreaths of flowers, but only small cubes of stone about a half meter tall and inscribed with a number! The cemetery resembled a huge field filled with the kilometer markers that you see on French roads.

Wretched tombs, but wretched only in appearance! This uniform simplicity and cold austerity of the graves is only on the exterior.

Americans want comfort all the way to the afterlife and it is in the grave itself that luxury is found. Similar to Egyptian mummies, one can tell the fortune of an American by looking at his coffin.

Even the most modest laborer in America would not be satisfied with four panels of oak which are good enough for most of our French bourgeois. The simplest of American coffins is made of a very beautiful wood similar to mahogany, entirely lined in zinc and covered with a bright colored tufted fabric.

More expensive coffins are made of rare woods and incrusted with mother of pearl, ivory, gold, and silver. The handles are finely carved and the interior is lined with velvet and satin. Some coffins are even made of solid silver! But the funeral ceremony in America lacks the somber tone of our tradition in France. The first time that I saw a funeral procession in America I mistook it for a wedding. The horse-drawn carriages were not distinctive and were not draped with black. In fact, these were the same carriages used for weddings and parties. The women were wearing light-colored dresses and the men were animatedly discussing business. The respectful attitude that is observed in France was totally absent from the proceedings. The hearse, which moved along at a quick trot, was similar to that used by the lower classes in France. It was surrounded, however, by windows that allowed people to see the coffin from the outside and looked to me like a moving aquarium.

As the funeral procession passed, no one stopped to show respect.

This lack of respect, which is so shocking to us, can be explained by the practical sense of Americans. Why spend time on useless ceremonies when the dead person cannot even enjoy them? The living should spend their precious time another way. This same logic explains the abandonment of cemeteries. Not so long ago these fields of repose had many visitors. Since cemeteries are beautiful places with green paths and large trees, people would often meet there for picnics. However, these parties got out of hand and as a result, access to cemeteries is now reserved for families in possession of a number.

This lighthearted attitude toward death seems, at times, to border on indecent brutality. I witnessed one scene that was truly appalling and which I cannot call to mind without indignation.

In the house across the street from where we were living, a young family, that included a husband, wife, and baby, was found asphyxiated one morning following a gas leak that had occurred in their room during the night.

In certain areas of Chicago a very inexpensive gas is used for lighting. It is completely odorless and for this reason, very dangerous. Because people are afraid of this gas, owners of boardinghouses warn their renters to be careful due to its odorless nature.

Following the accident, the three victims were transported to the morgue. The vehicle used for this purpose is a kind of open red cart. By the time the wagon arrived at the house to pick up the bodies, a small crowd had gathered.

The morgue employees took blankets and went up to the young family's apartment. A few minutes later, one of the employees came down carrying the body of the husband which was barely covered by the blanket. Confused cries burst out from the crowd as people moved forward and tried to reach up and touch the body as it was thrown, instead of placed, in the back of the cart. The employees then sat on the side benches, their feet brushing the cadaver. Two other employees came out carrying the bodies of the woman and the baby. The cover was not large enough and it was possible to see the poor woman's nightgown and her beautiful, long blond hair. I cannot express my horror and indignation when I saw people in the crowd reaching for her hair, trying to pull it out. There is a German superstition that touching a person who has died accidentally brings good luck, much like in France where touching the rope of someone who has been hung is considered lucky. This belief is in decline in France, but here in America it is very much alive and borders on the sacrilegious! Surprisingly, no one spoke out against the profanation that was being committed.

The bodies of the woman and baby were thrown next to that of the husband, and people in the crowd triumphantly waved clumps of hair that they had yanked out, as the cart headed to the morgue without any further ceremony.

This terrible drama made a painful impression on me. The image of the three victims haunted me all the more because the same kind of gas was used in Mrs. A.'s boardinghouse. I was constantly fearful that a similar incident would occur in our house and for this reason we decided to find new lodgings.

After having closely studied the behavior of our fellow boarders, their promiscuity had begun to bother me. It was only the kindness of Mrs. A. that kept us there. But now we had an excuse to leave and we seized the opportunity and moved to 44th Street, to the boardinghouse of Mrs. B.

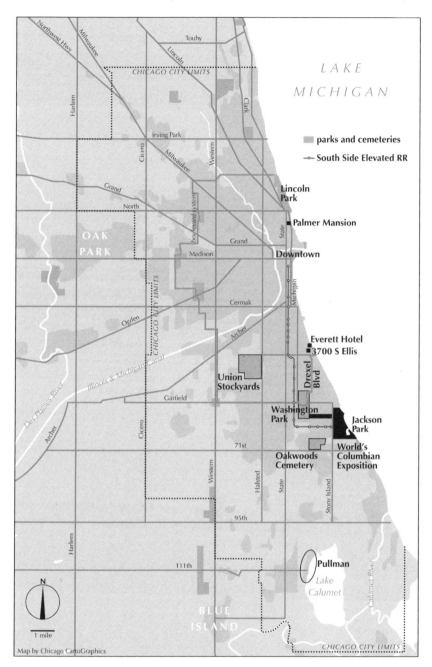

MAP 1. Chicago, 1892, including city limits and sites mentioned by Madame Léon Grandin.

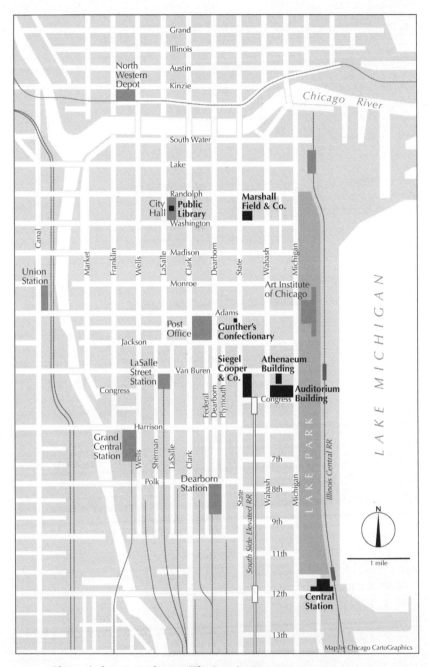

Grand

Illinois

North
Western
Depot

Austin

Kinzie

Chicago River

South Water

Lake

Randolph

City
Hall

■ **Public
Library**

**Marshall
Field & Co.**
■

Washington

Canal

Madison

Market

Franklin

Wells

LaSalle

Clark

Dearborn

State

Wabash

Michigan

Union
Station

Monroe

Art Institute
of Chicago

L A K E   M I C H I G A N

Adams
■
**Gunther's
Confectionary**

**Post
Office**

Jackson

**LaSalle
Street
Station**

Van Buren

**Siegel
Cooper
& Co.**

**Athenaeum
Building**
■

Congress

Auditorium

Congress **Building**

Federal

Dearborn

Plymouth

Harrison

**Grand
Central
Station**

Wells

Sherman

LaSalle

Clark

7th

L A K E   P A R K

Polk

**Dearborn
Station**

State

South Side Elevated RR

Wabash

Michigan

Illinois Central RR

8th

9th

11th

N

1 mile

12th

**Central
Station**

13th

Map by Chicago CartoGraphics

MAP 2. Chicago's downtown district (The Loop), 1892,
including sites frequented by Madame Léon Grandin

FIGURE 1. Postcard of the ship *La Touraine*. Private collection.

FIGURE 2. "Un coin de table à bord de *La Touraine*," in
Louis Mainard, *Livre d'or des voyages: L'Amérique* (Paris:
Les Grands Magasins de la Place Clichy, 1892), 9.

MICHIGAN CENTRAL

"THE

Niagara Falls Route"

And the Route of the
Fast Vestibuled Train

THE NORTH SHORE LIMITED

AND OTHER FAST TRAINS BETWEEN

CHICAGO AND NEW YORK, BOSTON AND NEW ENGLAND POINTS

—VIA—

NEW YORK CENTRAL & HUDSON RIVER

—AND—

BOSTON & ALBANY RAILROADS.

IT IS THE ONLY LINE running directly by and in full view of the WORLD'S COLUMBIAN EXPOSITION and the GREAT CATARACT OF NIAGARA.

It is Solidly Constructed,   Magnificently Equipped,

Vigilantly Operated,

And spares no pains nor expense to secure the Comfort, Convenience and Safety of its Patrons.

L. D. HEUSNER, CITY PASSENGER AND TICKET AGENT, 67 Clark Street, Corner Randolph, Chicago.

ROBERT MILLER, Gen'l Sup't., DETROIT.

O. W. RUGGLES, Gen'l Pass'r and Ticket Agent, CHICAGO.

FIGURE 3. An advertisement for the Michigan Central Railroad, in Frank M. Morris, *Morris' Dictionary of Chicago and Vicinity* (Chicago: Frank M. Morris, 1892–93).

ANDREWS' "GEM" FOLDING BED.

THE ONLY BED MADE WITH

| Special Provision for **Ventilation, Cleaning and Easy Moving.** | **No Bugs.** **No Dirt.** **No Breakage.** | **Elegant Designs.** **Moderate Prices.** **Occupies Small Space.** |

OPEN FOR DUSTING. NO. 1.

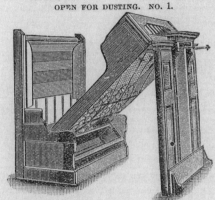

ADVANTAGES OVER ANY AND ALL OTHERS.

1. Any lady or child can easily open it, as represented in cut 1, for cleaning.

2. Or they can take it apart for moving.

3. While its length when opened is GREATER than any other bed, when closed its HEIGHT is 8 inches less.

4. It is the BEST ventilated of all Folding Beds.

5. It has in its base a very large box extremely useful night or day.

6. It is fitted with our adjustable cable spring, unequaled for comfort, simplicity and durability.

We are Sole Manufacturers and Guarantee Satisfaction.

Made in Birch, Oak, Walnut or Mahogany. See samples and get our catalogue. We also manufacture fine

Bank Fittings.
Commercial Furniture.
Office Desks.
Fine Brass and Wire Work.
School Furniture.

Office Chairs, Desks, Etc.

DESKS.
GLOBES.
CHARTS.
MAPS.
BLACK BOARDS.
Etc., Etc.

Church Chairs

Largest Variety,
Plain or Upholstered.
$50,000.00 worth like cut
furnished
CHICACO AUDITORIUM.
Pulpits, Pulpit Chairs, &c.

A. H. Andrews & Co.
215 Wabash Ave., Chicago.

FIGURE 4. An advertisement for an Andrews Gem folding bed, in John J. Flinn, *Chicago, the Marvelous City of the West* (Chicago: Flinn and Sheppard, 1891).

FIGURE 5. "Drexel Boulevard" (from Fortieth Street), in *Rand McNally and Company's Pictorial Chicago and Illustrated World's Columbian Exposition* (Chicago: Rand McNally and Company, 1893).

FIGURE 6. "The Columbian Exposition Dedicatory Ceremonies—The Grand Reception and Ball in the Hall of the Auditorium," drawn by B. West Clinedinst, in *Frank Leslie's Illustrated Weekly*, 3 November 1892, 309.

FIGURE 7. "Bird's-Eye View of the World's Columbian Exposition, Chicago, U.S.A., 1893," in *Rand McNally and Company's Pictorial Chicago and Illustrated World's Columbian Exposition* (Chicago: Rand McNally and Company, 1893).

FIGURE 8. The Potter Palmer residence, 1350 Lake Shore Drive, Chicago
(n.d.). Chicago History Museum, photograph by J.W. Taylor, ICHi-39490.

FIGURE 9. Main gallery of the Potter Palmer Residence,
circa 1900. Chicago History Museum, ICHi-01266.

FIGURE 10. "Lincoln Park, Looking South from the Palm House," in
*Rand McNally and Company's Pictorial Chicago and Illustrated World's
Columbian Exposition* (Chicago: Rand McNally and Company, 1893).

FIGURE 11. Cover of Chicago Athenaeum pamphlet (n.d.).
Chicago History Museum, ICHi-59763.

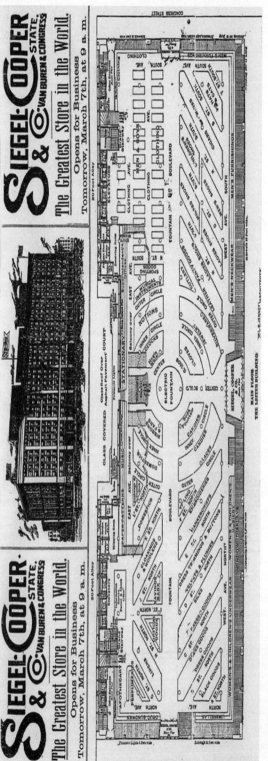

FIGURE 12. Layout of the Siegel Cooper and Company Department Store, *Chicago Tribune*, 6 March 1892, 40.

FIGURE 13. Postcard, "Gunther's Confectionery, 212 State St., Chicago." Private collection.

FIGURE 14. Reading Room of the Chicago Public Library, *The Graphic*, 8 February 1890.

FIGURE 15. Woman's Building, World's Columbian Exposition, 1893. Chicago History Museum, ICHi-02302, photograph by C. D. Arnold.

FIGURE 16. Interior, Woman's Building, World's Columbian Exposition, 1893. Chicago History Museum, ICHi-02291, photograph by C. D. Arnold.

FIGURE 17. Library in the Woman's Building. Chicago History Museum, ICHi-32385; taken from *Cosmopolitan*, September 1893.

FIGURE 18. Children's Building, 1893. Chicago History Museum, ICHi -13668, photograph by C. D. Arnold.

FIGURE 19. MacMonnies Fountain, World's Columbian
Exposition, 1893. Chicago History Museum, ICHi- 25181.

FIGURE 20. The "French Exhibit." In C. Graham, From
Peristyle to Plaisance: Illustrated in Colors by C. Graham,
with a Short History of the World's Columbian Exposition
(Chicago, 1893).

New Acquaintances

American Families—Art Institute of Chicago—
Election Celebration

The experience that I have just described cured me of my desire to cook in public; more than anything I wanted to have my own place. Mrs. B. agreed to rent us half of her apartment, dining room, kitchen, and bedroom, while she kept a bedroom and the living room for herself.[1]

Of French descent on her father's side, Mrs. B. spoke French quite well. She told me that this housing arrangement suited her very well as she no longer would she have to do all the household chores. She and her husband would be obliged, however, to take all of their meals in restaurants.

The appearance of the house gave us the impression that we were in a completely different world from that at Mrs. A.'s place. Although our bedroom was small and a bit dark, it was nicely furnished. I was very happy to see a large, French-style bed that would give us a welcome break from the folding armoire bed.

The dining room was larger, with a wide bow window like those that are so fashionable in Paris right now. The well-equipped kitchen had two large stoves, one of which was lit by gas, and contained two ovens for bread and pastry. Two spacious tables and laundry supplies completed the furnishings.

Since laundry services are very expensive, Americans often have their laundry done at home. They pay a laundress two dollars per day to wash and iron two weeks' worth of laundry. Like us, they use pearl ash and soap in the water and add ammonia which has an excellent whitening effect.

American women wear white petticoats, suits, and aprons but they do not wear a chemise.[2]

A corset of cotton, wool, or silk is worn instead of a chemise.

Slenderness is prized among American women and this undergarment molds the body without any lines.[3] In winter, women wear fine wool or silk corsets which are very warm. The few women who do favor chemises wear them over this corset in the French style.[4] Everything is then covered by one long petticoat.

In terms of their outfits they are always striking if not a bit eccentric. Unlike French women, American women love to show off their latest fashions and wear them whenever an occasion arises. The idea that a French woman has a skirt in her wardrobe that she only wears three or four times a year for social events seems funny to American women. They prefer to enjoy their clothing as much as possible before it goes out of style. American women are neither more elegant nor more charming than we French women, they are simply different.

They dress to please themselves rather than the public and seek only to satisfy their own personal taste. All sorts of whimsical touches are welcome and no one is criticized for this kind of originality, whereas in France, the proverb "the habit makes the monk" applies.[5]

Fewer people lived in our new residence than in our former one. A small, elegant private home, the owner and his family occupied the second floor and rented out the ground floor. As I mentioned earlier, Mrs. B. sublet half of her ground floor suite to us. A wide vestibule separated our respective lodgings. Instead of doors, draperies hung from the thresholds in the American style. In fact, there were no true doors, only pocket doors that slid into the walls. This is a very practical system, and given that the doorways are very wide it is possible to easily divide or join two rooms.

Mrs. B. kept the doorway between her bedroom and living room open in order to create one large room. The bedroom brought to mind a small salon or boudoir since the folding bed resembled a sofa.

Mr. and Mrs. B. were a charming couple. Though she was not very pretty, Mrs. B. was extremely gracious and had a friendly manner. Tall and thin, with dark hair and superb black eyes, she had a lively appearance. She dressed in a seemingly effortless way, with a bow here and there, but the overall effect was very elegant.

As blond as his wife was dark and as calm as she was vivacious, Mr. B. was a talented lawyer with a wonderful sense of humor. They were complete opposites and the only thing that they had in common was their love for one another.

As adoring of his wife as she was of him, Mr. B. was a model husband. Since Mrs. B., like many other well-to-do Americans, did not have a maid, Mr. B. took care of all the unpleasant tasks that would usually be left to a servant. Before going to the courthouse in the morning he brought up coal from the cellar, took out all the household trash, and put it in one of the large bins.

These garbage receptacles are found in the street and although they are not an artistic decoration, they are worthy of a digression.

Enormous green containers equipped with round covers are found on every street corner. They are only emptied twice a week by garbage carts. If they fill up before the designated collection day, people simply dump their trash next to the container.

From that point on, what a spectacle and what moldiness!

Many of our French husbands would make fun of this lawyer/house husband. The American man would be surprised to learn that on the other side of the ocean, a man allows a woman, regardless of whether she is his wife or a servant, to undertake chores that are too strenuous for her. An idea shared by all Americans is that a man is neither dishonored nor ridiculous when he finds it as natural to serve his wife as to be served by her. For Americans, this attitude is clearly linked to the superior and protective role of men.

Mr. B. spent his day in his office or at the courthouse. His evenings were devoted to accompanying his wife to balls, shows, or other kinds of amusements which she so loved.

Mr. B. was not only very American in his protective instincts but also in terms of his upbringing.

After several years of marriage, his parents divorced and Mr. B. was brought up by his father while his younger brother lived with his mother. Mr. B.'s father soon remarried but his first wife had no interest in getting married again. A perfect harmony reigned among these three adults: Mr. B. the father, Mrs. B. number one, and Mrs. B. number two.

The first Mrs. B. lived with her young son in a city that was quite far away from Chicago. Every year, she would bring him to Chicago to spend two months with her ex-husband and his wife. The new wife would receive them with open arms, and for twenty years there was no trouble in this relationship.

Such were our kind hosts. I would have been completely satisfied with our situation except for the fact that I had to do all of the daily chores myself. I tried, in vain, to find someone to help me with the harder tasks but this proved impossible. I had already seen the attitude of American maids and the very thought of them still makes me shiver!

For better or worse I quickly became accustomed to doing everything myself. Since it was extremely cold and I was stuck in the house, I had all of the time necessary to do my chores. My leisure time was spent with friends and seemed even sweeter, as these visits were such a nice change from the bustle of home.

One of my best friends at the time was Miss Lydia H.[6]

A distinguished painter, she had studied in Paris in the studio of one of our greatest masters and had been recognized at the Salon. Upon her return to her hometown of Chicago, she had been named professor of drawing at the Art Institute.[7]

Visiting my dear Lydia's class was one of my greatest pleasures and the time that I spent there is one of my fondest memories.

The Art Institute, which has a large number of both male and female students, offers courses in drawing, painting, sculpture, architecture, and even industrial arts.[8] It is, in fact, the equivalent of our École des Beaux Arts, but what a difference![9] From my first visit I was very surprised by what I saw there. I had gone to the Institute without much enthusiasm, somewhat obliged by circumstance. As a foreigner, I was curious but feared that it would be similar to our Parisian art studios where women feel uncomfortable and out of place. Not at all! On the contrary, this was not at all the situation. Instead of creating an uncomfortable atmosphere, the presence of young women was very appropriate in terms of their behavior and appearance. With the fervor of neophytes, the students worked diligently, thinking only of art!

They were so absorbed by their artistic work that there was no time for rude jokes or tricks. They were enthusiastic but also very serious. A true conviction for art was apparent and they approached their work with a certain reverence. These young people focused exclusively on their task and a sense of dignity reigned that even extended to the nude model who posed before them!

Let all the painters in France tell me that I am old fashioned or of the generation of 1830, but I had never experienced such a sense of admiration as I did in this setting.

Not one word or glance could be misinterpreted. The young ladies were protected by the men, who, I sensed, had a true respect for these women who were their friends, their sisters, and who one day might become their wives.

A dirty trick or suggestive joke, like those heard in the studios of Paris, would not be tolerated here and would elicit indignation.[10] Here the students work as if they are in a temple dedicated to art and hard work. Any outside interruption is viewed as sacrilege.

In addition, these young people have a practical goal, which is to make money. The phrase "time is money" rings in every ear.

From eight in the morning until the last light of day they work very hard.

In order to save time and money, most of the students bring their lunch in a steel container. After lunch, it can be folded up and put in a pocket. They eat lunch in a large refectory and for a reasonable price they can buy coffee, tea, bread, and cakes. In the library adjoining the Institute, courses are given in anatomy, art history, and perspective. All of the classes are taught by excellent professors, most of whom have spent years studying in Europe, especially in Paris.

Almost all of the Art Institute students will finish their studies in Paris.[11] This tradition is understandable since there are not yet many American masters with whom they can continue their studies. However, the day will soon come when America will not have to send her art students to Europe. They will no longer be content to study with our French teachers as they will study with their own masters. American artists such as Whistler and Sargent already have gained a reputation.[12]

I very much enjoyed visiting the Art Institute and began to get to know both students and teachers there.

Another teacher with whom I became well acquainted was Mrs. C. A French woman, she had met her husband in Paris.[13] He was a distinguished painter of military scenes and had come to France to finish his artistic training. After getting married, Mrs. C. left France and settled in Chicago with her husband, where they had been living for about five years. A student of her husband, Mrs. C. had a special interest in portrait painting. She also taught an elementary drawing class at the Art Institute. Mr. and Mrs. C. were a charming couple. They lived with some elderly relatives of Mr. C. and we often spent part of our Sundays with this lovely family.[14]

I say "part of our Sundays" for a reason. Since maids have the afternoon off, it is possible to invite friends for lunch but not for dinner. After lunch and a visit or a walk, everyone returns home to eat something that has been prepared in advance.

These family lunches at Mrs. C.'s gave me a much more positive impression of American cuisine. I had never tasted such perfectly cooked roasts, such delicate pastries, or such delicious ice cream.

After lunch, we would always take a walk. One of the most beautiful routes was along the aristocratic Lake Shore Drive in the northwest section of the city where the "kings of gold" live.[15] With marble facades and monumental staircases, every aspect of these homes is elegant, including antique doors and massive turrets. A large, square turret distinguishes the home of Mrs. Potter Palmer. The house is a veritable feudal manor which everyone in Chicago calls "the castle" [figs. 8–9].[16]

Lincoln Park, a superb public garden filled with tall, shady trees and statues, also lines the banks of sparkling Lake Michigan [fig. 10]. The majority of the statues are not very good, an exception being one of General Grant done by Antonin Mercié.

Another sculpture that attracted my attention was a monument dedicated to American Indians in recognition of their help in introducing business and industry to the region. What! These brave Indians were even sociable and welcoming to the strangers who stole their land.

What has become of this kind native race? What an ironic tribute!

The park also houses a small zoo that includes a rich assortment of animals native to the region. The variety of animals is as great as that of plants, as the zoo has an outstanding collection of reptiles, multicolored birds, and some animals not found in Europe.

A pit similar to the one in our Jardin des Plantes houses the bears.[17] One Sunday evening, an incident occurred in which one of the bears played the role of both hero and victim.

The magnificent white bear was enormous and powerful. We had viewed it with both admiration and sympathy. Obstinately perched high in his tree, disdainful of the bread crumbs on the ground, the bear seemed to be dreaming. We thought that he was in a philosophical crisis, preoccupied by an intellectual question. On the contrary, this American bear was not dreaming of metaphysics but rather of independence!

A citizen of free America, he intended to exercise the same liberty enjoyed by his fellow citizens. During the night, he bravely jumped from the top of his tree into the park.

Wandering in the moonlight, he strolled through the park and then onto millionaires' avenue! Was he admiring or critical of what he saw? Who knows what he thought of these sumptuous homes. He finally chose a doorstep where he settled in for the night. His pleasant dreams of freedom were interrupted by a group of policemen who were surprised to find the bear there. Ten officers surrounded him and led him back to his prison with a rope. The poor bear had awakened too late and was captured.

The brave bear fought violently for his freedom and the policemen had to pull the rope so hard that they practically strangled him! Poor bear!

Not far from Lincoln Park is an unusual house open to visitors. It is a kind of German tavern entirely composed of materials from the fire of 1871 that destroyed Chicago.[18] The walls are made of fragments of calcified stone combined with bits of metal, melted glass and porcelain, and all kinds of residue. Twisted steel beams serve as columns in the large room and mediocre paintings of the fire hang on the walls.

After returning from one of our walks with Mrs. C. and her family, we were invited to stay for dinner.

We were going to finish up the leftovers from lunch, including an enormous turkey that we had barely touched, at least half of a filet of beef, hors d'oeuvre, fruit, and pastries that would surely satisfy us.

Mrs. C.'s offer was so kind and she was so insistent about inviting us that we accepted. Once we arrived at the house, Mrs. C. quickly went to the icebox to get the food.

I must say a word about American iceboxes, which are far superior to the primitive cages that we use in France. Here, the iceboxes are about as large as the bottom section of a buffet. Made of very solid wood, the interior is lined with a sheet of white steel. The cover is designed as a container that holds ice. Gradually, the ice melts and trickles down the side tubes into a basin under the icebox. Sealed from air and light and refrigerated by the ice, this machine lives up to its name.

So Mrs. C. hurried to the icebox and soon let out a cry of distress!

All that remained of the turkey was the carcass! The large filet of beef was not even the size of a small steak. All of the other dishes were gone! Not even any pastries!

"Ah! Really." said Mrs. C., more disappointed than she was angry. "I would never have thought my maid's guests capable of reducing us to famine. I specifically told that girl to leave enough for us to have dinner!"

Friends of the maid! I was aghast. However, inviting friends over is yet another privilege enjoyed by American servants. They receive guests at their employer's expense, as if it were their own home.

Thanks to the maids' big appetite, we wondered if we were going to have to go without dinner since it is impossible to buy food on Sunday. All of the markets are closed from Saturday evening until Monday morning. Any business that breaks this rule pays a large fine.

After scavenging in the kitchen, we were able to find eggs, butter, cheese, and fruit that had escaped the voracity of the maid and her guests, and we managed to put together a dinner.

Don't even imagine that the maid was reprimanded.

"To what end?" Mrs. C. declared. "This girl does a reasonable job and we hope to keep her as we are afraid that we would not be able to find someone as capable."

Mr. and Mrs. C. had an art studio in their house but my friend Miss Hess had hers in the large Athenaeum building where the Art Institute is located [fig. 11].[19]

Painting and sculpture studios line the wide hallways and the doors are often left open.

Over time, I became acquainted with many of these artists. Often, we would go with Miss Hess to the Institute in the evening to pay a friendly visit.

Once a month, Mr. F. invited all of the professors from the Institute along with some outside visitors and I had the pleasure of being one of the invited guests.[20]

These "five o'clock" gatherings were intimate and charming. We would drink tea and discuss every subject, but mostly art, of course. The discussions were not at all pedantic and the Institute hierarchy faded as we freely expressed our opinions.

At that point the Columbian Exposition was foremost in everyone's mind. The architects, both male and female, were warmly congratulated for their buildings. Music accompanied our discussions and then, at seven o'clock, we all left as the building closed at that hour.

The Athenaeum, like other commercial buildings in Chicago, has no residential apartments.

By that time the election crisis had finally come to an end. Harrison was beaten and Cleveland was named president of the Republic by a great majority.

After seeing how heated the discussions preceding the election had been, I expected that brawls would break out following the results. Not at all! As if by magic spell, all political debate ceased, and the losers acknowledged with resignation and dignity the boisterous victory of their adversaries.

Cleveland's supporters were preparing for the victory celebration that started the very evening when the results were announced.

By dusk, every street corner had a victory fire which was surrounded by a chain of men of all ages.

Fireworks displays sparkled from the roofs of the tall buildings belonging to newspapers that had supported Cleveland. They also projected images of Cleveland that were visible to the people gathered in the street. This heavy president was known as the only man in the United States who could remove his collar without unbuttoning it! This flattering image was contrasted with that of poor Harrison, who had the unattractive features of a pig.

These antics went on throughout the night. At nine o'clock there was an enormous parade, beginning at The Auditorium. The musicians were first in line, followed by a wide array of costumes and accessories including red umbrellas, unusual hats, and head dresses resembling roosters. The people wearing these head dresses had whistles that imitated the "cock a doodle do" of a real rooster!

Leading this noisy fanfare was a stretcher decorated with greenery, holding a bust of the president. The stretcher was carried by men bearing torches and symbolic branches of laurel. There were so many people it seemed as if the entire population of Chicago had gathered downtown. Near the end of the parade, another stretcher appeared that bore an image of the former president and his cabinet dressed as pigs.

A musical instrument designed to imitate the snorting of a pig was activated by pulling a cord. The hilarity bordered on delirium! The projections continued showing caricatures and injurious remarks about Harrison that made the crowd laugh even more. The procession ended as it had begun, with an infernal band that would be pleasing only to the most untrained of ears.

The parade participants gathered in a central plaza with their victory torches and the pig music maker was thrown into the fire, as were all of the tri-colored umbrellas that could be found.

Dancing followed, with the roosters continuing their jig into the early hours of the morning.

Social Life

At Home in Chicago—Clubs and Dances— Gas Accident

Before leaving France, I had received a letter of introduction to Mrs. Potter Palmer from a charming American woman who lives in Paris and is a distinguished art critic.[1]

Knowing that Mrs. Palmer was very busy, I had not wanted to introduce myself until after the Inauguration festivities for fear of inconveniencing her. Once everything had calmed down, I went to the office of the Board of Lady Managers, which occupied two floors of a large building on Adams Street, where part of the exposition was being installed.

Needless to say, there were only women in the office since the exhibition of women's works was going to be organized entirely by women. A female architect had designed the building, and women sculptors and painters were in charge of decorating it.[2]

Mrs. Potter Palmer received visitors every morning even though it was an extremely time consuming task. Since the exposition was approaching, however, her many responsibilities as organizer did not allow her to hold these receptions.

Attractive and witty with a Parisian sort of distinction, even our most sophisticated women would envy her elegance. Her skin has an exquisite freshness that is rare in America and that brightens her magnificent black eyes. In short, Mrs. Potter Palmer is the very incarnation of charm.

She welcomed me with the same grace and friendliness that she shows toward all. We chatted for a long while and she invited me to visit her at home. By circumstance, I soon became one of the habituées of the house which was fit for a prince. I also became a very good friend of her companion, Miss Laura H.

For several years, Miss Laura had been Mrs. Palmer's secretary. She had accompanied Mrs. Palmer on her trip to France and, once back in Chicago, she had written and published an interesting account of their trip.[3] Since Miss Laura loved France and admired Paris and Parisian society, she enjoyed conversing in French with me.

Unlike Mrs. Palmer who has a very French appearance, Miss Laura H. has the look of a pure American.

Tall and well proportioned, with elegance and good manners, her appearance goes beyond pretty.

Her lively face, crowned with golden hair, expresses intelligence and energy.

Miss Laura is a woman of action and energy.

A descendant of one of the most illustrious American families, she has experienced some difficult times.

Parents, fortune, she lost everything! After having been surrounded in her childhood with all the luxury imaginable, Miss Laura found herself poor and alone. She was obliged to earn a living for herself and her younger sister, for whom she was responsible.[4]

She accepted this duty courageously and without any bitterness. Adversity did not darken her spirit as she threw herself into battle.

In Miss Laura's current social circle, she could, if she chooses, make a brilliant marriage and return to the status into which she was born.

Like a true American woman, she only wants to marry someone whom she truly loves. In the meantime, she lives happily and independently in her own place.

A pretty little nest that is a bit overdone, Miss Laura's home is charming.[5] Her home is very large and has seven rooms connected with sliding doors.

The largest room is the salon which is furnished with old family furniture, a few sketches, and two or three artistic little statues. A piano occupies a large corner of the room as Miss Laura's sister is a distinguished pianist. Several rocking chairs are scattered throughout and Miss Laura's banjo is attached to the underside of one.

Gifted with a pleasant voice and a musical sense, she sings Negro ballads which are sweet, full of poetry, and have a simple, monotone rhythm. She accompanies herself on the banjo, which is the Negroes' favorite instrument.

Adjacent to the salon, the bedroom is draped in white cotton. Miss Laura has painted wild roses and sparrows on the white fabric and pale-blue satin ribbons bring together the paintings in charming puffs.

The round ceiling is also decorated with roses and a white rug covers the floor. Completing the decoration is a folding bed in the form of a bookshelf and white lacquered furniture with blue details. Rose decorations and tufts of blue satin are everywhere. Painted branches of wild roses decorate the windows while rose garlands pull back the drapes and surround the tall mirror.

Pretty knick knacks decorate all the furnishings. A lamp with a large pink shade sits in front of the window but there are also gas ceiling lights covered with pale blue crystal globes. A profusion of both real and artificial flowers fills the room. Miss Laura is very dear to her friends and they take pleasure in giving her flowers.

Finally, there are a number of chairs, including blue and white armchairs with white satin heart cushions decorated with roses. A charming effect!! But why are the cushions in the shape of a heart!! A mystery!

I imagine that one is very comfortable when leaning against these little hearts and that one would enjoy staying in that spot indefinitely.

To take care of this adorable setting, Miss Laura has an excellent servant, an invaluable treasure in this country. Well versed in all of the household details, Mary is also a remarkable cook, or as we say a "cordon bleu."

The first time I saw her I mistook her for a true "lady." Had she not offered to help me take off my rubber boots, I do not know if I would have dared ask her to give my visiting card to Miss Laura. Her aristocratic manners were such that she seemed more like a duchess than a maid.

The daughter of a farmer in the west, she enjoyed serving others and took pride in the perfection of her service. An enthusiastic admirer of Miss Laura, she surrounded her with affection and devotion. Happy to live near such an intelligent and distinguished person, it would be impossible for Mary to remain among the uncivilized people who work on her father's farm.

Miss Laura was very sweet and respectful of Mary. She gave her free reign over the administration of the house and allowed her the freedom to do things as she pleased. When Mary wanted to go to a ball or to the theater, Miss Laura arranged her schedule to accommodate her.

"I would like you to see Mary in her ball gown," Miss Laura told me. "She is magnificent with a crown in her red hair and I am sure that her dresses cost more than mine do."

Just like her mistress, Mary went out in a carriage in the evening and her male friends were upstanding gentlemen.

Back at the house, she took up her role of model servant and was very pleasant to her mistress. One evening, Miss Laura invited my husband and me for dinner. Mary outdid herself in order to satisfy us by preparing exquisite American dishes that greatly improved our impression of that cuisine. Unfortunately, very few foreigners have a chance to try these delicacies.

The delicious meal was served on a beautifully decorated table, festooned with white roses and fine greenery. The crystal vase of roses in the center of the table, placemats and dessert napkins decorated with embroidery and French lace, bohemian glasses, and Saxe porcelain all created a sense of elegance and originality; one felt in the presence of an artist.

The food was worthy of these sumptuous containers! It was with true gluttony that I savored turkey stuffed with currant jelly and most of all, desserts which included salted nuts, candies in surprising colors, long blue and pink ribbons of spun sugar, and ice cream.

Miss Laura's table displayed small spoons that were true golden and silver jewels. No two were alike for this reason: each city creates a special spoon and decorates it with the name and attributes of the city. It is fashionable to offer these spoons as gifts and some collectors succeed in eventually collecting spoons from cities all over the United States.

These new friendships with people associated with the Board of Lady Managers did not lead me to abandon Mrs. B., my charming and lively landlady. On the contrary, I was very interested in her daily activities.

Tasks and preoccupations of a grave nature absorbed her from morning until evening as she prepared to host an upcoming meeting of her club.

The many clubs in Chicago are not at all similar to the kind of clubs we have in France.[6] These are familylike gatherings where members meet at each other's homes.

Once a week on a chosen day, people go to a member's home to play cards, listen to music, or discuss literature. The activity of the club depends on its focus. Since clubs in Chicago have many members, it is not very often that each member has to host the group.

Mr. and Mrs. B. were going to host the card game club and Mrs. B. was getting everything ready for this party. The living room and bedroom were opened into one room and game tables were set up everywhere.

An entire afternoon was devoted to cutting the club's initials out of cardboard. These letters would be used as tokens for card games. It was also necessary to fill candy dishes and prepare all cookies and sweets that would accompany the tea. They also had to buy a prize for the drawing which was purchased with money raised from the previous meeting. Mrs. B. had decided to give one of those small spoons that I mentioned earlier as a prize.

Then there was the organization of all the little details. Lunch was set up on a table covered with pink crepe paper, creating a pretty effect at little expense.

The entire apartment was decorated in pink, including lampshades, ribbons, and even the dress and face of the lady of the house.

Industrious and skillful, Mrs. B. made her own dresses. The dress she wore that evening, made of black silk with pink organza trim, was charming in its originality. Her model husband had thought to give her a box of beautiful roses. Although there were too many perhaps—but that is the style there—they beautifully complemented her outfit.

As soon as everyone had arrived, the players sat down at the tables and card games began. The games were played so seriously that one would have thought that these people were fulfilling a very important duty.

They were playing the card game "swinch," if I remember the name correctly.[7]

It is a game for four players and as soon as one set of partners has the number of points necessary to win, they ring a bell so that the others stop playing. Players start back up again and games continue until everyone agrees to stop. A prize is awarded to the player who accumulates the most points. Tea is then served along with cookies and candy. Before leaving, the guests decide where the next meeting will be held.

In Chicago, it is common to belong to more than one club. Mr. and Mrs. B., as well as some of the card players, also belonged to a dance club.

These dance meetings took place twice per week at the home of Professor Beek.[8] The first meeting was a rehearsal while the second meeting was a ball which friends of the dancers could attend as spectators.

This ball was to take place several days after Mrs. B.'s card party and she set about trying to preserve the roses that her husband had given her, so that she could wear them again.

Flowers are very expensive and thrifty people like Mrs. B. try to make them last as long as possible. Thanks to the precautions taken by Mrs. B. her flowers could be worn not only for the ball but for another evening out as well.

Her method for preserving them was simple and practical.

She placed a sheet of wet silk paper in the bottom of a cardboard box. Next, she placed the roses on this paper in layers, dampening them with cold water. The flowers were covered with more silk paper and hermetically sealed in the box which was then put in a cool, dark place. The next day she showed me the flowers and they were as fresh as if they had just been cut. Two weeks later, their beauty had not faded at all and she wore them for a third time. She finally put them in a vase in the living room. They were a bit pale, but still beautiful.

Dance in America is a carefully cultivated art form and dance schools are very popular.[9]

It is possible to study dances of different countries and time periods. During that particular year in Chicago, the minuet was in fashion.

Professor Beek's dance classes were among the most reputable and were popular with young ladies and gentlemen as well as with older people. A seventy-year-old man was one of the regular students. He never missed a dance and was able to do all the dances with a remarkable technique.

For the students who had worked all day, these evening dance sessions were less of a social activity and more of a gymnastic exercise for mind and body that both relaxed and strengthened muscles.

Americans go about dancing, like everything else, with seriousness and perfect calm. American mothers do not have to worry about their daughters going to the ball like French mothers do. The dancing is very evenly paced to the point where certain dances like the waltz seem to lose a bit of their character. Unlike our dips and twirls, the controlled pace and movement makes the dancers seem like two mechanical dolls

Mr. and Mrs. B. had invited us to attend the ball of Professor Beek and we accepted the invitation with pleasure. This ball was going to be one of the most brilliant of the season and Mrs. B. spent the entire week working on her dress of pale yellow silk trimmed with black velvet.

On the day of the ball the dress was not quite finished and needed a bow or a stitch here or there. For this reason, Mrs. B. requested that her husband not return until just before the ball. The plan was for him to come home at the last minute, quickly dress, and then the four of us would get into the same carriage that had brought him home.

Mrs. B., my husband, and I were ready to go when Fred arrived to get dressed among the chaos of fabric, thread, and pins. Fred quickly reappeared with an unhappy face. The poor man did not have a clean collar!

Mrs. B. had been so completely absorbed with her own outfit that she had not thought of this detail. Poor Fred stood there all dressed, with a dirty collar in his hand.

It was out of the question for Fred to borrow one of my husband's collars as he was so much taller and heavier than Fred that the collar would have had to be used as a belt. I was more annoyed with the incident than Mrs. B. was.

"Well," she said, "put on your dirty collar and we will stop at the laundry service to pick up a clean one on the way."

Since it was a Saturday, all the laundries closed at six in the evening and when Fred went to the door, it was locked.

"Pooh!" said Mrs. B. while poor Fred got back into the carriage with his dirty collar and we set off in search of a shirt maker.

It was going to be very difficult to find one at that hour and Mrs. B. finally realized this. "My dear friend," she said calmly. "I think that you will have to go without a clean collar this evening. It is getting late and we could spend hours looking for one. We have to go to the ball now. I know that it is very annoying but it is not my fault."

I was afraid that Fred, in spite of his good nature, would explode. Although he was visibly upset, he obeyed his wife and directed the driver to take us to the ball. Then, just in front of us in a quiet street, we saw a shirt shop that was open!

With two leaps, the lawyer was in the store trying on collars of all sizes while Mrs. B. giggled in the carriage, very amused by the adventure!

Finally, this excellent Fred, whom we were watching from the carriage, found a collar but in his rush, he dropped the diamond button used to attach the collar.

A new problem! Everyone in the store including the owner, the salesman, and the client started looking on the floor for the button. The three of us could see what was happening from the carriage and could not contain our laughter to the point where we were holding our sides.

It has been written that "all is for the best in the best of all worlds" and Fred eventually found his diamond, buttoned his clean collar, and got back into the carriage in a good mood.[10] He declared that we were truly lucky to have come across this shop and seemed to bear no resentment toward his wife.

I was practically stupefied by Fred's unbelievable patience and meekness. I told myself that in a similar situation this sweetness would have certainly touched me more than the most violent of quarrels. I fear, however, that this sweetness was felt only by me and was lost on Mrs. B.

When we finally arrived at the ball, we found the setting very charming. The room was filled with elegantly dressed men and women. No one dresses simply, not even the young girls who were attired in gowns as dazzling as those of the ladies. This love of luxurious outfits and the foolish purchases that it encourages is one of the most serious reprimands one can make regarding American women.

The dancers enthusiastically performed all of the dances of the repertory accompanied by an excellent orchestra. The ball ended with a cotillion. By the time we left, we were covered with flowers and colorful souvenirs.

The following day, November 21, was Thanksgiving Day. This is the day when Americans offer thanks to God for having helped them preserve their liberty. The date of this holiday is set by the President of the United States but it always falls in November. Since Thanksgiving is a religious holiday, Americans start the day by attending a church service and then spend the day with their families or friends.

That meant that we were going to be alone. In a foreign country, family holidays are sad days for foreigners away from home. You sense the joy around you but you are not taking part in the festivities. The distance from loved ones back home seems greater and dark thoughts swirl in your head. It was a very cold day, and despite the radiant sunshine we were not tempted to take a walk around the lake. Instead, we stayed home and my husband began to read while I worked on a sewing project that I hoped to finish in time for Christmas.

While I was pulling on my needle, I felt overcome by a strange uneasiness. My head became heavy and I thought that it was due to all of the melancholy thoughts I had been having. I tried to pull myself together and admired my husband who seemed completely absorbed in his reading of an English volume. Slowly but sadly, the hours passed. At twilight, I thought it was maybe time to see about dinner.

I stood up but my eyes clouded over and my head started to spin. I grabbed the tablecloth and pulled it down as I fainted and fell to the floor.

When my husband heard me fall, he was frightened and tried to come to my aid. But he could not stand up and fell and hit his head against the wall. The pain of the injury was such that it brought him to his senses and allowed him to think clearly for a second. Quickly, he opened the window wide and then, stumbling and feeling horrible stomach pains, he tried to run out into the courtyard to get help. He did not get that far but fell on the staircase, where he shouted in vain for help as everyone was out. Gathering up all of his energy, he dragged himself back to where I was lying and tried to get me up. After expending all this energy, he fainted next to me.

Asphyxiated! Yes! We were overcome by that famous odorless gas that had caused me to leave Mrs. A.'s house. It turned out that Mrs. B.'s house had the same type of gas. God only knows what would have happened if my husband had not had the presence of mind to open the doors and windows before he fainted.

For a long time we remained stretched out on the rug, where a glacial wind blew through the window.

When Mr. and Mrs. B. returned they were surprised that the house was so cold and sensed that something had happened. Mrs. B. immediately pulled back the tapestry curtain to our room.

When she saw our two bodies she cried out in distress, thinking that we were dead. Once she verified that we each had a pulse, she and her husband tried to help us.

They rubbed us vigorously with ammonia and cold water in order to combat the poisoning symptoms of the gas and they had us drink all of the milk in the house.

A doctor was sent for immediately but he was not able to come until the next morning. We were indisposed for about eight days.

No real harm had been done but it could have been otherwise. Our destiny could have been the same as those poor people who I had seen being taken away to the morgue. I could imagine our two bodies, rolled in blankets with the crowd grasping for our hair! I was very appreciative for all Mrs. B.'s care but I could not forgive her for not being honest with us regarding the quality of the gas used in the house. In fact, when we first moved in she was not using this type of gas, but since the boarders used a lot of fuel she had substituted this cheaper, odorless variety without telling us. She promised to change the type of gas but I only half believed her. A well-grounded fear of this gas had already caused us to move once before and also led us to give up our lodgings at Mrs. B.'s home.

Streets and Shops

Street Vendors—Dime Museum—
Department Stores—An Unusual Candy Shop

With each passing day the cold became increasingly intense, so intense that even Lake Michigan began to freeze. But what a lovely sort of cold! It never rained and the sky was always a splendid blue with sparkling sunshine. Even so, it was bitterly cold and our noses and ears were literally frozen. Gentlemen protected their ears with little black silk earmuffs while women wrapped themselves in large, warm shawls that covered their hats. This is not a very elegant look but when one is well covered up it is very pleasant to take a walk outside.

Bundled up like Eskimos, my husband and I enjoyed walking in the city and exploring eccentric neighborhoods and picturesque corners. This is how we came to discover the Dime Museum.[1]

The Dime Museum, a museum with a ten cent entry fee, does not have a very distinguished reputation but since it is a popular attraction, we wanted to see it for this very reason. Chicago has several establishments of this type. The exterior, from the ground floor to the top floor, is decorated with primitive frescoes representing the attractions of the museum. For the modest price of ten cents, visitors enter to the sound of deafening music and explore a whole series of phenomena: two-headed monkeys, mummies, strange animals, a man with no legs, a giant woman, and a dwarf princess. Other entertaining activities include games of skill. I admit that I was very amused by an exhibit of two bears boxing with their master. They did not spare him their blows and the public's joy reached its height when they gave him a few good punches.

On the ground floor, a theatrical performance was presented for an extra ten cents. It is easy to imagine the quality of this show with its bawdy songs accompanied by a jiglike dance.

We truly enjoyed one of the performances on the program, an authentic dance presented by a group of ten Negroes.

For visitors with a delicate constitution, a quick visit would suffice. However, a particular kind of spectator fills the Dime Museum from morning until evening.

Walking through the streets of Chicago was always a refreshing distraction for me. New ways of earning money seemed to be invented on the spot. Later that same day, we strolled into a boutique that sold paintings at auction. These oil paintings were executed right before the eyes of the buyer. The artist was seated on a kind of stage with an easel in front of him. He rapidly applied his brush and within five minutes, landscapes and sailors appeared on the canvas! Although the paintings were not masterpieces, they had certain artistic qualities. My husband confirmed my opinion and was particularly interested in this quick execution.

As soon as a painting was finished, it was passed to the hands of an individual who placed it in a frame. Finally, it was passed to a third person who auctioned it. In less than fifteen minutes, the painting was executed, framed, and sold. These three men appeared to be delirious, one with painting, the second with framing, and the third with selling.

They must have had some very good days as a number of these paintings sold for fifteen dollars. Others, of course, were sold for just one dollar. The boutique was always filled with people and I enjoyed the sight of happy buyers gingerly carting away freshly painted treasures.

Although these paintings were less impressive to naïve eyes than our bright chromos, the clients were charmed by the realistic quality of color and perspective.[2]

I saw a true instinctive artistic tendency and would be surprised if, in time, it did not develop.

In the streets of Chicago, the multitude of people hurrying, pushing, and pressing against one another provides a continual spectacle. People from all over the globe are part of the interminable procession including a large number of Negroes as well as Chinese, who add a bright note of color with their oriental dress.

Every now and then, we heard a strange sound associated with one of the many little traveling businesses. I had often heard the sound of three bells but did not know its source.

I finally discovered that the bells were attached to a rolling cart similar to the ones used by merchants in France. Affixed to the wheels, the bells rang when the wheels moved.

Another strolling merchant is the popcorn seller. This is a very American business. Popcorn is a type of corn with a fine, pointed grain. In the popcorn cart, there is a glass cage with a portable gas stove. The popcorn man heats and opens the kernels which are placed in a deep metal pan with a long handle. When heated, the little grains of corn begin to dance and jump from left to right as if they are avoiding contact with the pan. After jumping about, they burst and a beautiful white liquid comes out of their shell and covers the grain, like an exotic flower.

The merchant pours salt or sugar over the popcorn and shakes it for a few seconds. He then puts the popcorn in little striped paper bags that are sold for about five cents each to customers both young and old. Everyone likes popcorn so there is never a shortage of clients. Although I enjoy popcorn, I know that many Europeans find that it has no flavor and do not share my opinion.

Another snack that I enjoy even more are peanuts.[3] A type of tuber, they grow at the root of the plant, like potatoes. Peanuts are covered with a thin shell and inside there is a sort of red almond whose flavor, when cooked, is very delicate.

The peanuts have to be cooked in order to be eaten. This cooking takes place in an unusual way. A cylindrical iron pan equipped with a small tube, from which steam can escape, is placed over a flame. The interior of the pan is divided into two compartments: one is for water and the other is for peanuts. After being filled with water and peanuts, this steel box is sealed. The peanuts are cooked in this double boiler and are then packaged in small, multicolored bags similar to those used for popcorn, and are sold for five cents each. The peanuts are delicious and compete with popcorn in the streets and in the trams, where multicolored striped bags seem to be in everyone's hands.

In the commercial center of the city, all streets and avenues are lit with electric lights while gas lighting is used in residential neighborhoods. Lighting, however, is not quite the same as it is in France. The lamplighter is not a poor pedestrian but rather a nimble cavalier on a fierce horse who gallops about with a long lance. At the end of the lance is a flame which he uses to illuminate the neighborhood. He goes from one lamp to the next, so quickly that he does not even appear to stop. An apparition from another world poking holes in the shadows, he leaves a trail of fire behind him.

The department stores of Chicago are always dazzling and luxurious.[4] At that time, they were getting their windows ready for Christmas. One of the biggest stores, Siegel Cooper and Company, presented its "great attraction," which was composed of scenes arranged in the front windows, complete with live subjects [fig. 12].[5]

Children dressed in sumptuous costumes did dances and pantomimes from morning until night. In another window, two young girls washed fabric that was guaranteed to keep its color. Of course, the young girls were dressed from head to toe in the very same fabric.

In all of the department stores, one finds large crowds with almost as many men as women. Men go shopping and buy all of their own clothing and accessories.

You can find everything in these stores. In the basement there is a butcher shop and a grocery store. On the ground floor, counters exhibit every imaginable product. The fresh fruit section displays its oranges, pineapples, and bananas right next to the shoe department. The candy section is next to the silky fabrics while the jewelry department faces the spot where all sorts of liquors including whisky, rum, champagne and wines from France, Germany and Spain are found.

In the center of this enormous hall, a luminous fountain lights up a garland of colored glass. The area around the fountain is always very busy as this is a popular meeting place. Flowers are also for sale in this area.

Across from the fountain, three Negro men dressed in white prepare cold and hot soda waters at an enormous marble table. These drinks are served in large glasses similar to the ones we use for beer.

With extraordinary skill, they pour the contents of one glass into another. They also prepare a fountain drink called an egg phosphate.

To purchase a drink, you must buy a small metal token for twenty-five cents from the cashier. Near this bar, a man selling French brioche had set up his stand and sold his pastries all day long.

Other departments including the lingerie, ready to wear clothing, and book sections are found on the upper floors. The offices of dentists, doctors, and of a well-known divorce attorney are also located here. In addition, a restaurant and a resting area are available for women where they are assisted by chambermaids employed by the store.

The small, elegant salons are filled with beautiful furnishings and musical instruments including organs, harmoniums, and pianos that visitors are free to play. From morning until evening, a deafening concert of sonatas, caprices, waltzes, and musical fanfares was played with such enthusiasm and energy that they made me dizzy.

In the last of these small salons, the sight of a half-raised curtain piqued my curiosity. I was quite surprised by what I discovered inside.

Upon entering, I found myself in a large, darkened room. A mummy encased in a glass sarcophagus stood against the wall and seemed to smile at everyone through its grimace. More hideous mummies, who had perhaps been handsome thousands of years earlier, were also on display.

From this room, I discovered a passage to another large, brightly lit space. Here, Indian bones and the skulls of Negroes, Chinese, and Indians were displayed in glass cases and on tables. This macabre collection was complemented by an attractive collection of jewelry, embroidery, and pearl items. These handicrafts come from many different places.

Need I say that this fascinating part of the gallery is seldom visited by pretty shoppers?

The Siegel and Company store is not the only one that displays interesting objects. One of the largest candy stores in Chicago exhibits its collections as well.

Candy stores in America are generally decorated in a luxurious manner that surpasses that of the most well-known Paris confectionaries. They are temples to feminine desire that bring together the delicacies of the palate and visual pleasure. How to resist the temptation of these bonbons, so pretty to the eye, so exquisite in taste, and so reasonably priced?

Customers consume them in large quantities. There is no danger to the teeth or to the stomach. Since sugar is so inexpensive, no chemical products are used to replace it.

Mr. Gunther's candy shop is the largest in Chicago and his prosperity is entirely due to his energy and intelligence [fig. 13].[6] As a young man, he came to America from Germany and began to make his own candy that he sold in a little wooden stall. Energetic, persevering, and gifted with a rare intelligence, he promptly became a rich man.

"In less than thirty years," he told me, "I acquired my fortune which increases every day with little effort."

In spite of his age, he continues to run the store and to oversee all of the employees, activities that are important to his success.

Very erudite, he has always spent a lot of his free time studying but his true passion is collecting. Eclectic in taste, he has assembled paintings, stones, autographs, and old furniture which he displays on the second floor of his shop. Several of his beautiful paintings are of the Flemish school and are signed by masters. He also has autographed letters from George Washington to his wife and to Lafayette, and one letter from Napoleon.[7]

Although he is of German origin, good old Mr. Gunther really loves France and speaks French very well. In fact, I met him at the "French Club." He was one of its most zealous founders.

This "French Club" counts few French people as members. First of all, not many French people reside permanently in Chicago and secondly, of those who do, the majority do not have the social habits necessary for admission.

The club is primarily composed of Americans who meet once a week for musical presentations, poetry recitations, and theatrical presentations put on by amateurs.[8]

In America, advertising has taken off and has reached heights that the French will not attain for a long time.

Not far from our neighborhood, an entrepreneur rented a boutique and created a stage outside. Seven tall blonde women stood on the platform and showed off marvelous hair that trailed behind them like the train of a dress. These beautiful blonds were admired by all the ladies who passed by. Inside the boutique, hair pomade and a miraculous liquid were for sale that supposedly would make the baldest of heads grow hair as beautiful as that of the blonds. These products were selling very well.

A more modest kind of sign found throughout the city consists of a small piece of iron with hanging three golden balls which indicate that it is a pawn shop, known in France as the *mont-de-piété*.[9] This sad business is apparently one of the most prosperous and the number of establishments of this type seems to confirm that. I do not know exactly how loans are made or if they are done in an honest manner. I do know, however, that every week there is an auction in these pawn shops and that items are sold for very low prices. For example, I have seen gold watches sold for five dollars. If the lender sells the items for such a bargain price, the sum advanced by him to the client must have indeed been very low.

With Christmas approaching, the entire city became more festive and green. Streets were decorated with pine branches and holly, storefronts were framed with greenery, and everywhere there was a holiday air. The number of customers in the boutiques grew each day and carriages lined up outside stores in tightly packed lines. An often cited American proverb is that behind every white horse is a red-haired woman. I must say that I have seen a number of women with copper-colored tresses in carriages drawn by white horses. Perhaps they want to do justice to the proverb.

Everyone was shopping for Christmas presents.

It is surprising how often people give gifts in America! For holidays and birthdays, it is customary to give friends a gift. Usually, the gifts exchanged are not very expensive, for example a little frame, a small container to hold the contents of a pocket, or a picture. Silk embroidered handkerchiefs are very fashionable and can be quite expensive.

In homes, just like in stores, everyone is very animated and the house is cleaned from basement to attic in preparation for the joyous holiday.

Greenery everywhere! Miss H.'s family used cuttings from a magnificent pine tree for decoration throughout the house. Here and there, wreaths of holly decorated the doors and walls and framed the windows. A large bouquet of mistletoe hung from the ceiling. Young people were very preoccupied with the mistletoe since it means that a young man can kiss a young lady who finds herself under the flower.

It is easy to see the bouquet and I guess that young girls voluntarily position themselves in the right spot.

In our house, Mrs. B., with her usual taste, had decorated the salon in a very pretty manner. She was very kind to give me some holly. My kind friend Miss H. had sent me some branches from her tree as well as a bouquet of mistletoe. The poor mistletoe! It was going to be deprived of the beautiful tableaux that its fellow sprigs would witness.

During this season, there were many balls. Mr. and Mrs. B. attended many and often came home in the middle of the night. As a result of all this late night partying, poor Fred developed a terrible cold.

We were constantly awakened by their late night arrival and then for the rest of the night, were kept awake by his terrible cough.

During one of these nights, we heard him breathing with great difficulty and my husband wanted to summon a doctor. Mrs. B., however, did not move and did not seem worried. We thought that she might find our advice inappropriate so we did not interfere. Fred finally got better and fell asleep just as we did.

At exactly seven o'clock in the morning, we heard Mrs. B.'s voice: "Fred, get up. It is time for you to go to the courthouse."

The dear man, roused from a deep sleep, had several fits of coughing. He began to do all of his morning chores in the basement and in the street and finally left for the courthouse. When I saw Mrs. B. later that morning, I asked her how husband was. I could not help but add with just a nuance of reproach: "Are you not afraid that by going out in the evening with such a cough your husband might become seriously ill? With such a delicate constitution who knows what could happen?"

"Eh!" She responded without the least appearance of worry. "He is insured!"

I was stupefied by this response and imagined that I had simply misunderstood. Mrs. B. continued to give me a reassuring explanation about her situation but not that of her husband. Fred had life insurance and the sum that she would receive upon his death would allow her to live in the manner in which she was accustomed until she remarried. She would undoubtedly make a more advantageous marriage since now that she had experience, she would have the leisure of making a good choice.

This woman, who was surrounded by Fred's devotion and tenderness, considered his death an expected occurrence and had already calculated how to make a considerable profit.

I did not show my indignation as I realized that she would not even understand my feelings. Life insurance is so common that there is even speculation on it.

When you take the train, you can buy an insurance ticket in case a catastrophe interrupts the trip. All of the men get insured and their wives count on it. In France, all the husbands count on the death of their in-laws.

As the days passed, the weather became increasingly sunny and cold which was not favorable for Mr. B.'s cough. The household tasks became more numerous and tiring and I found that I hardly had enough time to complete them all as I lacked the necessary energy. With these frigid temperatures, hot air heating is absolutely necessary but our house was insufficiently heated with stoves and turned into a veritable icebox. In the kitchen, the oven compartment would have frozen during the night if my husband had not taken the precaution of emptying it each evening, a tiresome chore! We decided that in spite of all the agreeable aspects of the house, we would only stay at Mrs. B.'s through the last week of the year and then move.

On Christmas Eve, we attended a party given for children and members of an Episcopal church that was held in a large hall called the Douglas Club.[10]

A comedy was presented by a graceful group of amateurs, including Miss H., who played the role of a Negress. It was a very funny show and all of the actors played their roles marvelously. Once the play was over, Saint Nicholas appeared in the middle of all the applause.

Covered with snow and wearing a pilgrim's costume, he held a Christmas tree in his hand. He arrived on stage through an enormous brick chimney, made a short speech, and then distributed gifts to all of the children. After he had finished, he started tearing apart the chimney and the throwing the bricks, which were actually boxes of candy, to the audience.

The next day was Christmas! Christmas . . . that long-anticipated holiday. Joy was everywhere! Family celebrations were taking place! How were we going to spend the day? No museums, no theater, not even pretty windows to look at! This holiday can be very lonely for foreigners.

Despite the cold temperature, it was a nice day so we decided to take a walk in Washington Park. A large crowd of passengers, most of whom had ice skates, filled the tram cars. At the park, almost everyone got off the tram and walked toward the lake. It was terribly cold, never had I been so cold, yet the temperature was expected to dip even lower. Later in January, we had a week when the centigrade thermometer hit twenty seven degrees below zero for eight days straight![11] The fur trim around my neck seemed to be covered with snow, as my breath immediately froze.

How many frozen ears and noses!

The lake, however, was crowded with skaters and the skate rental place was packed. On the lake, the mass of skaters was so compact that it was almost impossible to move without bumping into someone. Two circles were established, each moving in an opposite direction. Almost all of the skaters skated well and we saw quick races as well as graceful waltzes. Small, heated cabins along the lakeshore provided refuge for them. All winter long, the lakes in Washington, Lincoln and Garfield Parks are crowded. Ice skating is so popular in America that the lakes are illuminated so that skaters can skate at night.

The Hotel Everett

Winter in Chicago—American Women—
Education and Schools

It was, I admit, with great regret that we left the place where we had lived for four months that was so peaceful and truly felt like our home. We ate what we wanted when we wanted and saved quite a bit of money in the meantime.

But ever since the gas accident, my strength had diminished and it had become impossible for me to continue to do all of the housework alone. I had tried to find a maid to help me, but in spite of all my efforts, I had no luck. As for American maids, ah! God knows we had already seen our share of them. It would be one hundred times better to stay in a hotel for the remainder of our trip! I would at least have the pleasure of observing a different clientele.

We decided to stay at the Hotel Everett on Lake Avenue.[1] The hotel resembled a barracks as it was made up of five square three-storey houses. In front of each house lay the typical patch of grass, surrounded by cemetery-like stones.

Each house had a monumental staircase leading up to the door, and all were topped by a large "Everett Hotel" sign.

The exterior appearance of the hotel was very acceptable and in keeping with the clientele. It was a well-maintained hotel for well-bred, middle-class clients but certainly not for millionaires.[2]

The rear of the hotel overlooked the lake and while the view was very charming, it was somewhat spoiled by the proximity of the railroad tracks and the frequent passage of trains all day and all night long.

In spite of this drawback, we were tempted by the magical view of the lake and chose a room on the ground floor in the rear section of the hotel.

It was not really on the ground floor but rather on the second floor.

In America, the ground floor is reserved for kitchens, pantries, dining rooms, and servants' quarters.

Our bright, spacious room was cleverly set up as a sitting room rather than a bedroom. Once again, we would have the pleasure of sleeping in a folding bed.

The cold that had chased us from Mrs. B.'s was not a problem here as the room was stifling hot. We had to open windows in order to get some sleep, or rather, to try to get some sleep as the constant passage of trains awakened us throughout the night.

To top things off, our room was located right above the kitchen. From four o'clock in the morning on, there was a horrible clanging of pots and pans as they began preparing for the six o'clock breakfast.

Our room was in the same area as the reception rooms and this presented another inconvenience. From morning until night, the piano was constantly in use. Children played scales or worked on sonatas, and the hotel owner, who was a virtuoso, also took his turn at the keyboard.

Mr. and Mrs. Everett, the loving couple who owned the hotel, were both relatively young, between thirty and thirty-five. Mrs. Everett was quite pretty but had a disagreeable facial expression. Her husband had a very content and satisfied air which made up for his wife's grimace.

His principal occupations were playing the piano and singing while his wife's only concern was her appearance.

Approximately eighty guests were staying at the Everett Hotel. Breakfast was served between six and eight in the morning. The schedule was very strict at the hotel and no meals were served outside of regular hours. If by eight o'clock you were still asleep, a maid would ring the bell. If you answered promptly, she would leave a piece of fruit or cake. How many times had I missed out on an orange that I would usually eat for dessert?

Although the food was not very refined, it was plentiful. In contrast to other boardinghouses and hotels, the Everett Hotel allowed guests to eat as much as they wanted. The roasts were delicious, the stews terrible, and the vegetables, which were cooked without butter, were horribly bland. There was a great variety of pastries but they were all very heavy—veritable lead cakes! Other guests, however, enjoyed the desserts. One evening, I noticed that a young man at my table ate four slices of rhubarb pie, a dessert so heavy that I could never have digested even half of a slice.

Only a few pensioners had lunch at the hotel, most preferring to take that meal elsewhere. At six in the evening, however, everyone reappeared for dinner.

By eight o'clock, all of the maids had left. If you needed something, you had to get it yourself or ask the owners.

All in all, we really had nothing to complain about at the Everett Hotel, and in many ways we realized that we did not miss our former lodgings.

We would have happily spent full days watching marvelous Lake Michigan. Indeed, one morning we admired the most splendid of spectacles.

All night long, a violent wind had begun to blow from the west and had swept ice from the banks of the lake into the water. The lake's surface, which was normally calm, began to foam. Fast and tumultuous, the waves seemed to be racing one another as they broke along the lakeshore. Throughout the night, the wind increased and the lake became so turbulent that our house trembled. In bed, we were so roughly shaken that it felt like we were on a boat. The night was so dark that unfortunately, we could not see anything. But in the morning, the storm, which had calmed down a little, was still going on and what an unforgettable sight!

The waves moved with a dizzy rapidity and were so high that they reached the walkway. The entire surface of the lake was agitated, with the depth higher in certain places and lower in others. The magnificent sun reflected the nuanced colors of the rainbow onto the foamy crests and intensified the green hue of the lake.

The birds flying overhead had piercing cries. Their large white wings seemed to bat the air in desperate movements.

This furious revolt by Lake Michigan was its final protest against the coming ice invasion.

By the next morning, frozen waves decorated the edges of the lake. A few days later, the lake resembled a brilliant mirror of ice and was frozen across a two-kilometer span at a thickness of seventy centimeters.

From that point on, there was a continual parade of skaters and ice-boats.

Iceboats resemble tugboats except that they have a sail and are spacious enough to carry four people plus the driver. They go very fast and if the ice gives in, the boat could disappear in a second.

One type of ice skating that I found amusing was a kind of wind surfing on ice. Holding the sail in front and moving it in different directions, the skater is able to go very fast. Nothing is more unusual than seeing a man, wrapped like a mast, moving as fast as lightning.

The street view was as picturesque as that of the lake. A great deal of snow had fallen and the whole city was veiled in white.

Sleighs were the only vehicles used as none of the streetcars were running. Simple sleds delivered goods while horse-drawn sleighs transported elegant ladies, bundled in fur, with a joyous air, sparkling eyes, and glowing cheeks.

Children were delighted to be able to indulge in one of their favorite games. As soon as they heard a sleigh approaching, they would hide behind trees or lie on the ground. Once the sleigh came near, they would jump out, imitate the cry of Indians, and pretend to attack it. This game was an imitation of the Indians' attacks on carriages. Usually, those in the sleigh pretended to be afraid which, of course, absolutely thrilled the children. If the passengers took offense, it did not really matter as a snowball fight would ensue and the young men would quickly outrun their pursuers. Even the police were lenient and often chuckled at this prank.

Cable cars continued to run but occasionally minor accidents occurred due to the fact that the frozen cables sometimes broke. They were filled with passengers and were, at times, so overloaded that the car could not move. This happened once while I was onboard. All of the seats were occupied by ladies while the men all stood in the center. The driver announced that was impossible to start the cable car. Immediately, all of the men calmly exited and began to push the car. As soon as the car started up, the most agile men among them jumped onboard while the others patiently waited for the next car.

To get back to the Everett Hotel, most of the pensioners were women and the hotel had a very respectable reputation. The most severe kind of temperance was observed and no one would be caught drinking even a drop of wine or beer in public.

Most of the women worked in department stores or as typists.

Typewriters are constantly in use in Chicago and are used almost exclusively by women. In all sorts of businesses and hotels, women type at this strange keyboard with incredible speed, from morning to night.

Some of the other women living at the Everett Hotel did not work. Some were married and others had large families. Their lifestyle was, for me, a constant source of fascination.

One of these ladies, who was on the older side, lived in the hotel with her husband and four children. The husband had to earn quite a bit of money to afford the expense of a hotel pension for six people.

This lady was very nice and became friendly with several pensioners, including myself. We spent time reading, taking walks, playing music, and doing needlework. The eldest of her daughters was eighteen and was still in school. She loved studying and wanted to continue until her marriage. Once married, she would live a life similar to her mother's at the hotel, busy with walks, reading, and needlework.

Another young lady, who was about thirty years old, had two children and led a similar existence. Yet another pretty blonde woman was even younger. Her husband frequently traveled on business and the young lady did not appear at all upset when her husband was away. During the day, she went shopping and in the evening, she invited her many friends in for card parties.

This idleness is a weakness in American women. I cannot understand how these women can accept living in public, in a hotel, with their husbands and children.[3]

I admit that this hotel lifestyle is practical for women who must work since it is so difficult for middle-class families to find servants. But for mothers of small children, how can they tolerate this detachment from a real home? The cause for this situation lies entirely in the education of young girls who learn absolutely nothing about their duties as homemaker and mother. The daughters naturally imitate their mothers' manner of doing things and cannot conceive of other ways. Although they attend school for many years, they do not learn anything about running a household.

In order to earn enough money to support a family living in a hotel, the husband must work like a Negro with no hope of ever relaxing. The tendency to save money, which is so characteristic of the French bourgeoisie, is unheard of among these families. They live from one day to the next, depending on the husband to make enough money to pay the bills in the present as well as the future. The wife is also consoled by the idea of life insurance, which protects her for the future.

The solid, brave woman whom we see so often in France—hardworking, industrious, thrifty, proud of the appearance of her little home, and ready to help her husband by working outside of the home—this woman is a myth in America.

It has not always been this way. Lazy American women should look to their ancestors as domestic virtues were a priority for the strict puritans.

The daughter of one of these ladies, an adorable little girl of six or seven, became a good friend of mine. Reasonable and calm, she loved to hear about France and asked me all kinds of questions.

"Mrs. Grandin," she asked me one day, "what are you?"

"I am French, darling!"

"That is not what I am asking," she said with impatience.

She repeated,

"What are you, Republican or Democrat?"

I was tempted to laugh but stifled it so that I could answer her. In fact, I evaded her question.

"And you Mary, what are you?"

"I am Republican and I regret that Harrison is no longer president."

This profession of faith was so firm and sincere that her beautiful eyes filled with sadness. I burst out laughing in spite of myself.

Offended yet dignified, she left my room without giving me her usual hug. I later showed her a beautiful French picture and got back into her good graces.

Her question was not, in fact, so unusual. In America, children talk about politics on a daily basis. Six-year-old boys already have political convictions and argue among themselves about the candidates. Reading the newspaper is unfortunately, one of their greatest preoccupations on Sunday. I am not sure if this habit of getting them interested in the country's affairs so early is good or bad. It certainly does encourage their love of American history. I have never seen French children speak of our famous patriots with the same enthusiasm.

I visited an elementary school and had the pleasure of discussing the point with a seven-year-old boy.

In elementary schools, it is common practice for each of the pupils to give a short presentation once or twice each week. The subject of the presentation is usually based on the life of a great man and the student is free to choose the specific anecdote. Only after the pupil has given the presentation does the teacher make comments. This is an excellent oral exercise since the child learns to express himself confidently, without the teacher having to drag the words out of him.

Both girls and boys do very well with this exercise and express their ideas simply and clearly.

The little boy was recounting the anecdote about George Washington's childhood when he received a new ax and tried it out by cutting down his father's favorite tree. When his father angrily asked him about it, he confessed and accepted his punishment.

This tale seems rather insignificant in itself, however the sincerity of the speaker and his obvious admiration for Washington made it very charming. I could not resist challenging the young enthusiast.

"So . . ." I told him, "Washington must not have loved his father if he destroyed something that was so precious to him."

"Ah! But he did! Ma'am, he was not paying attention."

"So he was not really a very good boy if he so easily forgot something that would upset his father."

"Oh," he said to me with a very sad expression. "I see that French people do not know the story of George Washington. He was, Madame, the best little boy in America. Thanks to all his good deeds, he eventually became father to all of us and we American boys love him as a father."

I could have hugged the little boy for all the enthusiasm he put into his declaration. I gave him a handshake and told him that I was joking. I explained that I was familiar with the story of Washington and that, like him, I loved and respected this great man.

This kind little boy was in the elementary class. He and his classmates were attentive, quiet, and hardworking and it was never necessary to reprimand them. The teacher was a very young woman and I was at first struck, then charmed, by the polite and friendly tone she used with her students. The typical disagreeable formula of authoritative command was replaced by a friendly invitation.

We were in the month of January, and even though the students had only been in this class since September they were already able to read the first elementary reader. Reading and writing lessons took place simultaneously, using the blackboard.

The emphasis was on pronunciation of words along with punctuation. I am certain that all Americans read well due to the fact that they have good instruction from the start.

In between each lesson, girls and boys, who share the same benches, stand up, walk around, sing, and play games.

The classrooms are much less attractive than ours in France. They are poorly lit, somber, and often, it must be said, dirty.

Most schools do not have playgrounds or courtyards so students play in dark classroom corridors.

These corridors are also used for physical education classes which consist exclusively of group exercises, sometimes using dumb bells, bars, or clubs.

Pupils perform the exercises perfectly and just like with their work bring exemplary attention and good will to the task. Their docility, however, does not diminish the inconvenience of such maneuvers done right outside classrooms where other teachers are giving lessons.

This is the biggest problem but not the only one. The layout of the school is not very practical, with corridors so dark and narrow that students can hardly move.

Though inferior in architecture and construction to French schools, American schools are far superior in terms of atmosphere. Since the pupils are very orderly, there is no need for an authority figure to impose order.

At the stroke of the clock, the young girls and boys immediately stop talking and line up so that the teacher does not need to intervene. Pupils walk into their respective classrooms where teachers are waiting for them. Punishment is never discussed. Rewards such as prizes and distinctions are not used either.

The pupils' only ambition is to learn, and with the knowledge they gain they hope to make their future easier. The best pupil in the class simply has the satisfaction of being the most respected among his peers and of being proudly introduced by his classmates to class visitors.

Visitors are numerous, as American schools are open to everyone—parents, friends, foreigners—so it is not necessary to obtain a special authorization to visit. Teachers and pupils greet visitors upon arrival and departure but otherwise they seem almost not notice their presence. Pupils are even allowed to leave the classroom without permission and are never forced to stay in their room like they are elsewhere. Americans are free.

Perhaps it is because they are not forced to go that American children enjoy and attend school regularly.[4]

A friend of mine wanted to have a portrait done of her little boy. She asked her son to stay home from school in order to pose. The boy obeyed his mother but was very upset at the thought of missing school. Upon the painter's arrival, the child's face was streamed with tears. They rescheduled the sitting for a Saturday and that time the boy was smiling.

All public schools are closed on Saturday. In these schools, regardless of social or economic class, boys and girls are in class together.[5] The boys are very obliging and respectful of the girls. In general, girls have more facility with learning and often continue their studies longer than boys do. Once boys finish primary school, they frequently start working. If they are interested in a liberal career, they go to special high schools in New York or Boston.

Most of the girls and a small number of boys go on to high school.

A French acquaintance of mine was a teacher at a high school near the Michigan border called the Hay School.[6] The school is nicknamed the "mausoleum" as it looks more like a funeral monument than a building for lively and carefree young people. Classes in the liberal arts, sciences, and foreign languages are offered.

Miss E. and I decided to spend a day there. We arrived in the morning, carrying our white metal lunch boxes just like the other students.

The morning classes began at nine and ended at noon. The stroke of the clock on the hour signaled to students and teachers that it was time for the next class. In a very orderly fashion, students would leave each classroom and continue onto their next class.

My friend taught French there, and I was particularly interested in observing her class. Once class began, the pupils spoke only French. All of the grammar explanations were given in French, while comparisons with English grammar were explained in English. This method results in rapid progress and even the young girls in the first year class were able to understand me and answer simple questions.

The teaching emphasis is on oral skills. Reading and writing lessons in the French classes were done as carefully as those I had observed in English classes.

There was much conversation as well. The pupils recounted anecdotes from French newspapers and tried to explain them as well as they could.

Americans like these little anecdotes but, unfortunately, they often recount the same ones over and over. In fact, in one week I heard the same anecdote nine times!

At noon, the stroke of the clock announces lunch time which pupils eat in their classrooms. Teachers and students alike take out their lunchboxes and eat at the tables. I was shocked that such a large school did not have a cafeteria, a place where one could conveniently have a simple lunch. They are accustomed to this and although all of the school personnel make do, I think that this habit flies in the face of the comfort that Americans hold so dear. Once lunch is finished, students go to the water fountain for a drink and then fold up their lunch boxes and tuck them in with their school books, everything kept together with a strap.

The students have a few minutes to walk and chat in the corridor before returning to classes. This central corridor is just as narrow and dark as the ones I had seen in the primary schools. It was used for physical culture classes that were under the direction of a male teacher.[7]

I asked the teacher why he did not use gymnastics apparatus in his classes. He responded that it would be impossible to install them in such a narrow space and that he did not really see the value of it. He felt that the exercises he used produced the same effects in terms of physical development over time and did not have the possible negative effects of more strenuous exertions. In addition, he noted that if the girls wanted more rigorous exercise they could play lawn tennis.

After visiting primary and secondary schools I had a great desire to see a kindergarten classroom. I had heard so much about these remarkable classes that sounded like they were one thousand times better than ours.[8] I had truly expected something magnificent and was disappointed from the start.

In a large, dirty classroom, four tables were placed haphazardly around the room, each surrounded by ten little chairs. The tables were so small that the chairs were tightly jammed next to one another. Children, including two little Negro boys, were seated at the tables.

The room contained two storage cabinets, their drawers overflowing with papers, balls, rags, pieces of cardboard, and wood. Black tracings of geometric figures covered the floor. In the corner, a woman played the piano and I assumed that she was the teacher.

A young assistant teacher sat at each table with the children. Dressed in white aprons, they resembled nannies.

And the garden? Where was the shady, flower-filled garden that I had imagined? The teacher showed me two green flower pots that sat in front of the windows. The plants looked as if they were desperately trying not to die under a thick layer of dust.

Another flower pot was filled with thin, pale herbs that would certainly never reach maturity. The teacher told me that this pot of herbs was the class wheat field!

What a pitiful wheat field! If the children did not have an opportunity to see a real wheat field one day what a curious idea they would have of the real fields where this precious cereal grows! The principle behind the project is good but the plants should at least bear some resemblance to the real thing. After seeing the pitiful wheat plants I prefer our habit in France of using sketches or colored drawings to teach children about nature.[9]

Rapidly abandoning the flower pots and their contents, I turned my attention to the children. Seated at their tables, they all seemed to be doing whatever they wanted, without any specific direction. Some of them were playing with wooden blocks, however they seemed more intent on making noise by letting the blocks fall rather than on building something. Others were doing the same thing with sticks.

Each teacher was responsible for a group of just ten children. What excellent results one should achieve with this number! Not there, however. I was astonished to see how dirty the hands and faces of the children were.

I asked the teachers if they did not put the issue of cleanliness before everything else.

"Yes!" they responded spontaneously. "But only for the dirty children!"

I am not sure what constituted cleanliness in the eyes of these ladies but every child looked unclean to me. I was interested in seeing the bathroom. What a disgrace! It was a dark little room with just one sink half full of black water. It made me wonder if the little black boys had been dyed! In the middle of the room, there was a chamber pot, but no consideration was given to privacy or odor. The children's clothing hung on the wall and lay scattered on the floor. Never would I have imagined such a sight in this country of comfort!

One can imagine the haste with which I left the bathroom. I was drawn back to the classroom by the off-key notes of the piano. With the same movement that an organ grinder would use, the teacher was doing a bearlike dance. At this signal, the children ran to the geometric lines on the floor and began to move their arms in epileptic-like gestures. They also made animal-like sounds and sang terribly, accompanied by the old piano. The teachers were all doing the same movements but they did them so quickly that they resembled mechanical figures, controlled by a spring mechanism.

We had apparently just witnessed the departure of sparrows, something that I would never have guessed from their movements.

Now that the sparrows had taken off, another exercise followed.

The teachers and children were sitting on the floor with their heads down and eyes closed.

This time I understood that they were pretending to be asleep and that it was a kind of charade. I must say, however, that as a live tableau it left much to be desired. Legs sprawled here and there, resulting in a ridiculous and sometimes immodest scene. A young assistant teacher was near me and was not able to comfortably fold her legs. Then, while everyone was pretending to be asleep, a child pulled out one of the teacher's hairpins. When she got up, she had to redo her hair. She did not look annoyed and did not scold the child.

After a few more of these silly exercises the piano struck its last notes and the children returned to their seats.

I ventured to ask a question regarding the lessons: in the midst of all these exercises, do the children learn to read? Just as in response to my question regarding cleanliness, the answer was affirmative. From time to time, the teachers drew the letters of the alphabet on the board and the students repeated them, but the lesson did not go any further. Essentially, the goal was to get the children to use their senses and to encourage physical development without taxing their young brains. I agree that teaching children material above their level is more harmful than helpful, however I believe that learning to spell words, put together letters, and count sticks is neither too abstract nor too fatiguing for children between the ages of four and six. I left the kindergarten in a very disillusioned state. I was not enthusiastic regarding the education principle, neither in theory nor in practice. The idea, as I have stated, is a very good one but a different mode of application is necessary.

I came away from this kindergarten visit with dashed illusions and not in the least enthusiastic about this approach to education. The idea, I repeat, is very good but it would require another mode of application.

A few days after these visits, I received an invitation from Miss B., the teacher at the Hay School. She invited me to an afternoon meeting with some of her students. It is customary for teachers to host students, from time to time, on Saturdays when school is closed.

Almost all of the students came to Miss B.'s home and were delighted to spend time with their teacher. I was immediately peppered with questions about Paris and our high schools. The girls thought that I had been impressed by the beauty of their school and seemed stunned when I described French schools: bright and airy, with well-maintained classrooms, large playgrounds with trees and benches, and cafeterias where children can get a hot meal for a few cents.

They could not believe their ears. To make them feel better I heartily praised their discipline, conscientious work, and behavior. In France, constant surveillance, calls to order, a system of good and bad grades, and prizes distributed as rewards do not achieve half as good of a result as what these girls did themselves.

The idea of being rewarded with a prize seems strange to Americans. I quickly explained that they should not jump to conclusions regarding the talents of young French girls. I told them that in fact, French girls' wealth of knowledge surpassed that of American girls. For example, sewing lessons in France go beyond simple embroidery. French girls learn to become good homemakers capable of doing what needs to be done, including mending, cooking, and overseeing a household.[10] I emphasized that food preparation should be considered by all women as the most serious of responsibilities.

After making this statement, the girls were on the verge of laughing in my face. They all exclaimed that, in terms of cooking, the only recipe that interested them was how to make candy! I tried my best to tell them about the duties of a good wife and mother. I described for them a modest but charming home run by an intelligent woman who was both educated and a good homemaker. She is interested in the intellectual pursuits of her husband, oversees the education of her children, mends their socks, and takes good care of her clothing. She also helps the maid in the preparation of stews and side dishes.

The American girls seemed to find my remarks pleasing but unrealistic. One of them asked me in a doubtful voice: "And you, Madame Grandin, do you know how to cook?"

My affirmative response surprised them, but they found the fact that I had been cooking in Chicago for the previous four months even more astonishing. I promised them that I would serve as their guide to the French exhibition of schools so that I could show them samples of the domestic talents of our young girls.

The conversation was accompanied by music and the afternoon ended with tea.

I was truly delighted to see the easy rapport between these young girls and their teacher. Their mutual affection charmed me.

The teacher was a great friend and more to her students, and I could only compare this amicable rapport with the stiff relationship our students have with their teachers in France. These little dears would love to open up and love us but instead there is a frigid dignity in the way that the French conceive of the rapport between student and teacher.

In France, the teacher is too distanced from the student and never deigns to come down to the student's level. In the end, the teacher is reduced to nothing more than a voice box that students listen to or pretend to listen to, with complete indifference.

We tolerate the teacher just as we do rain and bad weather, in the hope that they will soon go away. Once we finish our studies, the memory of both the teacher and the lessons completely disappears or simply brings to mind criticisms or teasing.

In America, on the contrary, the idea of finishing her studies is a sad one for a young girl. She stays for as long as she can, and once she leaves always happily returns. It is possible that the American student does not enjoy studying more than the French student does. Rather, it is the teacher who makes her studies so enjoyable. One day, perhaps, I hope that we will arrive at the same result.

Although they are frivolous in some respects, American women have nevertheless an instinctive desire to learn. This desire is not as strong in French women.

In certain social circles of the American upper class, ladies frequently get together to practice their French. They hire a French lady for ten or fifteen meetings and discuss a literary, historical, or artistic subject.[11]

During the time that I spent in Chicago, Americans were already a year ahead of us in their taste for anything associated with the First Empire. In discussion groups, topics included Madame Tallien, the Empress Joséphine, and, above all, Madame Récamier.

At four o'clock, everyone settled down and the speaker began her hour-long presentation. Afterward, tea was served and there was some musical entertainment. The French lady was always surrounded with attention and kindness until the very end.

It must be said that this kind of diversion is not always so intellectual. Another type of entertainment would be shocking to our French morals.

For example, it is common when families invite friends to dinner to prepare a pleasant surprise for them.[12] One evening, we were at a rather large gathering at Mrs. H.'s home. We were asked to go into a small room where we would see the curious spectacle of Madame Blue Beard.

I went in with others, expecting a projection of a magic lantern or something similar. When the door opened, I could not stop stifle a cry of terror! At the end of the room there was a green flame of sulfur. A white sheet was draped over the young girl and her head emerged from the opening. Her face had a bluish tint due to the green reflection of the flames, and her black hair was pulled straight up. One would have thought that the victim's head was hanging from the hair.

Truly petrified, I left the room only to be followed by the laughter of others who found my terror amusing. I quickly laughed myself but found that this macabre joke could produce harmful effects on a nervous person. At another gathering, the surprise came in the form of a competition.

Miss Eva and Miss Maude lay on the ground, completely covered by white sheets. As they lay side by side, they punched and kicked one another. These movements produced a very strange effect. The two young ladies continued and Miss Maude was victorious in the end. Miss Eva surrendered but was congratulated by the guests.

Calumet Lake and Pullman City

Calumet Lake—Pullman Factory—
Hospitals and Nurses

The bitterly cold weather only got worse. Everywhere a thick blanket of snow covered the ground, which was marked with trails and dappled with rays of sunshine.

Although winter in Chicago resembled a Siberian landscape, we would normally venture outdoors unless it was snowing. I had long wanted to see Calumet Lake, so one day we decided to take an excursion there.

Considered part of Chicago, Calumet Lake is located at the southern edge of the city. It takes about two hours to get there, passing through enormous plains of large cattle farms. Technically part of the city, it is not at all urban and is a bit like saying that the Parisian suburbs of Antony or Sèvres are in the city.[1]

The lake shore was completely deserted and its ice-covered surface was so vast that it was not possible to see the opposite shore.

This area does not attract many visitors at this time of the year. In the summer, however, it is a very popular place. Picnics are organized on the lake shore and races take place on the lake itself, including rowing competitions and regattas. Bleachers allow spectators to follow all the excitement of these nautical events.

The lake, however, was not the only goal of our walk as in such weather it was difficult to admire it for very long. We had promised ourselves that we would also visit the immense workshops of the large train manufacturer, Pullman, which are located near Calumet Lake.[2]

These factories are located in Pullman City, a town owned by Mr. George Pullman. In addition to the workshops, there are well-paved streets that are swept and bordered with houses, several churches, schools, and even a theater. Everything is powered by electric light and patrolled by police. The extremely wealthy owner finances all of this in the manner of a true feudal lord.

Mr. Pullman is not the only man of this sort in America. Twenty years ago, in the hope of encouraging railroad construction, the state gave large stretches of land to entrepreneurs. Today, the state still provides the land but holds on to parcels throughout the area so that the land remains part of the city.

Thanks to the liberal ideas of its owner, Pullman City is a model city. Let me quickly say that Mr. Pullman does not administer his lands with a feudal firmness. He only dreams of making the inhabitants who work in his factories as happy as possible.[3]

All of the inhabitants of Pullman City work in the factories. Despite the large number of employees who live there, many more commute from Chicago. The Pullman factory is one of the largest in the world.

The main factory building, where the company offices are located, resembles a monument and even has a small lake in front of it. Here in the offices, legions of women type or write all day long.

A simple letter suffices to get permission to visit the immense factory. Every item that will be used to construct the train cars enters the factory as a raw material. One can stroll through the factory and ask the workers questions. They respond politely, all the while continuing their work.

I will not attempt to describe these workshops or the functioning of their powerful machines, as it would be too long and difficult and would require mastery of a technical vocabulary that I do not possess. But seeing the colossal, vibrating machines with their rotating wheels and their steam whistles is a majestic and imposing sight. The rooms where they heat the materials have a Dante-esque quality with workers covered with coal and sweat, tending the fiery red flames in ovens that demand a constant supply of fuel.

In the buildings located next to the railroad tracks, a sawmill is used to cut up gigantic trees, and there is also a foundry, a carpentry shop, and glass, painting, and tapestry workshops. Trains arrive continuously to supply all of the materials needed by the workers. At the end of the process, other trains transport the finished luxury railroad car or the fast, powerful locomotive that the workers have constructed from the materials.[4] These trains will be shipped around the world as Pullman's has a worldwide reputation.

Although I was interested in all that I saw, some aspects of the factory were completely new to me. I was especially intrigued by workers who were loading an enormous container with cotton. In fact, this cotton was being placed on the floor of a railroad passenger car and would later be covered with a hardwood floor.

Our inspection of the workshops and the factories took up the entire afternoon and the clock showed that the workday had come to an end. As we exited the factory, we stood on the threshold, struck by surprise.

Snow had begun to fall again in such large, thick flakes that it resembled an accumulation of cotton, similar to what they were using to pad the railroad car. All of the walkways were filled with a compact crowd of workers whose footsteps were muffled against the blanket of snow. Under the electric lights, the snow appeared blue and created a silent, strange, and eerie scene.

Many of the workers were taking the train back to Chicago and we walked with them toward the train station where we found that the railroad tracks were covered with snow. Sometimes it is necessary to use two or three machines to clear off the snow so that the train can reach its destination. On the lake shore, the accumulation of snow was so great that a derailment followed by a cold bath in the icy lake waters was possible, a thought that I did not cherish. Fortunately, we managed, but our apprehension was warranted since train accidents are an eventuality that Americans have come to expect. Accidents are so frequent that in every train station you can buy an insurance ticket for twenty-five cents. If a railroad accident occurs, you receive a payment, the exact sum of which depends upon the seriousness of the injuries. In fact, the payment terms for all injuries, fractures, and medical expenses are indicated on the insurance ticket.

You can buy several tickets, and I have been told that in the case of a catastrophe, uninjured passengers often slip a ticket into the pocket of less fortunate ones.

Back in Chicago, we made plans to attend the annual costume ball of the Art Institute.[5]

This is a big event for all of the future great artists and the choice of costume is especially important. Traditional guidelines for appropriate dress did not seem to influence the gay youthfulness of the crowd, as originality, fantasy, and eccentricity won out over good taste and decency. Miss H., my blonde friend, transformed herself into a daisy. Another friend dressed as a yellow sunflower. Looking at the loges, the dressmakers who had worked on these outfits were without a doubt exhausted. As in France, many established dressmakers have their own businesses but their prices are very high.[6] The simplest of dresses can easily cost ten dollars and the most elaborate gowns go up to one hundred dollars!

Not everyone can afford to use these dressmakers but in addition to these fine workers, an army of excellent seamstresses who charge two dollars per day, plus meals, are available to come to the house. They are in great demand and have such a large clientele that it is necessary to book them one month in advance, if you would like to have them for several days. They cut, prepare, and fit the garments and almost all of them have sewing machines.

On the day of the ball, a great crowd hurried into the salons of The Athenaeum at nine in the evening. The rooms were decorated with large Chinese parasols which softened and tinted the bright gas lights. Flowers, especially cut blooms which were so expensive during that season, inundated the room to the point where the orchestra was completely hidden behind greenery.

The lavish costumes ranged from the grotesque to the coquettish, including Turks, marquis, flowers, pages, shepherdesses, and clowns that represented all of Chicago's youth. Few parents were present. Young ladies attended with brothers or friends and would make it home in their company without anyone worrying about them.

What was there to fear? At this ball like elsewhere, a sense of respect surrounded the young ladies, who behaved most appropriately in the middle of all the activity.

The buffets were crowded with guests, but the ice cream and lemonade did not tempt these young ladies, most of whom simply had a glass of water. The dancing was lively but not inappropriate.

All of this transpired in a familial kind of atmosphere, so the mothers of young ladies could in fact, sleep peacefully. Any kind of surveillance of young ladies is unknown here.[7]

From childhood, they learn how to behave and how to protect themselves, which is the best protection of all. Over time, they develop a sense of dignity.

For young ladies whose social condition requires that they earn a living, they hope that this situation will only be temporary. Through their behavior, they try to show that they are worthy of a good marriage.

This tendency toward social mobility is certainly one of the American virtues that I appreciate the most. Nothing is worse than for an intelligent person to be boxed in and limited. Nothing is worse than being stuck, as only a sense of powerlessness, silliness, and stupidity can come from caged rats.

Nursing is one of the professions embraced by women in America. Unlike in France, nursing is considered one of the most honorable professions here. Almost all of the nurses have had medical training.[8] When on duty, nurses wear an unflattering uniform that consists of a white cotton dress with an apron, a large gray cape, and a gray hat covered with a veil. In uniform, they resemble nuns and inspire kindness and respect as they cross the city from one end to the other.

From what people have told me, they earn a lot of money and are accepted into the most distinguished society.

They provide care both at home and in the many hospitals, which, unlike in France, do not exclusively care for poor patients.

Similar to our *maisons de santé,* American hospitals are private and are run by a doctor and a director who takes care of the finances.

American hospitals are always crowded. Since many Americans live in hotels or in boardinghouses, it is difficult to be cared for in a room when one has a serious illness. In the case of an epidemic, the ill person is transferred out of the hotel or boardinghouse immediately.

In the case of a less serious illness, a nurse can be summoned to the home. She stays with the patient and carefully carries out the doctor's orders. However, if the sickness gets worse, the patient is transported to the hospital.

Special hospitals exist for men, women, and children. Certain hospitals are for men who are alcoholics. After a rather long stay, they sometimes come out cured of their terrible passion.[9]

These hospitals are similar to boardinghouses, except that they provide very good care. Sick patients of different economic means are welcome. The difference in price is not related to the quality of care, which is the same for all, but rather depends on the number of rooms that the client occupies. For example, some patients have a large apartment where their relatives and servants stay. The poorest of patients share a room with one other person. Fortunately, these are not those large, sad rooms where human misery is on display, where the sounds of suffering and agony are present from morning until night, and where one often sees other patients die while awaiting one's own fate.

There are no operating rooms either since operations take place in the patient's room with as few terrifying preparations as possible. The surgeon is always assisted by the patient's nurses. Generally, there are two nurses for each patient so that there is no interruption in care from the beginning of the illness until the end.

Servants, who are few in number, perform all the tasks that our private nurses would never accept, even though American nurses are superior in terms of education and intelligence.

While visiting one of these hospitals with a woman I had met through mutual friends, I was surprised by the precautions taken by the young nurses as they made their patients' beds. The nurses are gentle and offer many kind gestures to their patients. They know how to sweeten long, painful days with interesting conversation and entertaining reading.

"It is impossible for me to be bored," I was told by the person I was visiting. "My two nurses are charming and I will miss them very much when I get well."

Many of the cures are the result of the devoted care provided by these nurses. We should envy Americans for their nurses who have both medical knowledge and a likable and gay worldliness.

Hospitals are not free but one should not conclude that charity does not exist in America. On the contrary, it is very substantial but practiced in a different way from in France and for a reason.

First of all, misery does not present itself like it does in France, an outstretched hand to receive alms. An American's dignity keeps him from this lowly practice. Instead, an American will do any kind of work as he seeks a salary, not a donation and does not consider any work beneath him. A ruined businessman will beat rugs or wash windows if he cannot find any other work. In a group of plasterers and masons, I have seen a doctor and a lawyer who did not feel dishonored by the mediocrity of their situation and were not worried about their future. However, in America, like elsewhere, orphans, sick people, and the elderly require care and these people are accepted into hospitals. Each church has a club that collects donations and distributes them.

Since Americans do not have to succumb to the extortion of beggars, it is possible to do a lot of good. The people who require help usually only need it for a brief time until they find a job and start to accumulate resources. In the case of illness or accident, the unfortunate person is placed in a hospital where the pension is paid by the church. Each individual is certain to find prompt and discreet help from his pastor.

Weeks passed, the weather turned mild, and a great thaw began. But what a debacle! It is impossible to imagine this when you have not witnessed it. The streets were transformed into veritable rivers. In order to allow pedestrians to cross the street, planks of wood were used to create walkways. The only people able to wade through the water were men wearing heavy boots. The unfortunate women who had to go to work sank down into the dirty water. To top things off, the thaw was interrupted for three days when a cold snap turned the surface back into a sheet of ice. Fortunately, Americans are very good ice skaters but, nevertheless, a large number of accidents occurred.

To make matters worse, a fine rain fell and covered the ice with frost. There was no private or public initiative to sprinkle sand or ashes on the ice on sidewalks or in front of houses.

During this time, there were countless broken limbs due to falls on the ice. Let us hope that the injured were insured! For more than a week, newspapers were full of sad stories of injuries and funny caricatures. Finally, the snow began to fall and blanketed the slips and falls. Traffic returned to normal to the great despair of shoemakers who had invented a shoe with a rubber sole that helped prevent injuries.

The less fortunate had already starting using Canadian-style snowshoes. Had the cold weather continued, it would have been beneficial to have these snowshoes.

This terrible weather annoyed me, as I took a very painful spill and was not able to go to the library to consult certain documents that were very necessary for my research.

Libraries are very numerous in Chicago. The largest library is found in City Hall while the other libraries are smaller branches [fig. 14]. It is not possible to compare the Chicago Library to our extremely rich Bibliothèque Nationale; however, the Chicago Library contains a considerable number of volumes and its reading rooms are very well designed.[10] They are similar to ours in France but have separate reading rooms for men and women. Foreign literature, including French literature, is well represented.

We were already coming up on the last days of April and the temperature was still not very warm. Not a leaf, not a blade of grass, not a bud! This eternal winter depressed me. I compared these cold, sad days to the mild days we have in France during this season. I remembered that even in late February in Paris, a few buds had usually already appeared. In March, trees start to turn green, their buds sprout white anemone stars, and violets decorate every Parisian lady's dress.

Suddenly, hot, suffocating weather arrived as if the earth had been heated from the interior by an enormous steam heater. Since the temperature the previous day had been less than zero, heaters were still in use indoors. The hot weather lasted for twenty-four hours and then the sky clouded over and the wind was so strong that I thought that snow would start falling.

It was, in fact, the beginning of a storm that struck with fury. The wind was so powerful that tree limbs broke and stones and debris swirled in its funnels. The lake had large waves and an eerie whistling noise could be heard. Suddenly, it became very dark and a hail shower created a terrible tapping noise.

During this hailstorm, pieces of hail weighing as much as three grams fell and windows shattered. In our hotel, twenty-five windows were broken and damage in the city was estimated to be an enormous sum. But the worst damage was at the exposition site where the tops of buildings were destroyed.

This terrible storm lasted for several hours and was the first greeting of spring.

It was a steam-powered spring, as it seemed that all of the vegetation had been waiting for this signal, ready to make its debut. The very next day we saw some greenery.

It was not at all timid and progressive like spring in France. Eight days later, all of the trees had leaves and the lilacs were flowering. Without exaggeration, it seemed as if you could watch the grass grow. In front of my window I noticed a spot that had been completely bare. By the next day it was covered with grass long enough to require mowing.

World's Columbian Exposition: A Tour

Woman's Building—Children's Building—
Other Pavilions

As May 1, the opening day of the exposition, approached, excitement in the city increased with each passing day. May 1 was also the day when people who rented apartments or houses moved into new lodgings.[1] Almost all the inhabitants on the south side of the city, close to the exposition, put even the most modest lodgings up for rent for unbelievably high prices. Hotel owners tripled their prices and reduced the size of their meals by half. All over, people were moving out in order to free lodgings for those on whom they hoped to make a colossal profit.

Many foreign visitors were expected to attend the opening ceremonies, however constant rain made travel difficult. Families continued to move, sometimes even staying in their home as it was placed on wheels and transported.

These houses were not light structures but two-story homes made of brick and stone, with seven or eight rooms. Placed on wheels, they were slowly guided to their destination. This technique was considered very normal. A seven-story stone building located across from the offices of the *Chicago Tribune* was moved back several meters using this technique. The renters did not have to move out and the building was brought in line with the regulation street alignment.

Slowly but surely, visitors began arriving but not in great numbers. At the same time, the price of everything from railroad tickets to laundry services continued to increase.

Rain continued to fall and the roads, which are composed of wood and mud, were in terrible shape. By May 1, road conditions were as bad as they had been during the melting of the winter ice.

The exposition, though scheduled to open on the indicated date, was far from finished. The most important and most visible buildings were ready.

The Court of Honor, which faced Lake Michigan, was the most beautiful area of the exposition if not the universe. For the opening ceremonies, a platform had been constructed in the Court of Honor where President Cleveland gave his speech surrounded by officials and spectators.

I was not able to hear the speech as the president's voice did not carry well. From his gestures though, I understood that he could only be talking about the glory of America and Americans.

A frenetic burst of "bravos" followed the speech. The flags of all the participating countries flew high above the crowd, while the hymn "My Country Tis of Thee" was played amidst an indescribable enthusiasm. The spectators around the platform began to disperse.

But how! But in what a state! And with such difficulty! The ceremony had been quite long and everyone's feet had gotten stuck in the sticky black mud. When all of the spectators attempted to leave, they found that their shoes were stuck to the ground. Many people had to leave shoes, umbrellas, and even raincoats behind.

We prudently stayed in our seats and watched this curious spectacle with amusement. Similar to the situation during the Milwaukee fire, bands of thieves arrived to pillage the items left behind. They then ran to the lake to wash everything and probably intended to sell the items, maybe even back to the legitimate owners.

In the afternoon, the inauguration of the Women's Exhibition took place.[2] With her usual grace and eloquence, the president, Mrs. Potter Palmer, gave a speech in which she addressed all women.[3] She began by discussing the great success achieved at the fair and thanked all of the participating women. Mrs. Palmer encouraged them to continue to persevere on the path toward activity and progress. According to Mrs. Palmer, they should not be satisfied with improvements that would allow them to work side by side with male colleagues. Their courage and intelligence made them deserving of an equal place. Even in America, which Mrs. Palmer accurately described as the "paradise of women," women's contributions in science and the arts are still regarded with a certain indulgence, if not disdain or scorn. In order to convince people that women can participate in every artistic and scientific activity throughout the world, it suffices to look at the Women's Exhibition of Arts and Industry.

Mrs. Palmer's speech was followed by numerous speeches given by representatives of foreign countries in their native languages. These were long and boring, as most people could not understand the language. Finally, Mrs. Palmer came forward to hammer the final nail of the Exhibition, which had come about in large part due to her initiative and devotion. Using a silver hammer, she pounded a thin gold nail into the Woman's Building and the structure was then complete and ready for visitors.

The Women's Exhibition was, without question, one of the most interesting places of the entire site. I spent many days there, fascinated and never bored as I always came upon an original or unusual display.

The two-story monument was the work of a woman [fig. 15].[4]

The interior was composed of a large hall illuminated by windows and was reserved for the exhibition of painting and sculpture [fig. 16]. At each end of the building, a large decorative mural had been installed. One mural was by Miss MacMonnies and the other was by Mary Cassatt.[5] It is not necessary to say anything about Mary Cassatt's talent as all of Paris knows her work. One of our Paris galleries recently had an exhibit of all of Miss Cassatt's works.

On the first floor of the building, various exhibition rooms were ingeniously divided into smaller spaces [fig. 17].

In the large room reserved for both committees from all over the United States and those from foreign countries, a very American exhibit was on display. It consisted of a series of boxes, each created by one of the committees. Each box contained a unique kind of propaganda for its specific region or country, including posters advocating temperance and anti-tobacco slogans. In addition, there were advertisements for products made by women, and even a description of a model school where American girls would learn household arts while having an opportunity to do canoeing, fencing, and cycling.

In another large room reserved for lectures and meetings, the walls were covered from top to bottom with portraits, paintings, sketches, and photographs of all of the women in the universe who are famous for their work or actions.

The Indian women's exhibition was located a bit off to the side and seemed to me to be one of the most interesting. On display were wool fabrics, items made of pearls, pottery objects in elegant shapes, and baskets that deserve a special mention. Nothing is finer, lighter, or prettier than these baskets made of grass and dyed different colors. While admiring these baskets, it occurred to me that if a primitive woman of modest means can achieve such results, women in our civilization should be able to create the kind of great works that Mrs. Potter expects from us.

Not far from the Indian exhibition was the display of works by women from Germany and Scandinavia. The Chinese women put together an exhibit that was exclusively composed of painting and embroidery on silk. Clothing, kimonos, fans, and parasols were all crafted with an unforgettable delicacy.

The exhibition of Californian women was next and its appearance was severe yet sumptuous. Large panels of beautiful California red mahogany alternated with panels of decorative painting that symbolized the principal industries of the state.

The women of California are, in general, very energetic. In that part of America, women are directors and workers in silver and gold mines. This situation, I am told, occurs in other parts of America but not as often as in California where the women seem to draw both a physical vigor and a great moral force from the earth and the luxurious climate.

Another very artistic and original exhibit was presented by the women of Cincinnati. Furniture and knickknacks that had been sculpted from precious woods, polished like jewels, and decorated with marvelous parquetry were on display. Many miniature items were also exhibited. Although the decoration of this room was much admired by Americans, it was too elaborate for our French taste.

All of these rooms were located on the second floor. Charming little boutiques set up in between the rooms offered a variety of items were for sale.

One of these boutiques belonged to Mrs. Palmer's secretary, Miss Laura. She had great success selling the "nail of Mrs. Palmer" which was a reproduction of the nail hammered into the Woman's Building by Mrs. Palmer. This was an ingenious idea and a French woman of the same social class as Miss Laura would not have thought of creating such a souvenir.[6] This project provided a nice income for my charming friend.

On the ground floor, exhibits of great nations such as England were presented. England and Italy rivaled one another in their splendid lace, however it is necessary to recognize in all sincerity the success of the French exhibition.

One particularly interesting display was organized by a young lady, Miss X.[7] She is a veritable heroine in terms of charity work as she has devoted herself to the care and cure of lepers. Accompanied only by a devoted servant, she has ventured to the extreme north in order to locate the poor victims of this terrible disease. She has braved all dangers and nothing stops her.

The display is an exact reproduction of the buildings she has constructed to lodge and care for these pariahs. Her goal is to obtain charitable donations to expand her work.

Next to the Woman's Building, of course, was the Children's Building [fig. 18]. This graceful and delightful monument was as lovely as those for whom it was constructed, a land of toys and a complete encyclopedia dedicated to the happiness of little ones. Mechanical dolls, stuffed animals, Lilliputian houses and furniture, as well as countless regiments of toy soldiers were found there. All of these toys were familiar to me and a few of the simpler ones attracted my attention.

Quite simple, yes. One toy was made of two pieces of painted cloth sewn together and stuffed, with one side representing the face of a person or an animal while the other side represented the back. In Paris, all the shops that sell American sewing machines have this kind of machine-made cat in the window. These stuffed animals delighted me. They were so inexpensive that I bought dozens in all types and sizes.

Even the youngest and most awkward child could handle them without running any risk of hurting himself. They are very light and their dimensions are similar to the animal in nature. Even the poorest child could enjoy them, just as the richest child would.

In the hotel where we were living, my little friend Mary had one of these dolls that was as big as a four year old child. She walked around with it as though it were a friend.

In the center of this palace for children, a large space was reserved for a variety of sports including tennis, football, and rhythmic gymnastics. All children were welcome to come and participate in these activities.

Two large rooms served as dormitories. One room contained bassinets where babies slept under the watchful eye of the women who worked there. The other room was furnished with beds where toddlers could rest, watched over by older children. Finally, in a third room, which had glass walls like a greenhouse, a young woman played with a happy group of small children.

"Where did these children come from?" I wondered and I quickly found out. At that moment, a family entered the office near the game room.

"Madame, we would like to leave two of our children here," the mother said to the employee.

"For the entire day?" asked the employee.

"Yes," answered the mother.

"Very well. It will be ten cents for each child, including lunch," explained the employee.

At the same time, the lady in charge put a sort of necklace with a number on each of the children. She then gave the parents tickets that corresponded to the numbers on the necklaces. Having settled this, the parents were free to explore the exposition while their babies took their place in the happy group.

The idea of this service was brilliant and the person who organized it must have turned a good profit. What an easy solution for parents and how much fatigue the children were spared!

In France, many people would be horrified at the idea of leaving children like one leaves raincoats and canes in a coat check area. Those people are the ones who are not afraid of dragging tired children around with them to unhealthy, dangerous places. At our Paris Exhibition of 1889, I saw crushing crowds where grown men had a hard time making their way out. Parents with children risked having their little ones smothered. Why couldn't these children have stayed in a childcare facility?

Women, children, flowers, this is a logical progression. The Horticulture Building, whether by chance or design, was right next to the Children's Building.[8]

A heavenly garden, an Eden-like forest, the building was enveloped with greenery from the floor to the dome ceiling. Palm trees festooned with ivy stood out in this stunning display.

Daffodils and tulips from Holland, radiant in their princely robes, arrived in America to open their calyx next to hibiscus from China and chrysanthemums from Japan. French rhododendrons, sent by the Tuileries and Luxembourg Gardens, were superb and their blossoms were admired by all of the visitors. This display paled, however, in comparison to the exhibits of Turkey and the state of Florida, which featured giant trees with dramatic greenery and intensely fragrant flowers.

Among the exhibits, the Virginia jasmine triumphed. Each evening, its flowers were removed and given to visitors and the next day it was as filled with sumptuous flowers as it had been the previous day.

Herbariums were for sale, which contained examples of American flora that had been carefully collected. An immense pyramid of greenery stood in the center of the building. A sparkling fountain surrounded by flowers and illuminated by electric light made this a magical setting.

The next building was the Palace of Transportation. Heavy and massive, the exterior had a pretentious decoration. Inside, the walls disappeared under a profusion of paintings in gold and silver frames. The frightful scrawl of these works would discourage even the most zealous admirers of decorative painting.

In this building, so vast that it would take weeks to visit it carefully, the railroad was the central focus with all of the different locomotives displayed in succession. Aerial projects for trains were suspended above our heads. Challenging nature, the rails hung in the air without bridges or supports. The boat display revealed that none were superior to French ships in terms of beauty, but other boats were better ventilated. (I came to New York on the French ship *La Touraine* and a terrible odor was present throughout the entire crossing. When I returned to France on the American steamer *Le Paris*, I found that the air was always pure and constantly refreshed!)

Finally, there was a display of vehicles, from the most primitive wagon to the glass-enclosed carriage that seems to be a disagreeable means of transportation.

The Palace of Mines resembled the scene in the novel A *Thousand and One Nights,* where Aladdin is astounded as he enters the genie's cave and sees piles of gold, silver, and precious jewels. Compared to the shipments from California, Minnesota, and Iowa, how could other parts of the world compete with so much gold! Gold and more gold! Before these piles of riches, the idea of leaving immediately for these places of fortune begins to haunt you. This temporary drunkenness passes when you learn from the exposition how difficult it is to extract these materials. In addition, these rich resources have either been stripped down to the last sparkle or have become the property of large companies. The image of gold diggers, isolated and discovering rich mines, is now the stuff of legend.

In addition to gold, silver, platinum, copper, iron and zinc, another substance occupies an important place: coal! Mineral oils, which spring from the ground, are part of the incalculable richness of America and no country rivals it in terms of its production. Besides displaying the raw materials, techniques for extraction and purification were also presented.

The Palace of Electricity was one of the most elegant and artistic buildings. Unfortunately, it was not finished in time for the opening of the exposition. It opened much later and contained only some of the marvels that it was supposed to display.

This was not by any means the only unfinished building at the exposition. Some of the buildings were only in the early phases of construction a month after the opening.[9] One of our friends arrived in Chicago at the end of May, firmly believing that his exhibit had been installed. A myth! In fact, the frame of the building that was to house it had not even been constructed.

They got to work and I hope that it was finished by the time of the closing ceremonies but I cannot say for sure.

Although these delays and unfinished buildings were unfortunate, one should not conclude that the exposition was a failure. Those who returned home and criticized the exposition seemed to be too eager to judge without giving it the attention it deserved.

Even though the Electricity Building was not complete, it was no less of an attraction. Constructed entirely of bricks, a hole had been drilled in each brick where an Edison lamp was then placed. This luminous building was startling as it was impossible to guess how the effect was achieved.

Inside the building, the same lighting effect was used. This would not be very practical for private homes but would be marvelous for a party.

Leaving the Palace of Electricity, one would end up in the Court of Honor which was the most beautiful spot one could imagine due to its dimensions, architecture, and above all, its location. This magic spectacle was somewhat spoiled by the Administration Pavilion which stood across from the Electricity Building. The heavy, round structure brought to mind a fancy nougat cake, which someone had had the bad idea to cover with a golden dome! To add to this display of bad taste, there was a colossal Statue of Liberty in gold. The statue crushed the delicate colonnade with its size and obstructed the view of the lake.

Apart from these small mistakes, what splendor there was in the ensemble of the decor! The enormous Palaces of Machines and of Agriculture stood on the right while the Palaces of Mines, Electricity, and Liberal Arts were on the left. The majestic canal led to the lake which provided an incomparable backdrop. The monumental MacMonnies fountain, "America Triumphant," emerged from the water of the canal [fig. 19]. The fountain was surrounded by symbolic figures including a tumultuous group of children, nymphs, soldiers, tritons, and sea monsters. Graceful gondolas and elegant electric boats chimed in with their joyful whistles as they glided across the lake.

The Palace of Machines featured inventions created by human genius, including wheels, cylinders, and windmills. Powered by gasoline, they were monsters of steel and I would have found out more about them had their force not frightened me.

The Palace of Agriculture was calmer and more enjoyable. Naturally, all of the products grown on American soil were represented and corn held the place of honor. An interesting display regarding farms was complete with an army of windmills that would have resuscitated Don Quixote. These windmills are indispensable for farms, especially those in the west. Isolated in the middle of prairies, it is absolutely necessary that they be self-sufficient.

On the lake shore, an unusual reconstitution of Mexican ruins, palaces, and temples covered with vegetation had been installed. In these sanctuaries, Aztec gods and wooden sculptures of idols were painted in primitive colors. In order to complete the illusion, elegant, artistic boats modeled on those of the Aztec period floated on the lake.

A bit farther up on the lake shore was an Indian village with tents made of wood and leaves. The women did basket weaving and made pearl-encrusted cloth, which they then sold to visitors. I was eager to visit their village school.

A kind of coeducational professional school, it resembled other American schools but only during the school day. Outside of school hours, girls were kept separate from boys.

Several boys greeted me at the entrance to the classroom. They were tall adolescents but it was difficult to guess their age as they had the facial expression of serious men. This severe expression was in marked contrast to the modern uniforms that they proudly wore, consisting of blue trousers and a jacket with copper buttons.

An eighteen-year-old-boy served as my guide. He did a marvelous job and responded to all my questions with good humor, patience, and a gentle manner. This behavior contrasted greatly with the hard, almost cruel expression on his face and his ferocious gaze. All of the boys had such similar features and expressions that one would think that they were all members of the same family.

In all of the Indian residences, a school similar to this one exists. It is open to young people but they are not required to take classes there. My Indian guide had been taking classes for a while and seemed very proud of the Indian civilization.

In general, the students make quick progress in their studies of the English language. In just a few months, they are able not only to speak but also to write more or less correctly. Their aptitude for drawing is even more surprising. After a few lessons, the student understands the relationship between lines and his hand can trace with surprising accuracy. I firmly believe that art is a strong characteristic of this race. The pottery that they create is proof of this aptitude in both the beauty of its form and the originality of the decoration.

Professional workshops are located next to the classrooms and include training in leatherwork, saddle-making, and metalwork. The most popular of these was the leather workshop. I watched a young Indian who was finishing a woman's boot. When it was finished, it would have attracted the admiration of Polish women, who are by reputation the most demanding when it comes to shoes.

Indian girls, like boys, seem to be intelligent and easily learn the English language. They all wear a very simple, dark-colored dress covered with a white apron. The young men's heads are completely shaven but the girls have such an abundant mass of hair that it seems like a caricature.

The girls are not very attractive. Although they do not appear seductive, they have from childhood a kind of instinctive coquettishness. This quality can often lead to provocation which must make it difficult for the administration in these schools.

In terms of handiwork, sewing, crochet, and tapestry are all done with great skill but the girls have a frivolousness of mind that makes them put aside their work quickly. Once they have given a task a certain amount of attention and work, it is impossible to make them continue.

A museum was the final part of the school visit. The collection on display included tribal relics, coats of arms of former chiefs, war headdresses, and statues of gods crudely sculpted in stone. Photographs of the principal chiefs who had been captured as well, as of students in their former Indian clothing, hung on the walls. They were much more beautiful with their long hair and native dress than they were with shaven heads and wearing blue tunics with copper buttons.

Another area where America easily showed its superiority over all other nations was the forestry exhibition. There, the giant trees of California regally dominated. A plaque of red mahogany that measured three meters in diameter was one of the curiosities on display.

The re-creation of the Rabida Convent, where Christopher Columbus lived for many years, was very interesting and touching. A massive and rather gloomy structure, it resembled both a church and a prison. The tranquility of this building favored the genius of Columbus. For many years, he worked on his plan away from any disturbances. The dark rooms were arranged as they were when Columbus inhabited them. In the tall, cold chapel, a case held the ashes of this great navigator.

The authenticity of these ashes was questionable. Americans almost lost them in a robbery attempt on the very day of the inauguration of the exposition. A bold criminal had the idea of stealing them in order to resell them. Fortunately, he did not have time to arrange the deal. He was arrested and the ashes were returned to the front of the altar. The ashes were placed next to the anchor which Columbus used to touch down in America and which was, for the first time, on American soil. Furniture, clothing, and various objects that belonged to Columbus were displayed along with a collection of portraits showing him at different times during his adventurous life. These paintings were used as models for a series of postage stamps for the centennial celebration that will be in circulation for one year.

The largest building at the exposition, and perhaps the largest ever constructed, was the Palace of Liberal Arts and Manufacturing. The building was an immense rectangle measuring 1,687 feet long and 787 feet wide. This is the equivalent of a half-kilometer in length and two hundred meters in width. The height of the building reached about forty meters. Situated on the lake shore, it is impossible to describe the sense of majesty created by the dimensions of the building. It was inside this colossal building that three thousand people were seated for the inaugural ceremony. Constructed almost entirely of iron, the bold use of gigantic metal arcs to support the rest of the building was impressive. The central part of the building contained an enormous hall covered with a glass roof that was similar to the nave of a cathedral. In this gallery, the places of honor were reserved for the exhibits of France, Germany, Russia, Belgium, and Switzerland. France easily surpassed all of her neighbors [fig. 20]. The proof came in the number of visitors and their obvious admiration for the French splendors on display, including Gobelin and Aubusson tapestries, Sèvres porcelain, gold work, furniture, bronzes, and delicate feminine items. The visitors' enthusiasm made me proud.

The German exhibit was also very beautiful. Although the artistic quality was not as evident as in the French exhibition, this great country is making constant progress.

Italy had naturally filled its allocated space with marble statues that were sold for very low prices but not low enough considering their artistic value. Everything is fair in business for these former great artists. Neither the pillage of other people's work nor outright plagiarism stops them. Among their "works," I noticed the *"Rieuse"* by Carpeaux, dressed in whimsical clothing and audaciously signed with an Italian name.[10]

Elsewhere in this building, in a section of the American exhibit, I was captivated by a display of petrified wood.

Underground for thousands of years and affected by chemical elements in the soil, this wood had acquired the hardness and coldness of marble. In certain parts of America these deposits are numerous and machines have been invented in order to extract them.

Monumental fireplaces, tabletops, paneling, and all sorts of objects are made from these petrified woods. Their colors vary and the concentric circles indicate their age just like those in a freshly cut tree trunk.

The graceful architecture and proportional dimensions of the Government Pavilion made it one of the most interesting buildings for foreign visitors. The display consisted of a kind of archives of the country and included all the documents and souvenirs of its birth as a free nation. The authentic Declaration of Independence was featured as well as contracts between England and the American people from the same era. Both official and personal letters of George Washington and other great American men were exhibited as well. Among these national relics were two portraits of Lafayette and various objects that had belonged to him. This display seemed to be proof of American's recognition of France's help during the American Revolution.

The next section presented the history of the army and showed successive uniform styles and artillery. This history was quite short in comparison to ours! A series of pictures representing American fauna showed marvelous collections of strange insects, multicolored butterflies, birds, flowers, monstrous reptiles, and enormous stuffed snakes that seemed like they were about to jump on their prey. With the exception of the lion, all of the large animals were displayed. Smaller animals that are native to American soil were represented but I was not familiar with all of them.

Finally, the Fisheries Exhibition was very well organized and included a special installation to show the hatching of salmon eggs. A thousand other displays included collections of minerals, letters, and photographs of admirable sites.

Not far from the building, the Artillery Exhibition was set up in the gardens. This was not a very impressive exhibit and demonstrated that America does not desire to become a warring country. On the lake, the naval exhibition was set up on the brick boat *Illinois*. This boat had a very pleasing construction and gave an exact idea of a warship. It differed very little from the beautiful vessels of the French fleet. A special building called the Fisheries Building was devoted to the inhabitants of salt and fresh water and its decoration was based on water and marine images. Enormous alligators filled a huge aquarium. They were not languishing like they do in the basins of the Jardin des Plantes in Paris but instead, they were moving around as rapidly as if they were free in the Mississippi River or in the swamps of Florida. Other aquatic displays showed a world of interesting individuals, including a very large white skate. Its body was very flat and its head was humanlike and horrible. When it exhaled, it opened its languorous eye and the resemblance to a human face was striking and disconcerting.

Throughout the gardens, water from the lake circulated through canals. One could stroll on the flowering banks and see groups of wild ducks who had made their home in the middle of the exhibition. They amused visitors with their quarrels as two different groups of ducks would attack one another.

Close to the Fisheries Building, three graceful Japanese pavilions had been installed on an island.

Decorated with Japanese art and surrounded by flowering gardens, the pavilions were maintained by Japanese workers in traditional dress.

Facing this island was the Palace of Fine Arts. To do it justice, it would be necessary to write an entire volume on both the building and its contents.

Each of the American states had its own building and the architecture and contents of some of the buildings were more interesting than others.

The California exhibit was an exact reproduction of a mission constructed near the Pacific Ocean. Florida had constructed a copy of the old Port Marion. The Iowa Building was decorated with grains of corn in various colors that were arranged on the walls and the ceilings displayed corn mosaics. The New Hampshire Building consisted of a wooden house similar to those found in the mountains of that state. One of the greatest attractions, especially in the eyes of Americans, was the Pennsylvania Building that displayed the Liberty Bell.

It had been transported from Philadelphia with great care and its arrival in Chicago had inspired an enthusiastic reception. Covered with flowers, the bell was carried triumphantly to the exposition, where it was decorated with fresh greenery and rare flowers. A reproduction of George Washington's house in Mount Vernon also drew a large number of visitors.

The European nations had constructed beautiful pavilions as well. England was the exception as neither its architecture nor its interior displays were very significant. The British Pavilion served primarily as a meeting room. The German Building was a reconstruction of an old feudal castle and its bell could be heard throughout the exposition grounds.

The French Building was one of the most admired, but the true success was the display contributed by the city of Paris. This exhibit was doubly attractive to Americans since it was a faithful reproduction of the room at Versailles where Louis XVI had signed the Act of Protection, demonstrating the French and American alliance against England.

The series of buildings that I have just described constituted the "official" exposition, meaning that all of these buildings were open free of charge to the public. Another section of the exposition called the Midway Plaisance had attractions of every kind and the entry fee varied from ten cents to one dollar. There were Eskimo villages, Turkish houses, Moorish cafes, Cairo Street with its spectacles and its dances, various panoramas, and establishments of every type.

Among the commercial exhibits was a glass company called Libbey Glass. This exhibit attracted as many visitors as the Venetian glass display did in Paris in 1889. The young girls who sold the products wore berets and aprons woven from glass. On the second floor, a display of all of the fabrics made out of this glass thread was installed and a demonstration of the weaving took place.

A huge, unusual structure stood in the center of The Midway. According to Americans, the Ferris wheel was one of the greatest attractions of the Fair and easily surpassed the Eiffel Tower.[11] An enormous wheel was positioned vertically and was similar to those structures that we have all seen at our country fairs. Seating compartments are loaded and the machine moves very slowly in order not to scare the riders. This construction may have been remarkable in the eyes of the engineers but I see neither the charm nor the utility of this circular ride.

In conclusion, I am not afraid to say that this exposition in Chicago, which was so criticized, was marvelous and superior to all of previous ones. With our meager resources, we could never equal its splendor.

There were a few problems, including transportation. Although there was a train that made the fifteen-minute trip from the center of the city every five minutes, it would have been helpful to have a shuttle train that took passengers to different sites of the exposition.[12]

In fact, there was a shuttle but it simply made a loop and did not provide the necessary service. Small carriages were available to transport visitors unable to walk.[13] Young boys dressed in blue pushed them but they were expensive and not very practical.

Finally, another weakness in my opinion was the lack of spirit and liveliness that was perhaps due to the large surface of the exposition and to the coldness of the national character.[14]

Final Impressions

*Stockyards—From Chicago to Washington—
Philadelphia—Departure*

For a number of reasons, including those I have mentioned, the exposition was not as successful as had been anticipated. First of all, the space was too large and many of the enormous buildings were never finished. Secondly, visitors from all over the world did not flock to the exposition as expected.

Within just a few months, an entire neighborhood was constructed in the area of the exposition; buildings made of massive stone contained up to three hundred rooms to house visitors. They were constructed in the middle of winter on frozen ground and had no solid foundation. For those like me, who had watched them go up, we wondered how they would stand. In fact, several of these buildings collapsed suddenly, burying numerous victims.

To the great dissatisfaction of small business owners who had hoped to make a fortune during the exposition, business in this neighborhood did not increase.

The only businesses that always seemed full were pharmacies. These establishments are generally located on street corners and sell not only medicines but also postage stamps, cigars, stationary, and many other items. Pharmacies are even open on Sunday. Besides pharmacy services, they have a room where people can wait for the streetcar, consult commercial directories similar to our *Bottin*, or use the telephone booth.[1] A soda fountain provides hot and cold drinks as well as small glasses of whiskey for ladies with ailments.

All of these services explain why these establishments are so prosperous.

A most unusual place that I wanted to visit before we left Chicago was the stockyards.

Chicago is the center of meat processing and the city's wealth is due in large part to this profitable business of fresh and preserved meat.

Located in the western part of the city, the stockyards are surrounded by enormous prairies where all types of cattle are naturally raised and graze. The cattle are enclosed in vast parks surrounded by wooden fences, each of which contains approximately 14,000 sheep, 25,000 cows and 150,000 pigs. A walk through these funereal places is very interesting. The cattle are simply waiting their turn to die as cowboys round them up.

These sturdy and vigorous men live on the prairie and are the heroes of many adventures. In order to round up the cattle and lead them to Chicago, the cowboys have to engage in the dangerous process of lassoing. Dressed in the Mexican style with wide pants and large felt hats, they stand next to their beautiful horses, the lasso hanging in the saddle.

The cows in the enclosure do not have horns and seem to have a much more intelligent expression than our French cows. The sheep are as peaceful as those found elsewhere.

The pigs are resplendent in their extraordinary stoutness. They are as fat as they are long, to the point where they can hardly support themselves on their legs. It is quite a spectacle to see them run towards the ears of corn, crashing into each other and rolling on the ground.

These slaughterhouses, like everything else in America, are models of organization designed to save time and energy.

Several railway companies have installed tracks that lead right up to the area where the animals are kept and open up into the slaughterhouses. The poor animals go in one door alive and well and come out the other, cut up in quarters, ready to be shipped to the corners of the globe.

Twenty thousand men work in the slaughterhouses. One company, Armour, employs four thousand. Visitors can tour the facility but the faint-hearted are advised to stay away as the spectacle is quite horrible.[2]

Puddles of blood are everywhere as well as all kinds of hideous debris. The sight of intestines being transported in wheelbarrows, which moved up and down the sloped walkways from the top floors to the courtyard, was repugnant. This temple of carnage raises questions about our level of morality. One striking aspect is the rapidity with which the slaughter takes place.

The way in which the pigs are killed and the different processes performed on the individual animals are fascinating.

The animal is placed on an inclined slab and one of its feet is attached with a chain which pulls it along the processing line. First, the pig is stabbed with a large knife. The executioner, who is covered with blood, stabs one pig after another from morning until night.

The pig, barely still alive, is then pulled by the chain into a huge cauldron of boiling water. After this hot-water plunge, the pig passes under large scraping machines that clean him off. The animal then passes through a series of stations. First, a worker scrubs the pig, then another worker chops off his head. At the next stage, a worker empties the organs of the pig. Another worker cuts the animal into four pieces that are subsequently divided into smaller sections at other stations. Some of the meat goes to the salt house and some goes to the smoke house to be transformed into ham. The intestines continue on another route, where they undergo various preparations.

In just a few minutes the process is over and the meat comes out, still quivering. In the slaughterhouses of the Morris, Nelson Company, they kill and process ten thousand pigs per day.

Although it is hard to believe, the process described above is not the most repugnant aspect of a stockyard visit. Of course, visitors do not always see these practices and it was by chance that we happened to learn about them.

When animals arrive at the slaughterhouse already dead, or if they die of a disease in the fields where they are raised, the corpses are abandoned in the yards despite the most elementary laws of hygiene. They remain roasting in the sun for a few days and are finally dragged into the furnace.

I witnessed this process while in front of one of these furnace rooms. The door was partially open, and out of curiosity I pushed against it. The sickening odor practically knocked me over and I could not believe what I was seeing!

Cadavers in varying states of decomposition were piled on top of one another. Some animals had recently died while others were practically skeletons. A whole gamut of putrefaction was on display, with rotting corpses infested with flies and putrid insects swarming around the flesh.

I finally understood why the wind coming from the west brought such a horrible odor to Chicago. The inhabitants of the city claimed that they did not know the source of this odor and showed no concern for it. This nonchalance regarding a situation that could spread terrible illnesses would not be acceptable even in a primitive culture. Here, in this country of constant progress, I found it revolting and inadmissible.

The visit to the stockyards, which I did not regret making, was one of our last excursions in Chicago.

Our departure date had been set long in advance, so at the end of June we boarded the train in Chicago and headed for Washington, passing through the mountains of Ohio.[3]

I was leaving Chicago!

Dare I admit it? Even knowing that I was returning home and would see the dear friends and family from whom I had been separated for more than a year, I felt profoundly sad at the prospect of departing. I was leaving the place where I had lived freely in terms of both my thoughts and actions. Some of these freedoms would not be tolerated on French soil where narrow prejudices, ridiculous etiquette, and absurd conventions still flourish. I was leaving the country where the laws, institutions, and morals fit so well with my natural sentiments, hopes, and inclinations.

I had tasted the fruit of independence, of intelligent activity, and was revolted at the idea of assuming once again the passive and inferior role that awaited me! I had enjoyed the consideration and respect given to all women and I was going to rediscover the disdain and scornful pity that masculine superiority imposes on women in France.

After having seen American women, my sisters, treated with respect, their burden lightened by their husbands and helped and admired by men, I was going back to a place where women are all treated like animals, delicate animals whose moral value and intelligence are not taken into consideration.

An old proverb declares that Paris is the ladies' paradise.

No, Paris is hell for any woman and the true feminine paradise is America!

There the husband is neither a sultan nor a tyrant. The American man's only demand is that his wife allow him to make her and their children happy. He dedicates himself to her happiness and makes it the goal of all of his hard work.

The founder of the family and the household, he is the born protector of his wife. If any aspect of the family is to be criticized, it is the American wife.

She is so accustomed to her pleasant life that she does not appreciate her husband enough. He gives her love, well-being, and tranquility and makes sure that she is spared fatigue and worry. Even so, it is rare for the American wife to show her gratitude. In fact, she does not even know how to create the sweetness and intimate warmth of a home. An American husband would find such comforts delightful, especially since his "home" is often just a room in a boardinghouse where his wife indulges in the lazy habits of American women.

Why doesn't she have a few of those French *pot-au feu* virtues?[4] I am not making fun of our well-known bourgeois reputation. On the contrary, I am proud of it. I wish, in good faith, that American women would emulate French women a little in household matters. They would have nothing to fear in modeling their behavior on ours and would not have to suffer the negative consequences that we do.

The American man is intelligent and has a lot of common sense. He understands the true essence of superiority so he would not denigrate his wife like French men do. In terms of French men, I am speaking of them in general, as I believe that when an individual French man is superior, he is superior to all men.

Unfortunately, this elite type is an exception in our day and making generalities does not do much about it!

Self-centered and heartless, the modern man in France has only one preoccupation: himself. As a result, he suppresses anything around him that could be an obstacle or nuisance. A wife and children are a burden that scares him and that he tries to avoid. He accepts them with regret and is determined not to sacrifice everything for his family. He will often marry not for the desire to give his chosen wife a sense of well-being but to receive her dowry! The fortune is what he has desired all along and the fiancée just comes along with it. A loving marriage? It is out of the question! A French husband who loves his wife and dares to say it would be ridiculed! Of course, everyone knows that to be ridiculed in France is even worse than death.

These were the thoughts that flooded my mind and saddened me as I closed our suitcases. But it is necessary to resign one's self to what one cannot prevent. Resignation is among the virtues which with women have been inculcated.

Several railroad lines run from Chicago to Washington and we had chosen one that crosses the mountains of Ohio.[5] The terrain is uneven, making the trip difficult and tiring. The marvelous beauty of the landscape, however, compensates for this hardship. We took an overnight train in order to reach the most beautiful spot on the trip at dawn. We would not arrive in Washington, D.C., until eight in the evening.

It was not necessary, however, to wait until dawn to see the most unforgettable landscape. In the middle of the night, an abrupt stop allowed us to see an enchanting spectacle. We were in the middle of the forest and all of the trees appeared to be blazing from top to base with thousands of little fires. They were fireflies that magnificently illuminated the entire forest. It is impossible to imagine a sweeter sight than this gentle light suspended on every leaf of the trees.

Following this lovely scene, the train continued on its way, with the decor changing in our mobile panorama. The darkness of the night was dotted with red patches similar to the reflection of a fire. We were crossing an area dominated by the metal industry, where metal is forged all day and all night long. The large ovens glow and resemble the mouth of a volcano.

When we emerged from this area, which brought to mind part of Dante's inferno, we found ourselves in Pittsburgh, the city of oil.[6]

Unfortunately, the stop was short so we did not have enough time to visit the outskirts of the city, which are more unusual than the city itself. A river divides Pittsburgh in two and railroad tracks run the entire length of the city. Railroad tracks are even found on city streets, without any fence or protection for pedestrians. Heavy trucks carrying oil ride alongside or cross in front of the train. Enormous factories process the oil which is then shipped to all points of the globe. Natural gas deposits are also extracted from the ground using wells.

Leaving Pittsburgh behind, we followed the banks of the Ohio River. The landscape became increasingly beautiful and heavenly.

As the river rolls gently toward the wide Mississippi, its waters seem to have been thickened by all the metals contained in its bed. The river appears to reflect the yellow tones of gold and copper and the gray blue of silver and iron. Along the river banks, mountains rise up, one taller than the next. Some of the mountains are rocky and made up of red stones while others are green with luxurious vegetation. The train accelerated its pace up the mountain as we meandered through a labyrinth of curves. The constant jolts made it impossible to stand, as one risked being thrown to the ground by their severity. However, the indescribable beauty of the mountain panorama made the trip less taxing. The train moved faster and faster, at a feverish pace that seem to be one of a German ballad. At one point the train was squeezed between the mountain and the river and there was barely enough room for the rails. Although there was no danger of running into another train, the possibility of a derailment or of a fall into the deep waters of the river loomed. When the passengers leaned out the windows, they could only see water, not even the narrow strip of land on which the railroad tracks were installed.

A catastrophe seemed all the more imminent as the terrain became increasingly unpredictable. In some spots the train was encased in such a narrow gorge, with high mountains surrounding us on both sides that the sky disappeared above our heads. In other places the train passed over the river, following a natural ramp of rock. Finally, we would come upon a valley and the view would extend over immense plains, surrounded by mountains. Occasionally, we would see some Indian encampments but these were the only evidence of life.

There was no trace of industry or civilization, just primitive, virgin, wild, sublime nature.

We enjoyed this ecstasy for seven hours and then the pure beauty of the landscape changed as we approached Washington, where we arrived an hour early.

From the train station, it is possible to see the Capitol.[7] It is clear from the first glance that Washington is very different from other American cities.

The houses are taller and there are museums, parks, and statues everywhere. The cobblestoned streets are very clean and relatively quiet as the noise generated by street cars is absorbed by the pavement.

We arrived on a Saturday and finding a hotel that would serve us the kind of dinner we desired was not easy. Eventually, we found a hotel willing to accept and serve us a substantial though cold meal. The Negroes who served us had beautiful black skin and were dressed in white outfits as usual. I was displeased when one of these servants brought me a yellowish liquid as a drink. I pushed it away and requested water. Water! But that was water, right from the Potomac River!

Having eaten, we left the restaurant in order to visit the city. In spite of the late hour, many people were strolling. Since it was stifling hot during the day, it was natural that people would want to take an evening walk in the cool air. The crowd was made up primarily of Negroes.

Many of the men and women were holding large baskets and heading in the same direction. We were amused by the colorful nature of this crowd in contrast to others that we had seen in the United States. We followed them and arrived at a marketplace, similar to those in Paris.[8]

It was the first time that I had seen a market like ours, where all sorts of items are sold. This market stayed open until midnight on Saturday so that workers could do their shopping for Sunday.

The following day, we started exploring the city very early. However, the quiet nature of Sunday in this aristocratic city meant that all of the museums, monuments, and other interesting sites were closed. We decided to go to Mount Vernon to visit the home and grave of George Washington.

In the stifling heat, we thought that the boat trip would be charming. A little later we found ourselves cruising on the Potomac, a wide river with yellowish waves due to its bed which contains a large quantity of ochre. On the bridge of the boat, an orchestra played a national hymn. My husband and I were enjoying the gentle movement of the boat and the music when all of a sudden we heard someone speaking French.

The purity of the accent led us to believe that some of our compatriots were on board. We soon made their acquaintance and discovered that they were young Russian naval officers whose ship was stationed in New York. They would soon leave for the French port of Toulon.

Both of the young men were very charming and the trip began pleasantly thanks to their company. We thought that it would be nice to visit Mount Vernon with our new friends. When the boat stopped, we were a bit confused. We were not at Mount Vernon, as it was closed on Sunday. Instead, the boat had brought us to a park where it was possible to play tennis, do archery, and even ride horses.

Annoyed by the misunderstanding, we took the next boat back to Washington and wondered how we were going to spend this long day. One of the sailors remembered that there had been a terrible accident two days earlier. A ceiling had collapsed at the Ministry of War in Washington, D.C., that had killed a number of officials.[9] The funeral was to be celebrated that day. Several important dignitaries were among the victims and were going to be buried at Arlington National Cemetery. We decided to attend this event, and as soon as we got off of the boat we rented a carriage to take us to Arlington.

The cemetery was open due to the ceremony.

Located on top of a hill, it is the only cemetery in America that holds several monuments, including one dedicated to the memory of 2,111 unknown soldiers who lost their lives in the Civil War. In addition, the house of General Robert E. Lee stands in the middle of the graveyard. The house is quite beautiful and offers a marvelous panoramic view. From the house, we could see the golden Potomac flowing between its green banks, graceful hills, and a white spot against the greenery which was the city of Washington. The monuments are free of the colors that decorate the exterior of buildings across America. Arlington Cemetery has beautiful trees and flowering rose bushes. Among the foliage, we could see a family of squirrels daintily jumping from branch to branch. They animated this embalmed solitude with their cries and movement.

We had arrived a little late for the ceremony so we took the carriage back to Washington.

We had planned to spend several days there and were able to visit the city and the outskirts. On Monday, we visited Mount Vernon and discovered an adorable cottage shaded by hundred-year-old trees. This is the house where Washington spent the greater part of his life with his family.

His tomb is very modest, consisting of a sort of chapel constructed in brick. It contains a tomb that can be seen through two tall iron doors. Several granite pyramids surrounded by ironwork are dedicated to members of Washington's family. There are no flowers, just an austere simplicity.

Washington's house, which is made of wood, has a unique style of architecture. In the "colonial style," it is at once rustic and graceful. The house faces the Potomac and is located in the most delicious spot one can imagine. Inside, nothing has been changed since the death of Washington. The furniture and all of the other items are exactly as he left them. In the salon, the decoration is extremely simple. A music book lies open, and the flute on which he accompanied his step-daughter on piano appears ready to vibrate under the breath of its illustrious owner. Aside from the rooms where Washington and his family lived, a large reception room has been transformed into a museum. There one can read the voluminous correspondence between Lafayette and Washington and see a number of portraits. The letters that Washington sent to his beloved wife during the war are also on display, and eloquently demonstrate that he was a model husband. Many other items are exhibited under glass, including the famous key to the Bastille prison that the Estates General sent to Washington to pay homage to this great apostle of liberty.

In the city proper the most important monument is the Capitol, which is located in the center and visible from every point. In terms of its architecture, the Capitol has a main section, which is an enlarged copy of our Pantheon, and is flanked by two other buildings in the Greek style.

These two wings are for the House and the Senate and they are laid out exactly like our Legislative Palace.

The presidential palace, known as the White House, has a quite simple style of architecture and welcomes visitors. Upon requesting permission, it is possible to visit a series of rooms, none of which is very interesting. Once a week the president holds a reception for visitors who wish to meet with him.

All of the other monuments resemble ours in terms of the architecture. The statues in the parks and plazas have an artistic quality, more or less.

One monument that is more unusual than the others is the enormous obelisk dedicated to the memory of Washington.

Five hundred fifty-five feet tall, approximately 130 meters, it cost $1,187,710, which is the equivalent of about five million francs. It was begun on July 4, 1848, and was inaugurated on February 22, 1885. The monument is a marvel in terms of the stone work. From the base to the summit, stones are simply juxtaposed and positioned without any cement. In the center of the monument there is a staircase and an elevator. The staircase is sufficiently wide and lit by electric lighting. At the top, there are four openings, one on each side, but from the bottom of the monument one would not imagine they are there.

Overall, Washington is an aristocratic and calm city that is pretty, artistic, and well maintained.

I learned there of an American profession of which I was ignorant, that of the leader of drunks. These professionals are more numerous in Washington than elsewhere, as nowhere else are whiskey lovers harassed by policemen as much as they are here.

Paid by business owners, these men lead drunken clients back to their homes.

There are two excellent reasons for this situation. First, the business that provided the liquor can incur a steep fine. Second, drunks are the best clients, and in order to protect them they need to be accompanied home, sometimes even in a carriage.

I imagine that in France, business people who followed this example would lose money.

From Washington, we headed to Philadelphia. A very American city, its large homes resemble army barracks and enormous monuments.

The largest public building is City Hall. A statue of William Penn, which is as tall as the building, stands in the courtyard. The streets of Philadelphia are wide, nicely paved, well maintained, and resonate with a joyous animation. All of the houses have a wrought iron staircase on the exterior in case of fire. Sometimes, instead of a staircase there is a pulley with a cord that resembles a gallows.

With its museums, a historical society, fine arts, music, and scientific academies as well as several colleges, Philadelphia is one of the premier cities in the United States from an intellectual standpoint. The city is most proud of the Liberty Bell, which at the time was on display at the exposition in Chicago.

Philadelphia is also the American city that seems to have the most churches. Almost all of them are pretty but, of course, they were built fairly recently.

The city has many parks, including beautiful Fairmont Park which extends over 2,750 acres. According to Americans, it is the largest park in the entire universe.

The 1876 Exhibition took place there and several buildings from that period remain. A number of other buildings in the park have been preserved as relics, including General Grant's little hut, William Penn's house, and Tom Moore's cottage. Several other monuments have been erected in memory of great men.

We left Philadelphia and arrived in New York several hours later, where we found ourselves back in the green nest of Morissania in the middle of our dear family. The two weeks that we spent there flew by like minutes. Onboard the American steamer *Paris*, which would take us back to Europe, I had the same sad feeling that I had experienced when we left Le Havre.

It was the same scene as well, with handkerchiefs waving goodbye, the anchor raised, and land fading into the distance. That beautiful American land of proud independence, which I feel is the great country of all those who deeply love freedom, began disappearing into the distance.

As hard as it was for me to leave France, it was just as hard to leave America.

As the coast became faint, I saw the colossal Statue of Liberty in the fog. Addressing her as if she were a friend who could hear me, I cried out:

"I will come back!"

Notes

INTRODUCTION TO CHICAGO

1. Bourget, "A Farewell to the White City," 138–40.
2. "The Columbian Exposition," *Engineering*, 5 December 1890, 667.
3. "A City Elevated," *Chamber's Journal*, 26 January 1861, 49.
4. Blanc, *The Condition of Women in the United States*, 56.
5. Villiers, "An Artist's View of Chicago and the World's Fair," 51; Kendall, *American Memories*, 182.
6. de Rousiers, *American Life*, 436.
7. Dernburg, *Aus der weissen Stadt*, 28.
8. Steevens, *The Land of the Dollar*, 151.
9. "Rapid Building in Chicago," *American Architect*, 10 September 1892, 172; M. "Ueber die ausserordentilich rege Bautätigkeit," 412; Sauvin, *Autour de Chicago*, 97; Emperger, "Eiserne Gerippbauten," 526; Jaffe, "Die Architekturausstellung," 2:1145.
10. "Knows No Parallel," *Chicago Tribune*, 17 January 1892, 27.
11. Hermant, "L'architecture aux États-Unis," 343.
12. Bocage, "L'architecture aux États-Unis et à l'exposition universelle," 334.
13. Pierce, *As Others See Chicago*, 276.
14. Hesse-Wartegg, *Tausend und ein Tag*, 1:160–61.

INTRODUCTION

1. Grandin, *Impressions d'une parisienne*, 313. Subsequent citations are to this edition.
2. According to *La bibliographie de la France, 14e année*, 16 February 1895, 99, Madame Grandin's book appeared in bookstores in February 1895 and sold for 3.50 francs. No subsequent editions were published.
3. See Smart, *A Flight with Fame*, 112–25, 291, for a description of the plans, execution, and transportation of the fountain segments from Paris to Chicago.
4. A dossier at the Service de Documentation at the Musée d'Orsay in Paris

contains information regarding Léon Grandin's submissions to the Salons de la Société des Artistes Français between 1885 and 1901 and to the 1889 and 1900 Paris Expositions.

5. No information is available regarding the subject or whereabouts of this bust.

6. In a letter written to his friend Helen Foote, dated September 3, 1901, Frederick MacMonnies expressed grief over Grandin's death: "Poor old Léon died suddenly and I am broken hearted. His idiot sister took him out in a push wagon and he died the same evening . . . It was a terrible blow to lose my big, bullying affectionate elder brother. . . . Poor kindhearted chap and devoted heart and soul to me for twelve years." Beinecke Rare Book and Manuscript Library, Yale University.

7. See Smart, *A Flight with Fame*, 153–54, and Gordon, "The Expansion of a Career," 59–81, for descriptions of the artistic community in Giverny in the 1890s. Grandin is listed as a frequent visitor to Giverny in the exhibition catalog *Impressionist Giverny*, ed. Bourguignon, 207. He was definitely acquainted with the American artists Conrad Slade (1871–1949) and Paul Burleigh Conkling (1871–1926) because he did busts of both that were exhibited at the 1897 and 1899 salons.

8. Madame Grandin's account is listed in Karel, *Dictionnaire*, 361. Several scholars mention her account and situate it in the context of other French and European travelers of the time: Anon., "The Gay Nineties in Chicago," 341–88; Monicat, *Itinéraires de l'écriture au féminin*, 24, 86; Lewis, *An Early Encounter*, 162–64; Broca, *Dictionnaire illustré*, 156–57; Portes, *Fascination and Misgivings*, 158; and Lapeyre, *Le roman des voyageuses françaises*, 91–96. In addition, the Chicago Historical Society has in its collection an insightful introduction and unpublished English translation of portions of Madame Grandin's text by Margaret Scriven.

9. Léon Grandin lived at 26, rue Didot, and Marie Lédier resided with her parents at 5, rue Brezin.

10. French elementary school teachers in the 1880s received training in academic subjects and pedagogical techniques in a three-year normal school program. Mayeur, *L'éducation des filles en France*, 148–59; Offen, "The Second Sex and the Baccalauréat," 262; Clark, *Schooling the Daughters of Marianne*, 17–18; Lelièvre and Lelièvre, *Histoire de la scolarisation des filles;* 155–60; and Heywood, *Growing Up in France*, 248, all contain discussions of the educational opportunities available to young women and the preparation of female elementary school teachers in late-nineteenth-century France.

11. Minutier Central des Notaires Parisiens, 14 November 1884, National Archives.

12. Madame Grandin's title was very much in keeping with other late-nineteenth-century French travel narratives. The terms *voyage, promenade,* and *impressions* were frequently used in titles of this period. Portes, *Fascination and Misgivings*, 13.

13. Grandin, *Impressions d'une parisienne,* 136.

14. Ibid., vii–xi.

15. For example, in *Une française chez les sauvages*, Jeanne Goussard de Mayolle repeatedly uses *nous* (we) to describe her adventures in North and South America

with her husband. The Belgian writer Madame Arthur de Cannart d'Hamale (*Un voyage de noces*) also favored *nous* in her account of her honeymoon in America. A discussion of the ways in which French women writers frequently evoke their husbands and families in nineteenth-century travel narratives appears in Monicat, "Autobiography and Women's Travel Writings," 61–70 .

16. Grandin, *Impressions d'une parisienne*, 8.

17. For discussions of early French travelers to America see Echeverria and Wilke, *The French Image of America*. For an annotated listing of the hundreds of French visitors to the United States between 1765 and 1932, see Monaghan, *French Travellers in the United States*. Broca's *Dictionnaire illustré* contains biographical information and travel routes for French travelers who visited North and South America during the nineteenth century. Rémond's, *Les États-Unis devant l'opinion française* discusses travel accounts as well as articles that appeared in the French press concerning the United States during this time. In *Fascination and Misgivings*, Portes analyzes the French fascination with America between 1870 and 1914.

18. Among the eighteenth-century French travelers to America who published accounts were Brissot de Warville, *Nouveau voyage;* Ducher, *Nouvelle alliance à proposer;* and Pagès, *Nouveau voyage autour du monde*. See Roger, *The American Enemy*, 37–48, for a discussion of the anti-American tendencies of some French eighteenth-century studies of America.

19. Grandin, *Impressions d'une parisienne*, x.

20. François René de Chateaubriand, *Atala* (1801), *René* (1802), and *Les Natchez* (1826). See Liebersohn, *Aristocratic Encounters*, 39–60, for a thoughtful discussion of Chateaubriand's trip to North America and his subsequent publications.

21. Grandin, *Impressions d'une parisienne*, 53.

22. Liebersohn, *Aristocratic Encounters*, 96.

23. Tocqueville, *Democracy in America*.

24. Volume 2 of *Democracy in America* focuses on the influence of democracy on American society, and the chapter titles include "Influence of Democracy on Mores," "Raising Girls in the United States," "How the Traits of the Girl Can Be Divined in the Wife," "How Americans Understand the Equality of Man and Woman," and "Some Reflections on American Manners."

25. Three unusual accounts published by French women in the 1850s reflect that nation's interest in racial, social, and gender issues. The earliest account of a French woman's journey to America is Madame de Saint-Amant's *Voyage en Californie, 1850 et 1851*. The wife of Charles de Saint-Amant, a former naval officer and wine dealer, she headed to California in July 1850 to set up a business in anticipation of her husband's arrival. Written in the form of letters to her husband, Madame de Saint-Amant described her four-month voyage to San Francisco and focused primarily on the details of transporting commercial goods. Upon arrival in San Francisco, she was struck by the diversity of its population and the small number of women, who, she felt, could be easily divided into two groups according to their moral values. Marie Fontenay de Grandfort, a lecturer on French history and literature, visited New Orleans in 1855 and wrote a controversial novel, *L'autre monde,* in which she described her negative impressions of slavery through the eyes of a fictional narrator. The novel was translated into English

soon after its publication as *The New World.* Fanny Loviot arrived in California in 1852, accompanied by her older sister. She lived there for eighteen months during the excitement of the gold rush before embarking on an eventful trip to China. In her account of her eighteen-month stay in San Francisco and surrounding areas, *Les pirates chinois: Ma captivité dans les mers de la Chine,* 21–60, Loviot described the various ethnic groups she encountered, including Chinese immigrants and African Americans. Another French woman, Jenny P. d'Héricourt (1809–75), a writer and midwife, lived in Chicago from 1863 to 1873, moving there following the publication of her book *La femme affranchie,* in which she criticized the theories about women's intellectual inferiority proposed by a number of writers, including Prudhon, Comte, and Michelet. While in Chicago she published several articles on women's rights in France in the journal *The Agitator.* Offen, "A Nineteenth-Century Feminist Rediscovered," 144–58.

26. See, for example, Carlier, *De l'esclavage dans ses rapports avec l'union américaine,* and Englebach, *L'esclavage.*

27. Liebersohn, in *Aristocratic Encounters,* presents a nuanced discussion of the French reaction to Native Americans in travel writing published between the late-eighteenth century and 1848.

28. Numerous British and European visitors complained in their accounts about the attitude of American servants. Trollope, *Domestic Manners,* 45–49; Bourget, *Outre-Mer,* 3, 22; Blanc, *The Condition of Woman,* 224.

29. Portes, *Fascination and Misgivings,* 12.

30. Ibid.

31. Jules Ferry, minister of public instruction, introduced legislation, which was passed in 1881–82, to make secular primary schooling compulsory and free for children aged six to thirteen. These laws applied to girls as well as boys although classes were not mixed. Clark, *Schooling the Daughters of Marianne,* 2; Margadant, *Madame le professeur,* 24–32.

32. French visitors expressed interest in all levels of American education, from kindergarten through university. For an overview of French reactions see Portes, *Fascination and Misgivings,* 228–53. For discussions of American elementary and high schools see Compayré, *L'enseignement secondaire aux États-Unis;* Vicomte de Meaux, "Les écoles aux États-Unis"; and Langlois, "L'éducation aux États-Unis." Descriptions of American colleges and universities are presented in Bourget, *Outre-Mer,* 276–325; Dugard, *La société américaine,* 229–300; and Blanc, *The Condition of Woman in the United States,* 165–224. For a discussion of European reaction to women's colleges see Albisetti, "American Women's Colleges through European Eyes," 439–58.

33. For late-nineteenth-century French perceptions of American women see Varigny, *The Women of the United States;* Bourget, *Outre-Mer,* 86–109; Soissons, *A Parisian in America,* 1–23; and Sauvin, *Autour de Chicago,* 102–23. For a summary of French reactions to American women see Portes, *Fascination and Misgivings,* 254–82.

34. Portes, *Fascination and Misgivings,* 12.

35. Bourget, *Outre-Mer,* 116, notes that the Chicago fire had occurred in October 1871, just after the Franco-Prussian War. The civil uprising known as the Paris Commune, which followed the signing of the Treaty of Frankfort, led to numer-

ous fires in Paris that destroyed important monuments, including the Tuileries Palace and the Hôtel de Ville.

36. Bruwaert, "Chicago et l'exposition universelle colombienne," 304. A translation of this article is included in Pierce, *As Others See Chicago*, 325–39.

37. Bourget, *Outre-Mer*, 120.

38. Sauvin, *Autour de Chicago*, 95, 97.

39. Soissons, *A Parisian in America*, 131.

40. Ibid., 132, 134.

41. Ibid.

42. See Lewis, *An Early Encounter*, 167–75, for a thoughtful discussion of the most striking differences between the 1889 Paris Exhibition and Chicago's World's Columbian Exposition.

43. See Flanagan, *Seeing with Their Hearts*, 57–58, for a discussion of Chicago women's participation in the fair. For an incisive study of the important organizational role of women in the Woman's Building see Gullett, "'Our Great Opportunity,'" 259–76. Bertha Palmer's speeches given before, during, and after the fair convey the excitement as well as the disappointments of the Woman's Building project. *Addresses and Reports of Mrs. Potter Palmer.*

44. See Webster, *Eve's Daughter / Modern Woman*, for an insightful discussion of the mural and of Cassatt's role in the project. See also Mathews, *Cassatt and Her Circle*, 235–47, for several letters exchanged among Cassatt, Palmer, and Sarah Hallowell regarding the plans for Cassatt's mural.

45. A special issue of *Libraries and Culture* 41 (Winter 2006) is devoted entirely to the Woman's Building Library and contains numerous articles that explore the historic importance of the library and its collection. See Weimann, *The Fair Women*, for an exhaustive and rigorous study regarding the planning, execution, and events surrounding the Woman's Building.

46. Grandin, *Impressions d'une parisienne*, 278.

47. See Badger, *The Great American Fair*, 120, for a description of the confusion provoked by the layout, sprawl, and eclectic exhibitions at the fair.

48. Ibid., 107–9.

49. Grandin, *Impressions d'une parisienne*, 304.

50. Two other travel accounts written in French by women who visited Chicago have not been included in this list because the authors were not of French nationality. A Belgian, Madame Arthur de Cannart d'Hamale, came to Chicago on her honeymoon in order to attend the fair and later published *Un voyage de noces à Chicago*. The Marquise de San Carlos de Pedroso was born in America but spent most of her life in France. In 1890 she published *Les Américains chez eux*, which included a chapter filled with statistics about life in nineteenth-century Chicago.

51. A number of critical works on women's travel writing have been helpful in thinking about Madame Grandin's account and those of other French women travelers: Foster, *Across New Worlds*; Mills, *Discourses of Difference*; Monicat, "Autobiography and Women's Travel Writings"; Monicat, "Problématique de la préface dans les récits de voyage au féminin du 19e siècle"; Monicat, *Itinéraires de l'écriture au féminin*; Stowe, *Going Abroad*; and Imbarrato, *Traveling Women*.

52. Audouard, À *travers l'Amérique*.

53. Audouard had been through a difficult separation and subsequently devoted herself to the cause of women's rights, specifically the right to divorce. For information about Audouard's political activities see Monicat, "Écritures du voyage et féminisme, 24–36; Moses, *French Feminism*, 178–79; and Lapeyre, *Le roman des voyageuses françaises*, 142–46.

54. At the time of Audouard's visit, discussions concerning woman suffrage were well under way in the United States because Wyoming Territory had approved full and equal suffrage for women on December 10, 1869.

55. Hartmut Keil points out that between the 1850s and World War I, German immigrants accounted for between 25 and 35 percent of the total population of Chicago. Keil, "Immigrant Neighborhoods," 25–58, quotation on 25.

56. Audouard, *A travers l'Amérique*, 53.

57. See Caplat, *Les inspecteurs généraux*, 478–80, for an overview of Marie Loizillon's career.

58. Loizillon, *L'éducation des enfants*.

59. Ibid., 59.

60. According to Pierce, *A History of Chicago*, 22–47, by 1890, 77.9 percent of Chicago's population was of foreign parentage. German-born immigrants made up the largest group, followed by Irish, Scandinavian, and Central and Western European immigrants.

61. Loizillon, *L'éducation des enfants*, 59.

62. Bernhardt, *My Double Life*.

63. Ibid., 277, 278. At the time, the Palmer House was located on State Street and considered one of the most elegant hotels in the city.

64. Bourbonnaud's husband, Étienne, had been a close associate of Baron Haussmann, who was responsible for Paris's vast urban renewal project during the 1850s and 1860s. Lapeyre, *Le roman des voyageuses françaises*, 36; Bourbonnaud, *Les Amériques*.

65. Bourbonnaud, *Les Amériques*, 43.

66. Monicat, *Itinéraires de l'écriture, au féminin*, 17, points out that this patriotic attitude is apparent in all of Bourbonnaud's travel writing.

67. Dugard, *La société américaine*. Before her trip to America, Dugard had already published *La culture morale: Lectures de morale théorique et pratique* in 1892. See the biographical entry for Marie Dugard in D'Amat and Limouzin-Lamothe, *Dictionnaire de biographie française*, 11:1480, for a complete bibliography of her publications, which include treatises on education, translations of Ralph Waldo Emerson's works, and novels.

68. Dugard, *La société américaine*, 30.

69. Ibid., 33.

70. Ibid., 38.

71. Ibid., 48.

72. World Congress sessions were held at the newly constructed building on Michigan Avenue at Adams Street that would become the home of the Art Institute of Chicago following the close of the exposition. Higinbotham, *The Report of the President to the Board of Directors*, 48. See Badger, *The Great American Fair*, 99, for a description of the wide range of topics discussed during the three-day

International Congress on Education held in July 1893. Marie Dugard was listed as a participant in an article on the event (*Chicago Tribune*, 28 July 1893, 8).

73. Dugard, *La société américaine*, 46.

74. Two important articles situate Blanc's account of her trip to the United States in the context of French opinions about American women: Chew, "Marie-Thérèse Blanc," 17–59, and West, "Th. Bentzon's Traveler's Notes," 29–33.

75. Bentzon, *Notes de voyage*; Blanc, *The Condition of Woman in the United States*.

76. Blanc, *The Condition of Women in the United States*, 21–22.

77. Blanc's primary target was Charles de Varigny, who had published a series of negative articles on American women in *Revue des Deux Mondes*. The articles were collected and published as a book, *La femme aux États-Unis*, which was translated as *The Women of the United States*.

78. Blanc, *The Condition of Women in the United States*, 42.

79. Ibid., 56.

80. Ibid., 43–55. See Martin, *The Sound of Our Own Voices*, 43, for a description of the Fortnightly Club.

81. Pierce, *A History of Chicago*, 465–66.

82. Blanc, *The Condition of Women in the United States*, 90.

83. Goussard de Mayolle, *Une française chez les sauvages*.

84. Batbedat, *Impressions d'une parisienne*, 43. Before her trip to America, Thérèse Batbedat had published two English translations of French texts, George Du Maurier's *Trilby* (Paris: Juven, 1894) and Ludovic Halévy's *L'Abbé Constantin* (London: Macqueen, 1897). A notice in the *New York Times*, 15 November 1902, 14, indicated that Brentano's Bookstore had received her book and described it "as a view of American customs." While living in Seattle, Batbedat joined the Club Français, which met once a week for French conversation (94–95). She studied the Squantum tribe and hoped to find descendants of Chief Seattle (128).

85. Ibid., 45. See Siry, *The Chicago Auditorium Building*, for a discussion of the origins and planning of the hotel within this multi-use building.

86. Ibid., 46.

87. Ibid., 48.

88. Vianzone, *Impressions d'une française en amérique*, 281. In her introduction, Vianzone describes the book as a collection of letters addressed to a dear old friend named Madame Le Paulmier. Vianzone's high-level contacts included President and Mrs. Theodore Roosevelt—to whom she dedicated her book—and wealthy New York families. The volume was favorably reviewed in the *New York Times* on March 31, 1906.

89. Ibid., 282.

90. Ibid.

91. Ibid.

92. Grandin, *Impressions d'une parisienne*, 35.

93. Ibid., 82. See Higinbotham, *The Report of the President*, 179–80, for a description of the state of Jackson Park upon Madame Grandin's arrival in August 1892.

94. Ibid., 90.

95. Miller, *City of the Century*, 490.

96. An expert discussion of this important building appears in Siry, *The Chicago Auditorium Building*.

97. Grandin, *Impressions d'une parisienne*, 101. The issue of woman suffrage was an important topic of discussion during the 1892 presidential campaign. Harrison was considered a supporter of woman suffrage because during his administration he had signed a bill on July 10, 1890, approving Wyoming's status as the nation's "Equality State." Wyoming Territory had approved suffrage for women twenty-one and older in 1869, and there was concern that it might lose this privilege upon becoming a state.

98. Ibid., 102.

99. Throughout her text, Madame Grandin expresses sympathy for the less-fortunate people she encountered. She was impressed, for example, by the energy and positive attitude of steerage passengers onboard the ship (10–12) and praised the noble attitude of Native Americans who had been displaced from their territory (80–81).

100. Grandin, *Impressions d'une parisienne*, 80.

101. Ibid., 233.

102. The routine and preoccupations of the ideal bourgeois homemaker were depicted in numerous nineteenth-century French etiquette books targeted at bourgeois women, including Delorme, *Les petits cahiers de Madame Brunet;* and de Bassanville, *De l'éducation des femmes*. Martin-Fugier describes the routine of the nineteenth-century French bourgeois wife and mother in *La bourgeoise*.

103. Grandin, *Impressions d'une parisienne*, 250.

104. See Clark, *Schooling the Daughters of Marianne*, 26–59, for a description of French primary school curriculum in late-nineteenth-century France.

105. Grandin, *Impressions d'une parisienne*, 278.

106. The World's Congress of Representative Women took place during the week of May 15, 1893, at the Art Institute and at the Woman's Building. Eighty-one meetings were held, during which 330 women presented papers on many different topics relating to women. Approximately 150,000 people attended. See Badger, *The Great American Fair*, 101–2, and Weimann, *The Fair Women*, 523–49, for descriptions of the planning and execution of these meetings. The official record appears in *The Congress of Women Held in the Woman's Building*, including the addresses of all the women who participated, among them Susan B. Anthony and Julia Ward Howe.

107. Grandin, *Impressions d'une parisienne*, 162.

108. In a letter to Madame Grandin dated April 13, 1893, Bertha Palmer indicated that Madame Grandin was giving her lessons, possibly French lessons. Palmer wrote that she would be too busy during the upcoming two weeks to have her lessons but that she "shall be very glad to recommence our talks at the end of that time." A letter containing the same information but written in French was sent by Palmer's secretary, Laura Hayes, to Madame Grandin on the same date. Chicago Historical Society, World's Columbian Exposition 1893, Board of Lady Managers Correspondence, President's Letter Books, 15:948.

109. Grandin, *Impressions d'une parisienne*, 313.

110. Ibid., 330.

111. Marie Gélon Cameron (1872–1949) was a student in the life class at the Art

Institute between 1891 and 1893. Her husband, Edgar, was a painter and art critic for the *Chicago Tribune*. Madame Grandin's description of her friendship with the Camerons appears in chapter 8 of this volume.

112. Edgar and Marie Cameron had rented an apartment and studio at numbers 9 and 11, rue des Fourneaux, which is today the rue Falguière, just west of Montparnasse. According to 1894 Paris Salon records, the Grandins lived at 48, rue Beaunier, several blocks south of Montparnasse.

113. Marie Gélon Cameron to Mrs. John R. Cameron, 1 February 1894, Edgar Spier Cameron Papers, roll 4292, 1019, Smithsonian Archive of American Art.

114. See Fink, *American Art at the Nineteenth-Century Paris Salons*, 137–42, for a description of artists' preparation for the salons and the judging procedures used by salon jurors. No images of this portrait have come to light. It seems likely that Madame Grandin was given the portrait following the salon competition. In a letter to his father dated April 2, 1894, Edgar Spier Cameron expressed disappointment that the portrait of Madame Grandin had not been accepted into the 1894 Salon but consoled himself with the fact that "I got some study out of it and as Madame Grandin pays for the frame, it was not an expensive experience." Edgar Cameron to Mr. John R. Cameron, Edgar Spier Cameron Papers, roll 4292, 1032–33, Smithsonian Archive of American Art.

115. Marie Gélon Cameron to Mrs. John R. Cameron, 20 March 1894, Edgar Spier Cameron Papers, roll 4292, 1027, Smithsonian Archive of American Art.

116. Marie Gélon Cameron to Mr. John R. Cameron, 18 April 1894, Edgar Spier Cameron Papers, roll 4292, 1038, Smithsonian Archive of American Art.

117. Both of Madame Grandin's children died at a young age. Her son, Sandy, served in the U.S. Navy during World War I and died at home on Staten Island following a gas accident in October 1917. Her daughter, May, whose death certificate indicated that she was employed as a musician, died during the influenza epidemic in January 1920.

118. The Ferrand family was living on Staten Island by October 1903. Madame M. A. Ferrand announced the first lecture and the start of free French courses at the French Alliance of Staten Island. *Staten Islander*, 17 October 1903.

119. Grandin, *Impressions d'une parisienne*, 313.

TO THE READER

1. These verses are from the poem "Ce que disent les hirondelles, chanson d'automne" (What the Swallows Say, an Autumn Song) by the French poet Théophile Gautier (1811–72). The poem was published in Gautier's collection *Émaux et camées* (Enamels and Cameos) in 1852. The poem describes a fall assembly of sparrows discussing their winter destinations, which include Athens, Rhodes, and Cairo. The verses Madame Grandin cites contain a reference to the German poet Friedrich Ruckert (1788–1866). Gautier published a French translation of one of Ruckert's poems, entitled "Les ailes" (Wings), in *La Petite Presse* on October 27, 1872.

CHAPTER 1: AT SEA

1. The French ship *La Touraine* was in service from 1891 to 1923 and known for its fine food. An article in the *New York Times* described the features of the ship upon its maiden voyage on June 20, 1891: "The interior of the vessel is elegantly fitted. Accommodations for 1,090 passengers are provided. The grand saloon is a model of elegance and comfort. The ceiling is designed in panels of blue and gold. The fireplace of the saloon is an artistic conception, constructed of mahogany relieved with gold and topped with red and white marble. A cozy little room, decorated in blue, white, and gold is set apart for the ladies. The smoking room is large and airy, and has walls of satinwood with panels of Japanese inlaid work." "Arrival of *La Touraine,*" *New York Times,* 28 June 1891, 8. An article in *The American Architect and Building News* on February 20, 1892, entitled "The Atlantic Steamship, 'La Touraine,'" provides a description of the passenger cabins ,which included twenty-one state rooms with two berths that were "simply but very conveniently furnished."

2. This is a description of a second-class cabin; the ship's manifest of *La Touraine* in the Ellis Island passenger records indicates that Marie and Léon Grandin traveled in second class.

3. For descriptions of condition of transatlantic travel and onboard activities see Portes, *Fascination and Misgivings,* 19–23.

4. Madame Grandin apparently confused the *Bismarck* with another ship. According to the *New York Times,* the *Bismarck* left Hamburg on July 15, 1892, and arrived in New York on July 23, 1892, so a sighting on the ocean would not have been possible.

5. According to Ellis Island records, *La Touraine* arrived in New York Harbor on July 30, 1892. The ship broke its record for a transatlantic crossing, arriving in six days, seventeen hours, and thirty minutes. "Another Record Breaker," *Washington Post,* 31 July 1892, 4.

6. After the opening of Ellis Island in January 1892, first- and second-class passengers were examined onboard ship. Burrows and Wallace, *Gotham,* 1111.

7. This is a reference to the smaller version of the Statue of Liberty that overlooks the River Seine in Paris.

8. Madame Grandin found this system efficient, but other visitors did not. Thérèse Vianzone, a visiting lecturer on French literature, arrived in New York in October 1903 and complained about the difficulty of locating both friends and luggage. Vianzone, *Impressions d'une française,* 15.

CHAPTER 2: NEW YORK

1. The Paris metro system would not begin service until July 19, 1900.

2. The Grandins' relatives lived in the suburban village of Morissania, which was located in what is now the southwest corner of The Bronx. Traveling from Manhattan, Madame Grandin would have boarded the Suburban Rapid Transit Company's elevated train that traveled north to the villages of Mott Haven, Melrose, and Morrisania. Burrows and Wallace, *Gotham,* 1054.

3. Madame Grandin alludes to the residential area on the Right Bank in Paris, near the Bois de Boulogne, where many homes have spacious yards.

4. The French text contains the spelling *Mankattan*.

5. The reference is to the Lower East Side. For a description of this neighborhood that housed recently arrived Jewish immigrants see Still, *Mirror for Gotham*, 216, and Burrows and Wallace, *Gotham*, 1117–118.

6. Burrows and Wallace, *Gotham*, 1126–131. Mathilde Shaw, a French journalist who married the American journalist Charles Shaw and lived in New York City in the 1890s, published an investigative article on Chinatown entitled "Scènes de la vie chinoise à New York," *La Nouvelle Revue* 91 (November–December 1894): 327–60.

7. Regarding tensions between Chinese immigrants and New Yorkers in the late nineteenth century see Burrows and Wallace, *Gotham*, 1130–33.

8. Ibid., 1138–40.

9. This is a reference to St. Mark's in the Bowery Church, which was completed in 1799.

10. The neighborhood of Les Halles, where the traditional central Paris market was located up until 1971, is on the Right Bank, a few blocks from the Seine.

11. Cheney, *Aprons*, 15–16, discusses the popularity of white decorative aprons among middle- and upper-class women in late-nineteenth and early-twentieth-century America.

12. The Lincoln Tunnel, which connects New York and New Jersey, was constructed between 1934 and 1957.

13. The official Festival of Connection celebrating the opening of the Brooklyn Bridge took place on May 24, 1883. Burrow and Wallace, *Gotham*, 937. The dramatic bridge is the subject of frequent commentary in nineteenth-century accounts of French visitors to New York. Portes, *Fascination and Misgivings*, 62–63.

14. The French cabriolet is a small carriage designed for two people. Burrows and Wallace, *Gotham*, 953, discuss Central Park's importance as a fashionable promenade in the late nineteenth century.

15. The Metropolitan Museum of Art was established in 1870 by a group of American businessmen and leading artists and intellectuals. It moved to its current location in Central Park in 1880. The present facade and entrance structure were completed in 1926. Tomkins, *Merchants and Masterpieces*. A description of the dedication of the museum's new building in March 1880 appears in Burrows and Wallace, *Gotham*, 1081–83.

16. Although Madame Grandin makes no reference to having formal art school training, her comments on sculpture throughout the text suggest her interest in the topic and familiarity with Parisian ateliers and art schools.

17. Augustus Saint-Gaudens (1848–1907) and Frederick MacMonnies (1863–1937) were two American sculptors who studied in France and later worked extensively on projects in New York City. Two letters from the Frederick MacMonnies's archive indicate that Léon Grandin worked on the Washington Square Arch in April 1894, but it is not clear if Grandin actually traveled from Paris to New York to assist with this project. For discussions of American art students in late-nineteenth-century Paris, see Wiesinger, "American Sculpture Students in Paris," 55–69; Weinberg, *The Lure of Paris*; and Adler, "'We'll Always Have Paris,'" 11–55.

18. Benoît-Constant Coquelin (1841–1909), a popular French actor in the late nineteenth century, was best known for his role of Cyrano in Edmond Rostand's play *Cyrano de Bergerac*. Victorien Sardou (1831–1908) was a French playwright who specialized in historical dramas and comedies.

19. The play *A Trip to Chinatown* was written by Charles H. Hoyt. It opened at Madison Square Theater on November 9, 1891, and ran for 657 performances, just under two years.

20. Maurice Hennequin (1863–1926) and Alexandre Bisson (1848–1912) were successful writers of French vaudeville plays in the late nineteenth and early twentieth centuries.

21. See Portes, *Fascination and Misgivings*, 258–60, for a discussion of the American female type called "the flirt" that so intrigued both male and female French visitors.

22. Madame Grandin seems to have confused Staten Island with Jersey City. According to Brown, *A History of the New York Stage*, 546, the impressive spectacle *Fall of Babylon*, presented on one of the largest stages ever erected in America, opened on June 22, 1887, at St. George on Staten Island. The Casino Theater was located on Broadway at 39th Street and featured a cafe, roof garden, and Moorish-style interior. It was constructed in 1882 and demolished in 1930.

23. Loie Fuller (1862–1928), an expatriot American dancer, first performed with the Folies Bergères in Paris in 1892. She created an immediate sensation when she danced across the stage wrapped in yards of shimmering cloth illuminated by multicolored spotlights. Current, *Loie Fuller*.

24. Madame Grandin uses the term *Peaux-Rouges* meaning Redskins.

25. Madison Square Garden II was located at 26th Street and Madison Avenue. Built in 1890, it was demolished in 1925. See Burrows and Wallace, *Gotham*, 1147–48, for a description of the building, which included an observation platform and a garden theater, ballroom–concert hall, and restaurant. The glass that enclosed the roof garden could be removed during the summer.

26. Late-nineteenth-century Parisian *café-concerts* were lively venues that presented musical entertainment without an admission charge. They attracted a mixed crowd of workers, artists, members of the bourgeoisie, and even the upper class. See Rearick, "Song and Society in Turn of the Century France," for an animated discussion of the role of these establishments in late-nineteenth-century Parisian social life.

27. The New York Juvenile Asylum opened in 1851 and was located at 10th Avenue and 175th Street.

CHAPTER 3: FROM NEW YORK TO CHICAGO

1. The Michigan Central Railroad, part of the New York Central Railroad system, advertised itself as the "only line running directly by and in full view of the World's Columbian Exposition and the Great Cataract of Niagara." Niagara Falls was a popular stop for travelers between New York and Chicago. See Portes, *Fascination and Misgivings*, 82–83, regarding Niagara Falls's status as a must-see destination for French tourists. A detailed consideration of the reactions of nine-

teenth-century European visitors to the natural spectacle appears in Dubinsky, *The Second Greatest Disappointment*, 55–71.

2. The monetary equivalent of $4 in 1893 would be approximately $86.56 in 2010.

3. Madame Grandin is referring to the French writer François-René de Chateaubriand (1764–1848).

4. This is a reference to the Chicago River.

5. Madame Grandin's train arrived at the Central Depot, which served the Michigan Central Railroad. The station was located at Michigan Avenue and Madison Street.

6. The Grandins arrived in Chicago in August 1892, and the World's Columbian Exposition opened nine months later, in May 1893.

CHAPTER 4: BOARDINGHOUSE LIFE

1. In Madame Grandin's French text, State Street becomes Stade Street, one of a number of misspellings of street names.

2. The Grandins arrived in Chicago during a heat wave.

3. This middle-class neighborhood was located on the south side of Chicago between The Loop and Jackson Park.

4. The French Legion of Honor, created in 1802 by Napoleon Bonaparte, is awarded for outstanding service to France. The medal is a five-sided, double-pointed star made of white enamel.

5. This is a reference to the sharp-witted Guignol, the main character in puppet shows held in the Luxembourg and Tuileries Gardens.

6. The Belleville funicular opened on August 25, 1891, and ran from the Place de la République to the Church of Belleville on the rue Faubourg du Temple and the rue Belleville. The funicular ran until July 18, 1924, when it was replaced by a bus. For a description of the features of this tramway see G. De Burgraff, "Tramway Funiculaire de Belleville," *Le Magasin Pittoresque* 8, no. 2 (1890).

7. The boardinghouse, located at the corner of Ellis Avenue and 37th Street, no longer exists, but a photograph in the collection of the Chicago Historical Society (Laughlin Master Prints, negative 14780) depicts a decorative detail on the support of one of its turrets.

8. The residential architecture of late-nineteenth-century Paris was very uniform due to the vast renovation of the city during the Second Empire (1852–70) under the direction of Baron Eugène Haussmann. The seven-story apartment building was the most common residential structure. Inside, the layout of each apartment was similar, the lower floors offering more spacious apartments. See Olsen, *The City as a Work of Art*, 35–57, 114–25, for a discussion of Haussmann's "New Paris" and the layout and features of nineteenth-century apartments in that city.

9. Boardinghouses were popular lodging places during the Chicago Exposition. *The Official Guide to the World's Columbian Exposition*, 170, and Morris, *Morris' Dictionary*, 20, 42, both provided information to visitors about all types of lodging, including boardinghouses. Both guides indicated that Chicago boardinghouses

charged between five and ten dollars per week. These guides also gave precise recommendations regarding the best neighborhoods: "Select some place, if possible, South of Twenty-Second Street and east of Wabash Avenue; north of Chicago Avenue and east of Welles Street; west of Ashland Avenue, or south of Madison to Jackson, or north of Madison to Park Avenue, the farther west the better" (*The Official Guide to the World's Columbian Exposition*, 170). Madame Grandin's Chicago lodgings were all located south of 22nd Street and east of Wabash Avenue.

10. Cromley, "American Beds and Bedrooms," 131–34.

11. According to David M. Katzman, the average weekly wage for servants in Chicago in 1892 was $4.23. Katzman, *Seven Days a Week*, 310.

12. Foreign visitors commented extensively on the relationship between American domestic servants and their masters. See, for example, Tocqueville, *Democracy in America*, 546–53, and Trollope, *Domestic Manners*, 45–49. Baronne Staffe, in *Usages du monde*, 206–14, described the ideal relationship between French servants and masters in late-nineteenth-century France. The master and mistress of the home, she advised, needed to be firmly in control at all times. A summary of French reactions to American servants is presented in Portes, *Fascination and Misgivings*, 267–69.

13. This is a reference to two characters in *The Marriage of Figaro* (1784) by Pierre de Beaumarchais.

14. See Morris, *Morris' Dictionary*, 43–44, for descriptions of lake cruises.

15. See Portes, *Fascination and Misgivings*, 104–36, for a discussion of French visitors' reactions to African Americans they encountered during their travels.

16. Madame Grandin, like many European visitors of the time, expressed great sympathy for the plight of Native Americans. See Liebersohn, *Aristocratic Encounters*, 111–12, for a detailed consideration of French reactions to Native Americans throughout the nineteenth century.

17. The "White City" of temporary exhibition buildings was constructed between September 1892 and the spring of 1893. Following the close of the fair, all the buildings were demolished except for the Palace of Fine Arts, which was transformed into the Museum of Science and Industry.

18. Madame Grandin is referring to the Columbian Fountain.

19. Appelbaum points out that "the winter of 1892–93 was extremely severe and made construction work difficult and dangerous." There were rumored to have been seven hundred accidents, eighteen of them fatal, during the construction of the fair buildings. Appelbaum, *The Chicago World's Fair of 1893*, 5.

20. Madame Grandin mistakenly refers to Hyde Park as "Jackson." Hyde Park was a separate town until it was annexed into Chicago in 1889. No town named Jackson ever existed in the area.

21. See Pierce, *A History of Chicago*, 3:455–60, for a discussion of the temperance movement in late-nineteenth-century Chicago.

22. Gamber, *The Boarding House*, 60–95, presents a thoughtful discussion of the complaints of both landlords and boarders. In Theodore Dreiser's *Sister Carrie*, set in late-nineteenth-century Chicago, tensions between tenants and servants are evident in boardinghouse conversations between Carrie and the housemaids (63, 97, 145–47).

CHAPTER 5: NEW LODGINGS

1. For information about the typical proprietors and boarders in Chicago board-inghouses in the late nineteenth and early twentieth centuries see Meyerowitz, *Women Adrift*, 70–73. The depictions of Carrie's room in a boardinghouse and her friendship with another boarder, Mrs. Hale, are similar to the rooms and interactions Madame Grandin describes. Dreiser, *Sister Carrie*, 54, 69, 77.

2. Following the defeat of France in the 1870 Franco-Prussian War, tensions remained between France and Germany.

3. See Calvert, "Children in the House," 75–93, for a discussion of the focus on exploration and child-directed play during this era.

4. Jean-Jacques Rousseau's treatise on education, *Émile*, was published in 1762. Rousseau advocated a natural approach to education, allowing the pupil to determine the subject, order, and method of study.

5. This is a reference to the social tradition of French bourgeois and upper-class women visiting friends and acquaintances on appointed days. See Martin-Fugier, *La bourgeoise*, 189–94, for a description of this Parisian custom.

6. See Mohun, *Steam Laundries*, 95–116, for a description of laundry technology during this period.

7. By the 1890s, Chinese laundries were well established in Chicago. Ibid., 67.

8. The nineteenth-century Parisian concierge typically lived on the ground floor of an apartment building and performed many domestic duties. Perrot discusses the important role of the concierge in urban apartment buildings in Perrot, ed, *L'histoire de la vie privée*, 176–77.

9. The monetary equivalent in 2010 would be approximately $22.

10. This reference to the "last war" is unclear. If Mr. H. was about thirty-five in 1893, he would have been too young to have served in the Civil War.

11. This is the first of Madame Grandin's numerous comparisons of American and French husbands.

12. Republican incumbent Benjamin Harrison's campaign particularly attracted women who were interested in pushing forward the suffrage movement. Harrison, as president, had admitted Wyoming Territory as a state in 1890. Wyoming, called the "Equality State," was allowed to retain its 1869 law that gave women over the age of twenty-one the right to vote.

13. In Madame Grandin's obituary, she was described as "an accomplished pianist who charmed many an audience at charitable entertainments as well as private functions." *Staten Islander*, 17 December 1905.

14. This is given as "Brexel Boulevard" in Madame Grandin's text (104).

15. The monetary equivalent of one French franc in 1893 would be about $5 in 2010.

16. The reputation of French cuisine was well established by the end of the nineteenth century. Amy Trubek describes the organization of culinary expositions held in late-nineteenth-century Paris and London that were designed to help promote French haute cuisine. Trubek, *Haute Cuisine*, 112–23.

CHAPTER 6: WORLD'S COLUMBIAN EXPOSITION:
DEDICATION CEREMONIES

1. The statue of Columbus was created by the Chicago sculptor R. H. Park and placed next to an elaborate drinking fountain on Washington Street. Several articles in the *Chicago Daily Tribune* describe the statue and its inauguration: "Statue of Columbus," 9 January 1892: 12; "Given to the City: Drake Fountain Is Formally Accepted by the Mayor," 27 December 1892, 9; and "Description of the John B. Drake Drinking Fountain," 22 October 1892, 16.

2. The schedule for Wednesday, October 19, indicated "Columbus Day in all the schools at 1:30 o'clock." Higinbotham, *The Report of the President*, 156.

3. This is the first of a number of schools that Madame Grandin would visit in Chicago. She had a strong interest in education given that she worked as an elementary school teacher in Paris.

4. In *The Report of the President*, Higinbotham notes that the reception and ball took place at 9 in the evening and were organized by Major General Nelson A. Miles and Messrs. Marshall Field, George M. Pullman, Philip D. Armour, and N. K. Fairbank. Higinbotham concludes that "the brilliant event elicited great praise for its faultless arrangements and the elegant completeness of its details" (156–57).

5. The Auditorium Building, a multi-use structure that at the time encompassed a theater, ballroom, hotel, and numerous businesses, was designed by Adler and Sullivan and attracted the attention of many foreign visitors. See Siry, *The Chicago Auditorium Building*, for an expert discussion of its planning, architecture, and spaces.

6. Siry, "Chicago's Auditorium Building," 145–46, compares the simple interior decoration of the Auditorium Theater to the more lavish decoration of opera houses in Europe.

7. The Auditorium Theater was designed so that it could be easily transformed into a ballroom. Siry, *The Chicago Auditorium Building*, 217.

8. An article in the *Chicago Tribune*, "Simple but Effective Decoration," 19 October 1892, 1, described the planned decoration of the Auditorium Theater for the ball. Descriptions of the actual ball also appeared in the *Tribune*, "Her Celebration Begins," 20 October 1892, 1, and *New York Times*, "Inaugural Reception,"20 October 1892, 2.

9. This is a reference to a fifteenth-century Indian fortress where jewels were stored. See "Costumes to Be Seen at the Ball," *Chicago Tribune*, 19 October 1892, 1, for descriptions of the gowns and jewels that the most distinguished women, including Madame Grandin's acquaintances Bertha Palmer and Laura Hayes, were planning to wear.

10. The Boston was a popular dance in late-nineteenth-century America.

11. "People will arrive in their own carriages but on leaving the ball they will purchase tickets in the lobby of the Auditorium according to the following tariff and take the first carriage in waiting." "Tickets to the Ball," *Chicago Tribune*, 2 October 1892, 11.

12. Rules and fares for cabs and hacks are given in Morris, *Morris' Dictionary*, 76–77.

13. The dollar equivalent in 2010 would be between $100 and $125.

14. Smiley, *Modern Manners and Social Forms*, 100, describes the difference between the French system of chaperonage and the relative freedom of American women.

15. The duties of an escort included sending a woman a bouquet during the day, ringing the bell when calling for her, escorting her in a carriage, and seeing her home at the end of the evening. Smiley, *Modern Manners*, 219, 220.

16. This is a reference to the Equal Protection Clause of the Fourteenth Amendment to the U.S. Constitution, which was ratified on July, 9, 1868.

17. The tradition of the bride's family making a payment to the groom in the form of a dowry was still in effect in late-nineteenth-century France. The historian Anne Martin-Fugier, however, points out that this custom came under attack in the 1890s because the dowry came to be viewed as an obstacle to the foundation of a good marriage. Criticism of the dowry tradition was motivated in part by growing concern about the declining birth rate in France in the last decade of the century. Fugier, *La bourgeoise*, 45–47.

18. "Address of Mrs. Potter Palmer," 7–18.

19. For accounts of Palmer's 1891 visit to Paris, where she publicized the upcoming World's Columbian Exposition and acquired numerous French impressionist paintings that would be displayed in the Fine Arts Palace, see "Work That Mrs. Palmer Is Doing," *Chicago Daily Tribune*, 25 July 1891, 12; Ross, *Silhouette in Diamonds*, 61–63, 147–63; and Webster, *Eve's Daughter* / Modern Woman, 49–67. It was during this visit that Bertha Palmer met with the painters Mary Cassatt and Mary MacMonnies and commissioned them to do murals for each end of the main gallery of the Woman's Building.

20. Almost all French visitors to the United States in the late nineteenth century condemned the treatment of Native Americans by the American government. Portes, *Fascination and Misgivings*, 99.

21. A common theme in French accounts was the probable extinction of Native Americans. Ibid., 102.

22. A description of the elaborate transportation system put in place during the exposition appears in Higinbotham, *The Report of the President* , 131–40.

CHAPTER 7: THE MILWAUKEE FIRE

1. Although the menu appears to be very elaborate, this meal, consisting of soup, a fish course, a meat course, and an offering of fruit and pastry, was typical of dinner parties in both late-nineteenth-century Paris and Chicago. See Bancquart, *Fin de siècle gourmande*, 14–15, for descriptions of Parisian dinner party menus. See Smiley, *Modern Manners and Social Forms*, 169–70, for a description of an elegant American dinner party that included oysters, soup, a fish course, a roast, game, salad, cheese, and sweets.

2. This is a reference to the fox's behavior in the fable by Jean de La Fontaine (1621–95), *Le renard et les raisins* (The Fox and the Grapes), in which a hungry fox

jumps in order to reach a bunch of ripe grapes. When he does not succeed, he bitterly concludes that the grapes must be sour.

3. The Great Fire of Milwaukee broke out in a factory in the city's Third Ward on October 28, 1892.

4. Charles Dickens, in *American Notes*, 103, commented on the large number of fires in America and the fact that some seemed of suspicious origin.

5. An *arrondissement* is an administrative neighborhood division in Paris.

6. This appears to be a reference to River Park, now known as Riverside Park. Designed by Frederick Law Olmstead, it opened to the public in 1890.

7. Oak Woods Cemetery is located at 1035 East 67th Street, just a few blocks south of Jackson Park and the exposition site. In Morris, *Morris' Dictionary*, visitors were advised that they could reach this cemetery via the Illinois Central.

CHAPTER 8: NEW ACQUAINTANCES

1. See Meyerowitz, *Women Adrift*, 73, for a discussion of the shift, which began about the time of the 1893 World's Columbian Exposition, from boardinghouses to rooming houses where renters had use of a kitchen to prepare their own meals. See Duis, *Challenging Chicago*, 82–85, regarding the different types of boardinghouses and the trend toward family hotels.

2. A chemise, a cotton shift with elbow-length sleeves, was worn either under or over a corset.

3. Steele, "The Corset Controversy," 161–91.

4. The American syndicated gossip columnist Margaret Cunliffe-Owen, writing under the pseudonym the Marquise de Fontenoy, published *Eve's Glossary: The Guide Book of a Mondaine*, 154, in which she advocated wearing a corset with a corset cover or chemise.

5. The French proverb "the habit does not make the monk" is usually translated as "clothes do not make the person." Madame Grandin stated the opposite, implying that in France women were judged by their clothing.

6. This is a reference to the American painter Lydia Purdy Hess (1866–1936). According to the archives of the Art Institute of Chicago, Hess was an instructor there from 1892 to 1895 and taught the "Antique" course. She was a former pupil of the Parisian painters Laugée and Delacluse. An article in the *Chicago Tribune*, 5 June 1892, 38, on the upcoming academic year at the Art Institute indicated that Miss Lydia Hess was on the teaching schedule.

7. At the time of Madame Grandin's visit, the Art Institute was located in The Athenaeum on the west side of Michigan Avenue at 18–26 Van Buren Street. The new Art Institute Building, located on its current lakefront site on Michigan Avenue, opened during the summer of 1893 in time to host many meetings of the World's Columbian Exposition Congresses.

8. See Pierce, *A History of Chicago* 3:495–99, for a historical overview of the Art Institute.

9. Léon Grandin had studied at the École de Beaux-Arts, which most likely explained Madame Grandin's familiarity with the classes there. See Martin-Fugier, *La vie d'artiste*, 32–36, for a description of the lively ambiance in the late-nineteenth-century classrooms and workshops of the school.

10. In *Modeling My Life* the American sculptor Janet Scudder describes the problems she encountered with models and male sculptors in the Parisian workshop of Frederick MacMonnies in 1894.

11. See W. M. R. French's article in the *Chicago Tribune*, 21 April 1889, 33, regarding the close relationship between the Art Institute of Chicago, of which he was director from 1882 to 1914, and the École des Beaux-Arts in Paris. He also discusses the importance of the Académie Julian and the Académie Colarossi, which accepted female students. The École des Beaux-Arts was not open to women until 1897. An important study of American painters and their experiences in Paris appears in Weinberg, *The Lure of Paris*.

12. James McNeil Whistler (1834–1903) lived in Paris in the early 1890s, and his paintings were much admired. John Singer Sargent (1856–1925) had studied in Paris. During the 1890s, Sargent frequently visited Paris and exhibited his paintings at the salons.

13. This is a reference to the painters Marie Gélon Cameron and Edgar Spier Cameron. Both husband and wife had studied painting in Paris under Cabanel, Constant, and Laurens. At the time of the World's Columbian Exposition, Edgar Cameron was an art critic at the *Chicago Tribune*. Sparks, "A Biographical Dictionary," 105, 319; Opitz, ed., *Mantle Fieldings's Dictionary*, 127–28.

14. Edgar S. Cameron resided at 558 Division Street, just south of Lincoln Park. *The Chicago Blue Book*, 477.

15. Lake Shore Drive was considered the most elegant street in the city; Potter Palmer had played an important role in its development when he decided to build his magnificent mansion there. Ross, *Silhouette in Diamonds*, 52–53.

16. The Palmer mansion was constructed between 1882 and 1885. Built of Wisconsin granite and Ohio sandstone, the sumptuous home had an eighty- foot-high tower and an octagonal hall that rose three stories. The interior was a mixture of styles, including a Louis XVI–style salon and a ballroom and picture gallery where Bertha Palmer hung art she acquired in Europe, which later formed the foundation of the Art Institute of Chicago's collection. The house was demolished in 1950. For a description of the eclectic decor of the Palmer home see Hoganson, "Cosmopolitan Domesticity," 5–14, and Ross, *Silhouette in Diamonds*, 52–56.

17. The Jardin des Plantes is a botanical garden in Paris that includes a zoo. The writer Bernardin de Saint-Pierre (1737–1814) started the zoo in 1795 with animals that had lived in the royal menagerie at Versailles.

18. This is a reference to the attraction known as Relic House. Duis, *Challenging Chicago*, 207.

19. Known as the "People's College," The Athenaeum offered instruction in science, classics, foreign languages, and art. The first floor housed a gymnasium, and the remaining five floors contained a library, reading rooms, and classrooms. Frank Morris described the building as "one of the most complete educational structures of the kind in the country" in *Morris' Dictionary*, 34. See Siry, *The Chicago Auditorium Building*, 36–37, 326, regarding the history of The Athenaeum as an important public educational institution. The opening of the new Athenaeum Building was described in "Warming Its New Home, the Chicago Athenaeum Throws Open Its Doors to the Public," *Chicago Tribune*, 10 May 1891, 13.

20. "Mr. F." is a reference to William Marchant Richardson French.

CHAPTER 9: SOCIAL LIFE

1. Madame Grandin was almost certainly referring to Sara Hallowell, who had met Bertha Palmer during her visit to Paris in 1891. Hallowell was assistant to the chief of the Department of Fine Arts for the Columbian Exposition. See Webster, *Eve's Daughter* / Modern Woman, 61–67, for a biographical sketch of Hallowell and a discussion of her role in recommending Mary Cassatt for one of the murals for the Woman's Building. Descriptions of Hallowell's services to Palmer during her Paris visit in 1891 appear in Smart, *A Flight with Fame*, 111, and Ross, *Silhouette in Diamonds*, 63.

2. Sophia Hayden, who had studied architecture at the Massachusetts Institute of Technology, submitted the winning design for the Woman's Building. Laura Hayes, Palmer's personal secretary and Madame Grandin's acquaintance, was one of the finalists. The competition is described in Weimann, *The Fair Women*, 144–56.

3. Laura Hayes coauthored a book with Enid Yandell about their experiences living in Chicago and Paris: *Three Girls in a Flat*. Chapter 2 describes Bertha Palmer's visit to Paris before the World's Columbian Exposition. For a discussion of Laura Hayes's role in the planning and execution of fair activities, see Weimann, *The Fair Women*, 107–9, 149.

4. Laura Hayes was under the guardianship of Harold Hayes until she attained legal age on February 27, 1885. *Chicago Tribune*, 19 July 1888, 6.

5. According to *The Chicago Blue Book*, 543, Miss Laura Hayes resided at 189 Cass Street, which ran parallel to North State and Rush Streets; its name was later changed to North Wabash Avenue. The flat would have been within walking distance of the Palmer home on Lake Shore Drive. Descriptions of the neighborhood and flat are given in Hayes and Yandell, *Three Girls in a Flat*.

6. Several French travelers visited women's clubs during their stay in America, including Thérèse Blanc, Marie Dugard, and Thérèse Vianzone. Frank Morris provided a list of Chicago social clubs in *Morris' Dictionary*, 57–58, and included the Douglas Club, which Madame Grandin frequented with her friend Lydia Hess.

7. The reference is to the card game Switch, also known as Crazy Eights.

8. Horace W. Beek was a well-known choreographer and dance instructor whose name appeared numerous times in the *Chicago Tribune* in 1892–93. According to *Morris' Dictionary of Chicago* (62), Beek's dance academy was located at 164 Warren Avenue.

9. See Duis, *Challenging Chicago*, 225–29, regarding the popularity of social dancing in Chicago throughout the nineteenth century.

10. This well-known quotation is taken from Voltaire's satire *Candide ou l'Optimisme* (1759). In this philosophical tale, the main character Candide frequently repeats "tout est pour le mieux dans le meilleur des mondes possibles" (all is for the best in the best of all possible worlds) even though everything seems to go wrong.

CHAPTER 10: STREETS AND SHOPS

1. See Duis, *Challenging Chicago,* 205–8, for the history of dime museums in that city. Morris, *Morris' Dictionary,* lists addresses for two: Epstean's Dime Museum at 111–117 Randolph and Kohl and Middleton Dime Museum at 150 Clark Street and 154 West Madison.

2. Chromolithography is a method used to make multicolored prints.

3. In Madame Grandin's French text, this word is spelled phonetically, *pinotses.*

4. In Dreiser's *Sister Carrie,* numerous descriptions are given of the new department stores, including Siegel Cooper and Company, where Carrie looks for work (16, 17, 51–52, 58, 185).

5. This is a reference to the Christmas display windows in the Siegel, Cooper and Company Department Store. See "Goods for Presents," *Chicago Tribune,* 11 December 1892, 6, for a description of the holiday displays in the department stores on State Street, including Siegel, Cooper during the 1892 Christmas season.

6. Charles F. Gunther's confectionary was located in an impressive six-story building at 212 State Street.

7. Gunther's eclectic collection of books, manuscripts, paintings, and relics was eventually divided between the Chicago Historical Society and the Field Museum of Natural History. Duis, *Challenging Chicago,* 239.

8. According to *Morris' Dictionary,* 59, the Club Littéraire Français was "the leading French club in the city," had been in existence for fifteen years, and had about two hundred members. Meetings were announced regularly in the *Chicago Tribune.*

9. Duis, *Challenging Chicago,* 309–12.

10. The Douglas Club was located at 3518 Ellis Avenue (Morris, *Morris' Dictionary*). An article in the *Chicago Tribune,* 21 December 1893, 4, reported that the club sponsored children's dances and entertainment events to raise money for charity.

11. The Fahrenheit equivalent is sixteen degrees below zero.

CHAPTER 11: THE HOTEL EVERETT

1. According to the list of hotels in the World's Columbian Bureau of Information's *People's Ready Reference Guide to Chicago,* 287, the Hotel Everett was located at 3619 Lake Park Avenue. This moderately priced hotel had forty rooms and offered the American Plan, which included room and meals for $2.50 per day. The hotel was listed in the category of hotels "especially constructed to accommodate World's Fair visitors."

2. See Groth, *Living Downtown,* 56–89, for an informative discussion of the popularity of residential hotels for middle-class American families in the late nineteenth century.

3. See Sandoval-Strausz, *Hotel,* 266–73, for a summary of the controversy regarding family residential hotels in the late nineteenth century.

4. In 1883 an Illinois state law was enacted requiring children between the ages of eight and thirteen to attend school for twelve weeks a year. This law, however, was not strictly enforced. Pierce, *A History of Chicago*, 3:383.

5. Coeducational elementary schools did not exist in France, and for this reason many French visitors were especially interested in observing the phenomenon in American schools.

6. No secondary school of this name is listed in Patterson, *Patterson's School and College Directory*.

7. Physical culture classes became part of the Chicago school curriculum in 1886. Pierce, *A History of Chicago*, 3:388.

8. Kindergarten classes were first introduced by Friedrich Froebel (1782–1852) in mid- nineteenth-century Germany. By the late nineteenth century, early childhood educators in America were establishing kindergartens in the principal cities. The kindergarten movement was prominent in Chicago, where several organizations, including the Kindergarten College, Chicago Free Kindergarten Association, and Chicago Froebel Kindergarten Association, offered free kindergarten classes. The Chicago Board of Education officially assumed responsibility for kindergartens in 1892. Pierce, *A History of Chicago*, 3:383.

9. Madame Grandin was clearly familiar with elementary school teaching methods in France since she had worked as a teacher prior to her visit to Chicago.

10. Girls' secondary school education in the late-nineteenth-century France emphasized the importance of developing moral values and practical skills that would enable them to fulfill their later familial and societal roles. Françoise Mayeur, *L'éducation des filles*, 148–80; Clark, *Schooling the Daughters of Marianne*, 17; Margadant, *Madame le Professeur*, 205–6; Quartararo, *Women Teachers and Popular Education*, 108–25; Heywood, *Growing Up in France*, 248.

11. Madame Grandin would later give similar lectures at the Alliance Française of Staten Island.

12. Smiley, *Modern Manners and Social Forms*, 244, describes tableaux as a form of late-nineteenth-century American parlor entertainment. For a discussion of the popularity of these live tableaux see *American Home Life*, ed. Foy and Schlereth, 150.

CHAPTER 12: CALUMET LAKE AND PULLMAN CITY

1. Antony is a suburb located approximately seven miles south of Paris; Sèvres, a suburb southwest of Paris, is about six miles from the city center.

2. See Morris, *Morris' Dictionary*, 115, for a description of Pullman City

3. In fact, Pullman employees were not particularly happy, as evidenced by the strike that took place during the summer of 1894. See Miller, *City of the Century*, 542–48, for a discussion of the strike and its consequences.

4. Although Madame Grandin thought that locomotives were manufactured at the factory, only railroad cars were made there.

5. Numerous descriptions of masquerade balls are found in the *Chicago Tribune* in the early 1890s, but there are no references to this specific ball.

6. See Gamber, *The Female Economy*, for a detailed consideration of the ser-

vices provided and situation of late-nineteenth and early-twentieth-century dressmakers.

7. Numerous other French women writers commented on the comparative social freedom of American girls, including Marie-Thérèse Blanc, Marie Dugard, and Thérèse Batbedat.

8. Several nursing schools in Chicago provided training, including the Illinois Training School for Nurses, which was founded by Dr. Sarah Hackett Stevenson in 1880. Duis, *Challenging Chicago,* 326.

9. This is a reference to inebriate asylums, several of which are listed in Morris, *Morris' Dictionary,* 84.

10. The Chicago Public Library was located on the fourth floor of City Hall at the corner of Lasalle and Washington Streets during Madame Grandin's stay in the city. Morris, *Morris' Dictionary,* 114.

CHAPTER 13: WORLD'S COLUMBIAN EXPOSITION: A TOUR

1. See Duis, *Challenging Chicago,* 75–81, regarding the Chicago custom of "moving day."

2. See Weimann, *The Fair Women,* for a comprehensive study of the background and execution of the Woman's Building and the activities held within it.

3. "Address of Mrs. Potter Palmer."

4. Sophia Hayden (1868–1953), who won the architectural competition held to select the design for the Woman's Building, was the first woman to receive a degree in architecture from the Massachusetts Institute of Technology. See Paine, "Sophia Hayden and the Woman's Building," 28–37, and Weimann, *The Fair Women,* 141–56 for discussions of the architectural competition and reproductions of Hayden's sketches of the floor plans for the building.

5. This is a reference to Mary MacMonnies, the American painter who was married to the sculptor Frederick MacMonnies. By 1893 the American painter Mary Cassatt was well known in both Paris, where she resided, and in America. Weimann, *The Fair Women,* 194–206; Webster, *Eve's Daughter / Modern Woman.*

6. An article in the *Chicago Tribune* of February 23, 1892, "Concessions to Fair Exhibitors," indicated that Laura Hayes had been granted a concession to sell "reproductions of the last nail in the Woman's Building in the form of a lead pencil."

7. This is a reference to Kate Marsden, who had a display at the Woman's Building concerning her charity work with lepers. Marsden, "The Leper," 213–16.

8. Madame Grandin began her description of the exposition with the Woman's Building and then continued in a counter-clockwise direction.

9. Some construction delays were related to the harsh winter and rainy spring of 1892–93. Badger, *The Great American Fair,* 87.

10. Jean-Baptiste Carpeaux (1827–75) was a leading sculptor of his time. He studied at the École des Beaux-Arts with François Rude and over the course of his career sculpted busts of many important figures of the Second Empire, including Napoleon III and his family. Carpeaux's marble bust of a smiling young woman, "La Rieuse," was created around 1873. Wagner, *Jean-Baptiste Carpeaux.*

11. An early plan for the Midway Plaisance was to build a steel tower similar to

the Eiffel Tower. The project was shelved, however, due to financial and time constraints as well as a concern about its lack of originality, and the Ferris wheel was chosen instead. Higinbotham, *Report of the President*, 87–89.

12. See Badger, *The Great American Fair*, 90–91, for a description of the train and boat connections to Jackson Park.

13. The Columbia Roller Chair Company had a concession "for the operation of light-running, comfortable wicker chairs, each pushed by a uniformed attendant who was trained to be an efficient and courteous guide. The corps was recruited from undergraduate students of colleges who thus secured, in addition to employment for their vacation, an opportunity for seeing the Exposition." Higinbotham, *Report of the President*, 93.

14. "A just criticism, frequently uttered during the first half of the season, was that there was a lack of effort to amuse the visitors and to instill life into the vast and beautiful expanse of grounds and buildings." Ibid., 251–52.

CHAPTER 14: FINAL IMPRESSIONS

1. This is a reference to the Parisian business directory, known as the *Bottin parisien*.

2. Morris, *Morris' Dictionary*, 141, provided directions for reaching the stockyards by train and offered this advice: "Wear your old clothes and when you are met at the entrance by a guide, do not scorn his assistance."

3. It appears that the Grandins left Chicago in early June, because they were already in Washington, D.C., by Sunday, June 11, when the funerals of victims of the collapse of Ford's Theater were held.

4. Madame Grandin referred to solid bourgeois values in a colorful way by evoking a hearty beef stew (*pot-au-feu*).

5. The Pennsylvania Railroad served the route between Chicago and Washington, D.C., crossing the Allegheny Mountains.

6. Pittsburgh was a center of oil production in the late nineteenth century.

7. This is a reference to Union Station in Washington, D.C.

8. Eastern Market in Washington had been in operation since 1873.

9. On June 9, 1893, Ford's Theater was the site of a collapse that killed twenty-one people and injured approximately fifty others. Most were employees in the Pension Department. "Twenty-One Killed," *Washington Post*, 11 June 1893, 1.

Selected Bibliography

The chapter endnotes provide an index of contemporary articles from the *Chicago Tribune* and the *New York Times* that give information about specific people, places, and events mentioned in Madame Grandin's account. The following list contains primary source travel accounts as well as secondary sources on travel literature, nineteenth-century Chicago, and American and French social history that were helpful in reconstructing what she observed in America and understanding how she interpreted it.

PRIMARY SOURCES

Audouard, Olympe, *À travers l'Amérique: Le Far West.* Paris: E. Dentu, 1869.

———. *À travers l'Amérique: North America, États-Unis: mœurs, usages, institutions, sectes religieuses.* Paris: E. Dentu, 1871.

Bassanville, Comtesse de. *De l'éducation des femmes: le monde, le chez-soi, la famille.* Paris: Charles Douniol, 1861.

Batbedat, Thérèse. *Impressions d'une parisienne sur la côte du Pacifique.* Paris: Juven, 1902.

Bentzon, Th. [Marie-Thérèse Blanc]. *Choses et gens d'Amérique.* Paris: C. Lévy, 1898.

———. "Impressions of the World's Fair." *Critic* 25 (November 1893): 331–32.

———. *Notes de voyage. Les américaines chez elles.* 2d ed. Paris: C. Lévy, 1896.

Bernhardt, Sarah. *My Double Life: The Memoirs of Sarah Bernhardt.* Trans. Victoria Tietze Larson. Albany: State University Press of New York, 1999.

Blanc, Marie-Thérèse. *The Condition of Women in the United States: A Traveller's Notes.* Trans. Abby Langdon Alger. Boston: Roberts Brothers, 1895.

Bocage, Adolphe. "L'architecture aux États-Unis et à l'exposition universelle de Chicago: La maison moderne et la situation de l'architecte aux États-Unis." *L'Architecture,* 13 October 1894, 333–39.

Bourbonnaud, Louise. *Les Amériques: Amérique du Nord, Les Antilles, Amérique du Sud.* Paris: Librairie Léon Vanier, 1889.

Bourget, Paul. "A Farewell to the White City." *Cosmopolitan* (December 1893): 133–40.

———. *Outre Mer: Impressions of America*. New York: Charles Scribner's and Sons, 1895.

Brissot de Warville, J. P. *Nouveau voyage dans les États-Unis de l'Amérique septentrionale, fait en 1788*. Paris: Buisson, 1791.

Bruwaert, M.E. "Chicago et l'exposition universelle colombienne." *Le Tour du Monde* 65 (1893): 294–304.

Cameron, Edgar Spier. Edgar Spier Cameron Papers, 1868–1968. Reels 4290–92. Smithsonian Archives of American Art.

Cannart d'Hamale, Mme Arthur. *Un voyage de noces à Chicago*. Brussels: J. Lebègue, 1895.

Carlier, Auguste. *De l'esclavage dans ses rapports avec l'union américaine*. Paris: Michel Lévy Frères, 1862.

Chambrun, René de, ed. *Un Français chez les Lincoln: Lettres inédites adressées pendant la guerre de sécession par Adolphe de Chambrun à son épouse restée en France*. Paris: Librairie Perrin, 1976.

Compayré, G. *L'enseignement secondaire aux États-Unis*. Paris: Hachette, 1896.

Cotton, L. de. "A Frenchman's Visit to Chicago in 1886." *Journal of the Illinois Historical Society* 47 (Spring 1954): 45–56.

Cunliffe-Owen, Margaret [Marquise de Fontenoy]. *Eve's Glossary: The Guide Book of a "Mondaine."* Chicago: Herbert Stone, 1897.

Delorme, Marie. *Les petits cahiers de Madame Brunet, gouvernement de la famille, hygiène, économie domestique, calendrier de la bonne ménagére; dialogues*. Paris: Armand Colin, 1888.

Dernberg, Friedrich. *Aus der weissen Stadt*. Berlin: Julius Springer, 1893.

Dickens, Charles. *American Notes for General Circulation*. 1842. Reprint. London: Penguin, 2004.

Ducher, G. J. A. *Nouvelle alliance à proposer entre les républiques française et américaine*. Paris: Ducher, 1792.

Dugard, Marie. *La société américaine, mœurs et caractère, la famille, rôle de la femme, écoles et universités*. Paris: Hachette, 1896.

Emperger, Fr.Von. "Eiserne Gerippbauten in den Vereinigten Staaten." *Zeitschrift des Oesterreichischen Ingenieur-und Architekten Vereins*, 6 October 1893, 526.

Englebach, H. *L'esclavage dans les États Confédérés*. Paris: E. Dentu, 1865.

Grandfort, Marie de. *L'autre monde: Lettres sur les États-Unis*. Paris: Librairie Nouvelle, 1855

Goussard de Mayolle, Jeanne. *Une française chez les sauvages*. Tours: Marne, 1897.

Héricourt, Jenny P. d'. *La femme affranchie*. Brussels: A Lacroix Van Munen et Cie, 1860.

Hermant, Jacques. "L'Architecture aux États-Unis et à l'exposition universelle de Chicago: L'architecture en Amérique et à la World's Fair." *L'Architecture*, 20 October 1894, 341–46.

Hesse-Wartegg, Ernst von. *Tausend und ein Tag im Occident*. 2 vols. Leipzig: Carl Reissner, 1891.

Jaffe, Franz . "Die Architektur-ausstellung Fremder Länder." In *Amtlicher Bericht über die Weltausstellung in Chicago 1893, 2:1145.* Berlin: Reichsdruckerei, 1894.

Kendall, John. *American Memories.* Nottingham: E. Burrows, 1896.

Loizillon, Marie. *L'éducation des enfants aux États-Unis: Rapport présenté à M. le ministre de l'instruction publique après une mission officielle.* Paris: Librairie Hachette, 1883.

Loviot, Fanny. *Les pirates chinois. Ma captivité dans les mers de la Chine.* Paris: A. Bourdilliat, 1860.

M. "Ueber die ausserordentilich rege Bautätigkeit und einige bauliche Sonderheiten in Chicago." *Centralblatt der Bauverwaltung,* 17 September 1892, 412.

Mainard, Louis. *Le livre d'or des voyages, L'Amérique.* Paris: Editions des Grands Magasins de la Place Clichy, 1892.

Mandat-Grancey, E. de. *En visite chez l'Oncle Sam: New York et Chicago.* Paris: Plon, 1885.

Nasatir, A. P., ed. *A French Journalist in the California Gold Rush: The Letters of Étienne Derbec.* Georgetown, Calif.: Talisman Press, 1964.

Pagès, Pierre Marie François. *Nouveau voyage autour du monde, en Asie, en Amérique et en Afrique en 1788, 1789, et 1790.* Paris: H. J. Jansen, 1797.

Passy, Paul Edouard. *L'instruction primaire aux États-Unis.* Paris: Delagrave, 1885.

"Rapid Building in Chicago." *American Architect,* 10 September 1892, 172.

Rousiers, Paul de. *American Life.* Trans. A.J. Herbertson. Paris: Firmin-Didot, 1892.

Russailh, A. Benard de. *Journal de voyage en Californie à l'époque de la ruée vers l'or (1850–1852).* Paris: Éditions Aubier Montaigne, 1980.

Saint-Amant, Mme Charles. *Voyage en Californie (1850–1851).* Paris: Garnier Frères, 1851.

San Carlos de Pedroso, Marquise de. *Les Américains chez eux.* Paris: Librairie de la Nouvelle Revue, 1890.

Sauvin, G. *Autour de Chicago: Notes sur les États-Unis.* Paris: Plon, 1893.

Shaw, Mathilde. "Scènes de la vie chinoise à New York." *La Nouvelle Revue* 91 (November–December 1894): 327–60.

———. "A travers la Nouvelle Angleterre." *La Nouvelle Revue* 93 (March–April 1895): 329–62.

Smiley, James. *Modern Manners and Social Forms.* Chicago: James B. Smiley, 1889.

Soissons, S. C. *A Parisian in America.* Boston: Estes and Lauriat, 1896.

Steevens, G. W. *The Land of the Dollar.* New York: Dodd, Mead, 1897.

Tocqueville, Alexis de. *Democracy in America,* 2 vols. Trans. Henry Reeve. 1835, 1840. Reprint. Cambridge: Sever and Francis, 1862.

Trollope, Fanny. *The Domestic Manners of Americans.* 1832. Reprint. London: Penguin, 1997.

Uzanne, Octave. *Vingt jours dans le nouveau monde.* Paris: May and Motteroz, 1893.

Varigny, C. "The American Woman." *Popular Science Monthly* 43 (July 1893): 383–88.

———. *Les États-Unis.* Paris: E. Kolb, 1892.

————. *The Women of the United States*. Trans. Arabella Ward. New York: Dodd, Mead, 1895.

Vianzone, Thérèse. *Impressions d'une française en Amérique: États-Unis et Canada*. Paris: Plon, 1906.

Villiers, Frederick. "An Artist's View of Chicago and the World's Fair." *Journal of the Society of Arts*, 8 December 1893, 49–54.

SECONDARY SOURCES

Adams, Percy G. *Travel Literature through the Ages: An Anthology*. New York: Garland, 1988.

"Address of Mrs. Potter Palmer, President of the Board of Lady Managers." In *Addresses Delivered at the Opening of the Woman's Building, May 1, 1893*. Chicago: Rand, McNally, 1894.

Address and Reports of Mrs. Potter Palmer, President of the Board of Lady Managers, World's Columbian Commission. Chicago: Rand, McNally, 1894.

Adler, Kathleen. "'We'll Always Have Paris': Paris as Training Ground and Proving Ground." In *Americans in Paris, 1860–1900*. London: National Gallery, 2006.

Albisetti, James C. "American Women's Colleges through European Eyes, 1865–1914." *History of Education Quarterly* 32 (Winter 1992): 439–58.

Anon. *Picturesque Chicago and Guide to the World's Fair*. Baltimore: R. H. Woodward, 1892.

Anon. "The Gay Nineties in Chicago: A French View." *Chicago History* 7, no. 11 (1966): 341–88.

Appelbaum, Stanley. *The Chicago World's Fair of 1893: A Photographic Record*. New York: Dover Publications, 1980.

Badger, Reid. *The Great American Fair: The World's Columbian Exposition and American Culture*. Chicago: Nelson Hall, 1979.

Bancquart, Marie-Claire. *Fin de siècle gourmande, 1880–1900*. Paris: Presses Universitaires de France, 2001.

Block, Jean F. *Hyde Park Houses: An Informal History, 1856–1910*. Chicago: University of Chicago Press, 1978.

Bourguignon, Katherine M., ed. *Impressionist Giverny: A Colony of Artists, 1885–1915*. Chicago: Terra Foundation for American Art, 2007.

Brady, Heather. "The Frontiers of Popular Exoticism: Marie Bonaparte's New Orleans Crossings." *Nineteenth-Century French Studies* 31, nos. 3 and 4 (2003): 311–23.

Broca, Numa. *Dictionnaire illustré des explorateurs et grands voyageurs français du XIXe siècle, Amérique*. Paris: Éditions du CTHS, 1999.

Brown, Thomas Allston. *A History of the New York Stage from the First Performance in 1732 to 1901*. New York: Dodd, Mead, 1903.

Burrows, Edwin G., and Mike Wallace. *Gotham: A History of New York City to 1898*. New York: Oxford University Press, 1999.

Cable, Mary. *Top Drawer: American High Society from the Gilded Age to the Roaring Twenties*. New York: Atheneum, 1984.

Calvert, Karin. "Children in the House, 1890–1930." In *American Home Life*,

1880–1930: A Social History of Spaces and Services, 75–93. Ed Jessica H. Foy and Thomas J. Schlereth. Knoxville: University of Tennessee Press, 1992.

Caplat, Guy. *Les inspecteurs généraux de l'instruction publique: Dictionnaire biographique 1802–1914*. Paris: Institut National de Recherche Pédagogique, Éditions du CNRS, 1986.

Cartwright, Derrick R. "Beyond the Nursery: The Public Careers and Private Spheres of Mary Fairchild MacMonnies Low." In *An Interlude in Giverny*, 35–57. Giverny, France: Palmer Museum of Art, Penn State University, and Musée d'Art Américain, Terra Foundation for the Arts, 2000.

Cheney, Joyce. *Aprons: Icons of the American Home*. Philadelphia: Running Press, 2000.

Chevalier, A. *Les voyageuses au XIXe siècle*. Tours: Alfred Mama et Fils, 1888.

Chew, William. "Marie-Thérèse Blanc in America: A Fin-de-Siècle Perspective of the American Woman." In *Re-Discoveries of America*, 17–59. Ed. Johan Callens. Brussels: VUB Press, 1993.

Chicago Blue Book. Chicago: Chicago Directory, 1893.

Clark, Linda. *Schooling the Daughters of Marianne: Textbooks and Socialization of Girls in Modern French Primary Schools*. Albany: State University of New York Press, 1984.

Colloques Internationaux du Centre National de la Recherche Scientifique. *Les botanistes Français en Amérique du Nord avant 1850*. Paris: Éditions du CNRS, 1957.

Cromley, Elizabeth Collins. "American Beds and Bedrooms." In *American Home Life, 1880–1930: A Social History of Spaces and Services*, 120–41. Ed. Jessica H. Foy and Thomas J. Schlereth. Knoxville: University of Tennessee Press, 1992.

Current, Richard Nelson. *Loie Fuller, Goddess of Light*. Boston: Northeastern University Press, 1997.

D'Amat, Roman, and R. Limouzin-Lamothe. *Dictionnaire de biographie française*. Paris: Letouzy et Ané, 1967.

Dennett, Andrea Stulman. *Weird and Wonderful: The Dime Museum in America*. New York: New York University Press, 1997.

Ditchett, Samuel Herbert. *Marshall Field and Company: The Life Story of A Great Concern*. New York: Dry Goods Economist, 1922.

Dreiser, Theodore. *Sister Carrie*. 1900. Reprint. Ed. Donald Pitzer. New York: W. W. Norton, 1970.

Dronsart, Marie. *Les grandes voyageuses*. Paris: Hachette, 1894.

Dubinsky, Karen. *The Second Greatest Disappointment: Honeymooning and Tourism at Niagara Falls*. New Brunswick: Rutgers University Press, 1999.

Duis, Perry R. *Challenging Chicago: Coping with Everyday Life, 1837–1920*. Urbana: University of Illinois Press, 1998.

Eagle, Mary Kavanaugh Oldham, ed. *The Congress of Women, World's Columbian Exposition*. Chicago: Monarch Book, 1894.

Echeverria, Durand, and Everett C. Wilke Jr. *The French Image of America: A Chronological and Subject Bibliography of French Books Printed before 1816 Relating to the British North American Colonies and the United States*. 2 vols. Metuchen, N.J.: Scarecrow Press, 1994.

Echeverria, Durand. *Mirage in the West: A History of the French Image of American Society to 1815.* New York: Octagon Books, 1966.

Fink, Lois Marie. *American Art at the Nineteenth-Century Paris Salons.* New York: Cambridge University Press, 1990.

Flanagan, Maureen. *Seeing with Their Hearts: Chicago Women and the Vision of the Good City, 1871–1933.* Princeton: Princeton University Press, 2002.

Flinn, John J. *Chicago, the Marvelous City of the West.* Chicago: Flinn and Sheppard, 1891.

———, ed. *Official Guide to the World's Columbian Exposition.* Chicago: Columbian Guide Company, 1893.

Foster, Shirley. *Across New Worlds: Nineteenth-Century Women Travellers and their Writings.* New York: Harvester Wheatsheaf, 1990.

Gamber, Wendy. *The Boardinghouse in Nineteenth-Century America.* Baltimore: Johns Hopkins University Press, 2007.

———. *The Female Economy: The Millinery and Dressmaking Trades, 1860–1930.* Urbana: University of Illinois Press, 1997.

Gemie, Sharif. *Women and Schooling in France, 1815–1914.* Staffordshire: Keele University Press, 1995.

Gordon, E. Adina. "The Expansion of a Career: Frederick MacMonnies as a Teacher and Painter." In *An Interlude in Giverny,* 59–86. Giverny, France: Palmer Museum of Art, Penn State University, and Musée d'Art Américain, Terra Foundation for the Arts, 2000.

Graham, C. *From Peristyle to Plaisance: Illustrated in Colors by C. Graham: with a Short History of the World's Columbian Exposition.* Chicago: N.p., 1893.

Groth, Paul. *Living Downtown: The History of Residential Hotels in the United States.* Berkeley: University of California Press, 1994.

Guentner, Wendelin. *Esquisses littéraires: Rhétorique du spontané et récit de voyage au XIXe siècle.* Saint-Genouph: Librairie Nizet, 1997.

Gullett, Gayle. "'Our Great Opportunity': Organized Women Advance Women's Work at the World's Columbian Exposition of 1893." *Illinois Historical Journal* 87 (Winter 1994): 259–76.

Hamalian, Leo. *Ladies on the Loose: Women Travellers of the Eighteenth and Nineteenth Centuries.* New York: Dodd, Mead and Company, 1981.

Hayes, Laura, and Enid Yandell. *Three Girls in a Flat.* Chicago: Knight, Leonard, 1892.

Heywood, Colin. *Growing Up in France: From the Ancien Régime to the Third Republic.* New York: Cambridge University Press, 2007.

Higinbotham, H. N. *Report of the President to the Board of Directors of the World's Columbian Exposition.* Chicago: Rand McNally, 1898.

Hoganson, Kristin. "Cosmopolitan Domesticity: Importing the American Dream." *American Historical Review* 107 (February 2002): 5–14.

Honour, Hugh, ed. *L'Amérique vue par l'Europe.* Paris: Éditions des Musées Nationaux, 1976.

Imbarrato, Susan Clair. *Traveling Women: Narrative Visions in Early America.* Athens: Ohio University Press, 2006.

Karel, David. *Dictionnaire des artistes de langue française en Amérique du Nord.* Quebec: Presse de l'Université de Laval, 1992.

Katzman, David M. *Seven Days a Week: Women and Domestic Service in Industrializing America*. New York: Oxford University Press, 1978.

Keil, Hartmut. "Immigrant Neighborhoods and American Society: German Immigrants on Chicago's Northwest Side in the Late Nineteenth Century." In *German Workers' Culture in the United States, 1850–1920*, 25–58. Ed. Hartmut Keil. Washington: Smithsonian Institution Press, 1988.

Kowalewski, Michael, ed. *Temperamental Journeys: Essays on the Modern Literature of Travel*. Athens: University of Georgia Press, 1992.

Langlois, C. V. "L'éducation aux États-Unis." In *Questions d'histoire et d'enseignement*, 97–122. Paris: Hachette, 1906.

Lapeyre, Françoise. *Le roman des voyageuses françaises, 1800–1900*. Paris: Éditions Payot, 2007.

Leask, Nigel. *Curiosity and the Aesthetics of Travel Writing, 1770–1840: From an Antique Land*. New York: Oxford University Press, 2002.

Lelièvre, Claude, and Françoise Lelièvre. *Histoire de la scolarisation des filles*. Paris: Nathan, 1991.

Lemonnier, Léon. *La ruée vers l'or en Californie*. Paris: Librairie Gallimard, 1944.

Lewis, Arnold. *An Early Encounter with Tomorrow: Europeans, Chicago's Loop and the World's Columbian Exposition*. Urbana: University of Illinois Press, 1997.

Liebersohn, Harry. *Aristocratic Encounters: European Travelers and North American Indians*. New York: Cambridge University Press, 1998.

Lowe, David. *Lost Chicago*. Boston: Houghton Mifflin, 1975.

Margadant, Jo Burr. *Madame le Professeur: Women Educators in the Third Republic*. Princeton: Princeton University Press, 1990.

Marsden, Kate. "The Leper." In *The Congress of Women: Held in the Woman's Building World's Columbian Exposition U.S.A. 1893*, 213–16. Ed. Mary Kavanaugh Oldman Eagle. Chicago: Monarch Book, 1894.

Martin, Theodora Penny. *The Sound of Our Own Voices: Women's Study Clubs, 1860–1910*. Boston: Beacon Press, 1987.

Martin-Fugier, Anne. *La bourgeoise: La femme au temps de Paul Bourget*. Paris: Grasset, 1983.

———. *La place des bonnes: La domesticité féminine à Paris en 1900*. Paris: Grasset, 1979.

———. *La vie d'artiste au XIXe siècle*. Paris: Éditions Louis Audibert, 2007.

Mathews, Nancy Mowell. *Cassatt and Her Circle: Selected Letters*. New York: Abbeville Press, 1984.

Mayer, Harold M., and Richard C. Wade. *Chicago: Growth of a Metropolis*. Chicago: University of Chicago Press, 1969.

Mayeur, Françoise. *L'éducation des filles en France au XIXe siècle*. Paris: Hachette, 1979.

Meaux, Vicomte de. "Les écoles aux États-Unis." *Le Correspondant*, 25 February 1891.

Mesnard, Jean, éd. *Les récits de voyage*. Paris: Nizet, 1986.

Meyerowitz, Joanne. *Women Adrift: Independent Wage Earners in Chicago, 1880–1930*. Chicago: University of Chicago Press, 1988.

Miller, Donald. *City of the Century: The Epic of Chicago and the Making of America*. New York: Simon and Schuster, 1996.

Mills, Sara. *Discourses of Difference: An Analysis of Women's Travel Writing and Colonialism.* New York: Routledge, 1991.

Mohun, Arwen. *Steam Laundries: Gender, Technology, and Work in the United States and Great Britain, 1880–1940.* Baltimore: Johns Hopkins University Press, 1999.

Monaghan, Frank. *French Travellers in the United States, 1765–1932.* New York: New York Public Library, 1933.

Monicat, Bénédicte. "Autobiography and Women's Travel Writings in Nineteenth-Century France: Journeys through Self-Representation." *Gender, Place and Culture* 1 (Winter 1994): 61–70.

———. "Écritures du voyage et féminisme: Olympe Audouard ou le féminin en question." *French Review* 69 (October 1995): 24–36.

———. *Itinéraires de l'ecriture au féminin: Voyageuses du 19e siècle.* Amsterdam: Rodopi, 1996.

———. "Les lettres d'un voyageur: Récit de voyage au féminin?" *George Sand Studies* 12 (Spring 1993): 11–17.

———. "Pour une bibliographie des récits de voyage au féminin." *Romantisme* 77, no. 3 (1992): 95–100.

———. "Problématique de la préface dans les récits de voyage au féminin du 19e siècle." *Nineteenth-Century French Studies* 23 (Fall–Winter 1994–95): 59–71.

Morris, Frank M. *Morris' Dictionary of Chicago and Vicinity.* Chicago: Frank M. Morris, 1892–93.

Moses, Claire Goldberg. *French Feminism in the Nineteenth Century.* Albany: State University of New York Press, 1984.

Offen, Karen. "A Nineteenth-Century Feminist Rediscovered: Jenny P. d'Héricourt, 1809–1875." *Signs: Journal of Women in Culture and Society* 13 (Autumn 1987): 144–58.

———. "The Second Sex and the Baccalauréat in Republican France, 1880–1924." *French Historical Studies* 13 (Autumn 1983): 252–86.

Olsen, Donald. *The City as a Work of Art: London, Paris, Vienna.* New Haven: Yale University Press, 1986.

Opitz, Glen, ed. *Mantle Fielding's Dictionary of American Painters, Sculptors and Engravers.* Poughkeepsie: Apollo Books, 1986.

Paine, Judith. "Sophia Hayden and the Woman's Building." *Helicon* 9 (Fall–Winter 1979): 28–37.

Patterson, Howell. *Patterson's School and College Dictionary for the United States and Canada.* Chicago: American Educational Company, 1905.

Perrot, Michelle. *Histoire de la vie privée: De la Révolution à la Grande Guerre.* Paris: Seuil, 1987.

———. *Histoire des femmes.* Ed. Georges Duby and Michelle Perrot. Paris: Plon, 1991.

Pierce, Bessie. *A History of Chicago, 1871–1893.* Vol. 3. New York: Alfred A. Knopf, 1957.

———. *As Others See Chicago: Impressions of Visitors 1673–1933.* Chicago: University of Chicago Press, 1933.

Portes, Jacques. *Fascination and Misgivings: The United States in French Opinion, 1870–1914.* Trans. Elborg Forster. New York: Cambridge University Press, 2000.

Pratt, Mary Louise. *Imperial Eyes: Travel Writing and Transculturation.* New York: Routledge, 1992.

Quartararo, Anne T. *Women Teachers and Popular Education in Nineteenth-Century France.* Newark: University of Delaware Press, 1995.

Rand McNally and Company's Pictorial Chicago and Illustrated World's Columbian Exposition. Chicago: Rand McNally, 1893.

Rearick, Charles. "Song and Society in Turn of the Century France." *Journal of Social History* 22 (Fall 1988): 45–63.

Rémond, René. *Les États-Unis devant l'opinion française, 1815–1852.* 2 vols. Paris: Librairie Armand Colin, 1962.

Roger, Philippe. *The American Enemy: A Story of French Anti-Americanism.* Trans. Sharon Bowman. Chicago: University of Chicago Press, 2005.

Rogers, Rebecca. *From the Salon to the Schoolroom: Educating Bourgeois Girls in Nineteenth-Century France.* University Park: Pennsylvania State University Press, 2005.

Ross, Ishbel. *Silhouette in Diamonds: The Life of Mrs. Potter Palmer.* New York: Harper and Bros., 1960.

Sandoval-Strausz, A. K. *Hotel: An American History.* New Haven: Yale University Press, 2007.

Schriber, Mary Suzanne. *American Women Abroad, 1830–1920.* Charlottesville: University of Virginia Press, 1997.

Scudder, Janet. *Modeling My Life.* New York: Harcourt Brace, 1925.

Sears, John F. *Sacred Places: American Tourist Attractions in the Nineteenth Century.* New York: Oxford University Press, 1989.

Sinkevitch, Alice, ed. *AIA Guide to Chicago.* 2d ed. New York: Harcourt 2004.

Siry, Joseph. *The Chicago Auditorium Building: Adler and Sullivan's Architecture and the City.* Chicago: University of Chicago Press, 2002.

———. "Chicago's Auditorium Building: Opera or Anarchism" *Journal of the Society of Architectural Historians* 57 (June 1998): 128–59.

Smart, Mary. *A Flight with Fame: The Life and Art of Frederick MacMonnies.* Madison, Conn.: Sound View Press, 1996.

Sparks, Esther. "A Biographical Dictionary of Painters and Sculptors in Illinois, 1808–1945." Ph.D. diss., Northwestern University, 1971.

Staffe, Baronne. *Usages du monde: Règles du savoir-vivre dans la société moderne.* Paris: Éditions 1900, 1989.

Steele, Valerie. "The Corset Controversy." In *Fashion and Eroticism: Ideals of Feminine Beauty from the Victorian Era to the Jazz Age,* 161–91. New York: Oxford University Press, 1985.

Still, Bayrd. *Mirror for Gotham: New York as Seen by Contemporaries from Dutch Days to the Present.* New York: New York University Press, 1956.

Stowe, William. *Going Abroad: European Travel in Nineteenth-Century American Culture.* Princeton: Princeton University Press, 1994.

Thibaudet, Alfred. "Le genre littéraire du voyage." In *Réflexion sur la critique,* 7–22. Paris: NRF Gallimard, 1939.

Tomkins, Calvin. *Merchants and Masterpieces: The Story of the Metropolitan Museum of Art.* New York: Henry Holt, 1989.

Trubek, Amy. *Haute Cuisine: How the French Invented the Culinary Profession.* Philadelphia: University of Pennsylvania Press, 2000.

Volo, James M., and Dorothy Deneen. *Family Life in Nineteenth-Century America.* Westport: Greenwood Press, 2007.

Wagner, Anne Middleton. *Jean-Baptiste Carpeaux, Sculptor of the Second Empire.* New Haven: Yale University Press, 1986.

Webster, Sally. *Eve's Daughter /* Modern Woman: *A Mural by Mary Cassatt.* Urbana: University of Illinois Press, 2004.

Weimann, Jeanne Madeline. *The Fair Women: The Story of the Woman's Building, World's Columbian Exposition, Chicago, 1893.* Chicago: Academy Press, 1981.

Weinberg, Barbara. *The Lure of Paris: Nineteenth-Century American Painters and Their French Teachers.* New York: Abbeville Press, 1991.

Weisberg, Gabriel, and Jane R. Becker, eds. *Overcoming All Obstacles: The Women of the Académie Julian.* New Brunswick: Rutgers University Press, 1999.

West, Joan. "Th. Bentzon's Traveler's Notes: Redefining American Women." *Selecta: Journal of the PNCFL* 16 (1995): 29–33.

Wiesinger, Véronique. "American Sculpture Students in Paris." In *Paris Bound: American Students in Art Schools, 1868–1918,* 55–69. Paris: Réunion des Musées Nationaux, 1990.

Wilson, Mark. "Mr. Clemens and Madame Blanc: Mark Twain's First French Critic." *American Literature* 45 (January 1974): 537–56.

World's Columbian Bureau of Information. *The People's Ready Reference Guide to Chicago and the World's Columbian Exposition.* Chicago: World's Columbian Bureau of Information, 1893.

Index

MADAME LÉON GRANDIN (1864–1905) was a
Parisienne who lived in Chicago with her husband from
August 1892 until June 1893. Her spirited reaction to
the city, *Impressions d'une Parisienne à Chicago,* was
originally published in France in 1894.

ARNOLD LEWIS, professor emeritus of art history
at the College of Wooster, is the author or coauthor
of several books on American architecture, including
*An Early Encounter with Tomorrow, American Victorian
Architecture, American Country Houses of the Gilded
Age,* and *The Opulent Interiors of the Gilded Age.*

MARY BETH RAYCRAFT is a senior lecturer in
French at Vanderbilt University.

The University of Illinois Press
is a founding member of the
Association of American University Presses.

Composed in 10/13 Fairfield LT Std
with Sloop display
by Barbara Evans
at the University of Illinois Press
Designed by Kelly Gray
Manufactured by Thomson-Shore, Inc.

University of Illinois Press
1325 South Oak Street
Champaign, IL 61820-6903
www.press.uillinois.edu